MEDIA in the 20th century

Copyright © 1997 Bluewood Books

All rights reserved. No part of this publication may be reproduced, stored in a retrieval system or transmitted in any form by any means, electronic, mechanical, photocopying or otherwise, without first obtaining written permission of the copyright owner.

This edition produced and published
in 1997 by Bluewood Books
A Division of The Siyeh Group, Inc.,
P.O. Box 689
San Mateo, CA 94401

ISBN 0-912517-24-7

Printed in USA
10, 9, 8, 7, 6, 5, 4, 3, 2, 1

Designed by Linda Wanczyk
Production by Eric Irving
Contributing Editors: Catherine DeSantis and Michelle Crowe
Copy Edited by Greg Aaron and Bob Juran
Edited by Richard Michaels and Barbara Krystal
Proofread by Barbara Krystal

About the Author:
Oscar W. Alexander was born in Levittown, NY. He earned a B.A. in English from University of Michigan and now lives in Rancho Mirage, CA where he is a freelance writer and editor.

The publisher wishes to thank and acknowledge the following for the courtesy of reproducing the following images:
American Radio Relay League, Inc. 70, 79, 157; Archive Photos: 86, 87, 88, 91, 101, 102, 113, 120, 128, 129, 135, 136, 137, 146, 150, 154, 156; Archive Photos/American Stock 66; Archive Photos/APA 64, 112; Archive Photos/CBS 115; Archive Photos/Consolidated News 162, 173; Archive Photos/Museum of the City of New York 38; Archive Photos/Reuters/Lee Celano 174; Property of AT&T Archives, Reprinted with permission of AT&T: 73, 74, 75; Bluewood Books Archives: 52, 107, 145, 182, 187; Capital Cities/ABC, Inc. 175, 183, 184; Dow Jones & Company 97; Copyright © Eastman Kodak Company 49(t); E.W. Scripps Company 48, 95, 103, 131; Franklin D. Roosevelt Library 80, 96; Used by permission, Gannett Co., Inc. 67, 110, 159, 166, 168; General Motors 155; The Hearst Corporation/Cosmopolitan Production Dept. 45; The Hearst Corporation 81; International Business Machines 82; KCBS Newsradio (74) 50; KPIX Channel 5 176; Library of Congress 6, 41, 54, 65;76 National Archives 36, 43, 44, 49(b), 51,56, 57, 58, 93, 100, 111, 117, 118, 121, 125, 130, 132, 133, 143, 144, 151, 161; Radio Corporation of America 62, 76; Reader's Digest Association, Inc. 69; The San Francisco Academy of Comic Art 35, 39; San Simeon State Historical Monument 40; Statue of Liberty National Monument 37; Sears, Roebuck and Co. 108; Sony Electronics, Inc. 126; Turner Broadcasting Systems, Inc. 167; Jerry Vanicek 61; Washington Post 147, 148; Westinghouse Electric Corporation 63, 71, 134; Zenith Electronics Corporation 72, 77, 105, 109, 122, 171, 185, 186.

Media Table of Contents

Introduction 4

Chronology 7

Chapter I. 1900-1909 35
Sensationalism, Muckraking and Social Reform

Chapter II. 1910-1919 51
Tabloids, Radio and Global Politics

Chapter III. 1920-1929 63
Jazz Journalism, Radio and the News

Chapter IV. 1930-1939 77
The Great Depression, Scrutiny of the Press, Radio's Dominance and World War II

Chapter V. 1940-1949 93
The War Ends: Radio Wins, Newspapers Lose

Chapter VI. 1950-1959 109
The Golden Age of Television

Chapter VII. 1960-1969 125
Social Activism and Counterculture, TV's Effects and New Journalism

Chapter VIII. 1970-1979 143
Investigative Reporters and the Advent of Television News Programs

Chapter IX. 1980-1989 157
Scandals, Mergers, and Cable TV

Chapter X. 1990-1999 171
The Internet, the Decline of Newspapers and the Emergence of Full-Service Entertainment Conglomerates

Index 188

Introduction

"Media" is defined by *Webster's Collegiate Dictionary* as something in the middle position; a means of effecting or conveying something; a channel of communication, especially a means of disseminating ideas or advertising; and an intermediary. Look around. Media is everywhere— it's on supermarket shopping carts, on buses and taxis, freeway billboards, sports stadiums, the schoolroom, and more. **Media in the 20th Century** examines the history of communicating news and information through print, radio, television, and the internet, with the potential to be the most important means of mass communication in our century.

In the United States media is protected. The First Amendment to the Constitution, adopted in 1789, states: "Congress shall make no law respecting an establishment of religion, or prohibiting the free exercise thereof; or abridging the freedom of speech, or of the press; or the right of the people peaceably to assemble, and to petition the Government for a redress of grievances." At the dawn of the 20th century, media had already established itself as a key growth industry in the U.S.

The story of media begins with the journalists, the institutions and traditions they established, and the regulations they challenged and continue to challenge to protect the First Amendment.

The chapters of this book explore each of the ten decades of the 20th century. Each chapter discusses the prevalent forms of media at that time, their influence on public opinion, and the factors that influenced how they chose to cover stories. The book surveys landmark events in media history, the issues that made news, and the personalities that shaped and delivered it. We have included numerous examples of how major news events were covered and interpreted by reporters, editors, publishers, broadcasters, producers, and others in media.

Media reflects and influences the views of the nation. Each chapter has a unique focus and demonstrates how technology aided the growth of media, and the developing responsibility of media as public informants, to provide objective reporting. What you will also discover in the chapters is the

Stamp commemorating Horatio Alger

INTRODUCTION

influence of profit in the news and the power that advertisers held in shaping media.

Starting at the beginning of the century with the sensational yellow journalists and muckrakers, media asserted themselves as instigators of social reform. Reporters such as Ida Tarbell exposed the oil barons and others who monopolized business and drove people into bankruptcy. In the second decade, the newspaper *Pravda* played an integral role in influencing people in the Soviet Union to pursue a revolution. In America, media's influence over public opinion was decisive in gaining support for the U.S. to enter World War I. In the Twenties, the newspaper press was challenged by radio, which established itself as an expedient news and entertainment source. The press accepted the challenge of radio by turning toward more sensational news stories and creating the tabloid, a new form of news entertainment.

In the Thirties, President Franklin D. Roosevelt used the power of radio to reach a vast audience and promote his reforms. Radio continued to expand as it brought World War II directly into the living rooms of the American people. Reporters such as Edward R. Murrow traveled to remote locations in order to obtain first hand accounts and submit their reports directly to the public. Television became the dominant medium in the Fifties, as fears of a nuclear war and Communist invasion began to grip America. The combination of image and sound provided by television had a greater power over the public than the radio.

The Vietnam War was telecast live to the nation during the Sixties, bringing the sites and sounds of war to America. Protests, scandals, and tragedies were the focus of media coverage and television provided live sound and pictures of them. The press would face legal challenges while attempting to expose government corruption and deceit in the Seventies, and emerge victorious. Along with the conventional forms of print, radio, and television, media would expand to electronic forms, such as the Internet and the World Wide Web, in the Eighties and Nineties.

Throughout the century media has evolved in many ways. We are now able to receive news, information, and entertainment almost instantaneously as events occur. Unfiltered and live news from around the world is accessible to almost anyone. With the advent of cable television's 500 channels and the endless reaches of the Internet, media has developed into a truly large and powerful industry. At the dawn of the 21st century are we at information overload?

New York newsstand, 1903

MEDIA chronology of the 20th century

MEDIA IN THE 20th CENTURY

1900-1909

1900

Apr 14 — Millions of visitors attend the Paris Universal Exhibition in France. Among the innovations featured was a early "Cineorama" with 10 projectors displaying film images on a circular screen.

Dec — American electrical engineer Reginald Aubrey Fessenden transmits the first human voice by radio to a receiver a mile away.

♦ Eastman Kodak introduces the Brownie camera, making photography easy and cheap enough for almost everyone: The Brownie camera's six-exposure film sells for 10-15 cents.

♦ Italian physicist Guglielmo Marconi patented an invention allowing wireless telegraphy stations to operate on different wavelengths without interference.

1901

June 29 — Reacting to what he felt were press-agency abuses and bad advertising practices, James B. Shale began the magazine *Editor & Publisher* in New York City, New York.

July 1 — Adolph Ochs, American newspaper publisher, becomes the majority stock owner of the newspaper *New York Times*. He boosted its 9,000 circulation in 1896 to 466,000 before his death in 1935, and coined its motto "All the News That's Fit to Print."

Oct 20 — The *New York Times* newspaper celebrates its 50th anniversary.

Dec 12 — Italian wireless inventor Guglielmo Marconi sends and receives the letter "S" by wireless transmission across the Atlantic Ocean, from Poldhu station in Cornwall, England, to St. John's, Newfoundland, Canada.

1902

May 4 — New cartoon, Buster Brown, by Richard F. Outcault, debuts in the newspaper *New York Herald*. Together with his trusty dog Tiger, Buster Brown will become more popular than Outcault's previous strip, The Yellow Kid, a cartoon which derived its name from a sensationalist style of reporting.

1903

Jan 1 — The Pacific Cable line links San Francisco, California, with Honolulu, Hawaii.

Jan 19 — Wireless inventor Guglielmo Marconi sends the messages of American President Theodore Roosevelt to Great Britain's King Edward VII via wireless telegraphy.

Jan — Investigative journalists Lincoln Steffens, Ida Tarbell, and others gain national attention in the U.S. as they assail big business and political bosses with articles in *McClure's* magazine.

CHRONOLOGY

Feb 22 Guglielmo Marconi publishes the first newspaper at sea, in the middle of the Atlantic Ocean on the ship S.S. Cunard. The paper features news accounts transmitted from Britain by wireless telegraphy.

Feb *Ladies' Home Journal* becomes the first American magazine to reach a circulation of 1,000,000 in paid subscriptions.

Mar 2 Regular news service between New York City, New York and London, England is enacted through the use of the invention of Guglielmo Marconi's wireless telegraph.

Apr 1 *New York World* newspaper publisher Joseph Pulitzer agrees to donate $2 million to Columbia University in New York City, to endow a school of journalism.

July 4 The Pacific Cable links New York, to Manila, Philippines. American President Theodore Roosevelt sends a celebration message from Oyster Bay, New York, to Governor William Howard Taft in Manila, which circles the globe in 9.5 minutes.

Aug 15 Joseph Pulitzer confirms gift of $2 million to Columbia University to begin plans for its journalism school, which opened in 1912. Of the $2 million gift, $500,000 will be set aside to establish the Pulitzer Prizes for "prizes or scholarships for the encouragement of public service, public morale, American literature, and the advancement of education."

◆ Lawyer Charles L. Knight buys a part interest in the Ohio paper, *Akron Beacon Journal*, which will later merge with the Ridder newspapers to become the Knight-Ridder newspaper chain.

1904

Mar 22 First color photograph published in a newspaper. The honor belongs to the *Daily Illustrated Mirror* of London, England.

Dec 31 The newspaper giant *New York Times* opens its new building in downtown New York City.

1905

May 5 Publisher Robert S. Abbott begins the first African-American newspaper, the *Chicago Defender*, which sells for 2 cents. It will become a daily in 1956.

Dec 16 *Variety* magazine begins publishing weekly in New York City, under former Morning Telegraph newspaper editor Sime Silverman.

◆ The newspaper *New York Tribune* purchases the first typewriter for its newsroom.

◆ *New York Journal* newspaper publisher William Randolph Hearst purchases *Cosmopolitan* magazine for $400,000.

1906

Feb On assignment from a socialist weekly magazine, journalist Upton Sinclair's fact-based novel, *The Jungle*, a classic forerunner of investigative journalism, exposes U.S. meatpackers disregard for consumers' health. The Pure Food and Drug Act is enacted on June 30, 1906, as a result.

MEDIA IN THE 20th CENTURY

Apr 14   President Theodore Roosevelt makes his famous "men with the muckrakes" speech, quoting form the novel *Pilgrim's Progress* by John Bunyan at the Gridiron Club, in Washington, D.C., criticizing investigative and crusading journalists and publications for focusing too much on the negative.

Oct 17   Arthur Korn of Germany and a team of scientists successfully send a photographic image over 1,000 miles via telegraph wire. Korn terms the technique telephotography.

Nov 21   American inventor Reginald Fessenden sends the first voice radio transmission 11 miles, from Plymouth to Brant Rock, Massachusetts.

Dec 24   Inventor Reginald A. Fessenden broadcasts the first voice and music program from Brant Rock, Massachusetts. The broadcast of "O Holy Night" is received by ships within a several hundred-mile radius, including the West Indies.

◆   Thomas A. Edison invents the "cameraphone" for synchronization of photograph and projector.

◆   Lee De Forest invents the "triode," a three-element vacuum tube, the basic component of radio, which generates, detects, and amplifies electric signals.

1907

Oct 18   Wireless telegraphy service begins between the United States and Ireland.

1908

Jan 17   The tower for the newspaper *New York Times* picks up a wireless message from Puerto Rico.

Mar 29   Mutt and Jeff cartoon by Bud Fisher begins in the *San Francisco Examiner*. Mutt and Jeff is the first daily comic strip and features the same characters.

May 5   It is ruled by the a U.S. Circuit Court judge that moving pictures fall under copyright law, requiring royalties to be paid.

◆   The *Christian Science Monitor* newspaper begins publication in Boston, Massachusetts.

1909

Apr 9   Singer Enrico Caruso broadcasts from Metropolitan Opera House in New York to home of Lee De Forest, inventor of three-element tube which makes modern radio possible.

May 3   First wireless press message sent from New York City to Chicago.

◆   KCBS, regarded as the legitimate oldest radio station in the world, based in San Francisco, California, begins broadcasting.

◆   The first newsreels produced by the French film company Pathe-Journal are publicly displayed. By the start of World War II, soundbites of information, called the newsreel, consisting of unrelated news stories lasting several minutes, and shown between screenings of feature films, had spread to all the industrialized countries.

CHRONOLOGY

1910-1919

1910

May 18 — Noting the return of Halley's Comet, the Washington state newspaper *Seattle Post-Intelligencer* reports: "The comet came, the comet went and this old earth is no worse and no better and thus far no wiser."

♦ *Women's Wear Daily*, a New York fashion newspaper, begins publication.

1911

Nov 19 — New York receives wireless message from its inventor Guglielmo Marconi in Italy.

1912

Mar 16 — A speed record is set for wireless transmission, at 55 minutes from London to New York.

Apr 10 — First wireless message received on an airplane in London.

Apr 14 — The ship Titanic sinks on maiden voyage; young David Sarnoff, future president of Radio Corporation of America, receives the distress signal and relays it to other ships. Sarnoff remains on duty for 72 hours relaying names of the survivors.

May 5 — First legitimate, state-approved issue of *Pravda*, daily Russian newspaper founded by Vladimir I. Lenin, published with Joseph Stalin as its editor. Until 1991, when the Soviet Union collapsed, *Pravda* was the official publication of the Central Committee of the Communist Party, and was one of the most widely distributed newspapers in the world. The paper is still in existence.

1913

Dec 21 — First modern newspaper crossword puzzle, the "Word Cross," published in the *New York Herald Sunday* supplement. Within a decade, crossword puzzles appeared in most American newspapers.

♦ Type composing machines for newspapers are invented.

1914

July 28 — World War I officially begins. The press is forced to address censorship issues between its role as public informants and government imposed security measures.

Sep 5 — President Woodrow Wilson orders Navy to open wireless stations for use by European powers.

1915

May 13 — Headline in *The Rural Weekly*, a St. Paul, Minnesota, newspaper, reads: "Giant Liner Lusitania Torpedoed and Sent to Bottom by Germans; 1,149 Lose Lives."

MEDIA IN THE 20th CENTURY

1916

Aug 20 — *London Times* newspaper assails U.S. neutrality in war, stating it will cost the United States post war rights.

♦ — American illustrator, Normon Rockwell, belonging to no genre, begins painting everyday scenes of American life and people, from visiting the doctor to gathering at the local drugstore, for the covers of the magazine *Saturday Evening Post*.

1917

May — First Pulitzer Prizes awarded for biography, history, and journalism.

♦ — Scientist Frank Conrad builds radio station in Pittsburgh, Pennsylvania, with Westinghouse radio manufacturers, known as KDKA.

1918

Nov 11 — Official end of World War I with the Armistice.

♦ — Robert LeRoy Ripley begins Believe It or Not newspaper cartoon series in the newspaper *New York Globe*. The series will eventually be syndicated into 326 newspapers in 38 countries.

♦ — *Stars and Stripes*, the official armed forces newspaper, starts publishing.

1919

Aug 14 — *Chicago Tribune* newspaper found guilty of libel by calling car manufacturer Henry Ford an anarchist, but pays just six cents in damages.

Dec 19 — First official tabloid picture newspaper in the United States begins with the New York City *Illustrated Daily News*.

♦ — Pulp magazine *True Story*, known for providing sensational and scandalous stories, begins publication.

1920-1929

1920

Jan 5 — Radio Corporation of America is formed.

Aug 20 — Radio station 8MK in Detroit, Michigan, opens first daily broadcasting with the show "Tonight's Dinner."

Oct 27 — First licensed radio station is KDKA in Pittsburgh, Pennsylvania.

Nov 2 — First commercial radio station in U.S., KDKA in Pittsburgh, Pennsylvania, broadcasts the Harding-Cox presidential election results.

1921

Apr 11 — The first boxing match broadcast in U.S. (Johnny Ray vs. Johnny Dundee) marks the first sports radio coverage.

Chronology

Aug 3 — *Collier's* and *Harper's* magazines announce a merger intent, thought to be one of the largest in publishing history.

Nov 11 — President Warren G. Harding broadcasts the Armistice Day address on radio live from the Tomb of the Unknown Soldier in Washington, D.C.

1922

Feb 5 — *Reader's Digest* is first published as a monthly magazine by Lila and DeWitt Wallace in New York City.

Feb 8 — President Warren G. Harding has the first radio installed in the White House.

Aug 3 — WGY radio station in Schenectady, New York, makes first radio sound effect, two wood blocks slammed together to imitate door slamming.

Aug 28 — New York's station WEAF, owned by American Telephone & Telegraph Company, carries the first radio commercial, broadcast for a price of $100 for 10 minutes.

Dec 6 — Italian dictator Benito Mussolini threatens Italian newspapers with censorship if they keep on reporting false information.

1923

Mar — Two Yale University graduates, Henry R. Luce and Briton Hadden, start *Time*, a new weekly magazine; in early days, the magazine simply summarized news from the major wire services.

Nov 25 — Transatlantic radio broadcasting from England to the U.S. is established for first time.

◆ — President Calvin Coolidge addresses Congress; radio carries U.S. presidential message for the first time.

1924

Jan — *American Mercury* magazine begins publication under editor Henry L. Mencken.

Mar 7 — A milestone in radio broadcasting is achieved as signals form WJZ in New York travel 7,000 miles to San Francisco, California, and then to Manchester, England.

Apr 7 — Newark, New Jersey, radio station heard in Tokyo, Japan, 9,000 miles away.

July 31 — C.O. Johnson becomes the first to broadcast from bottom of the sea on station WIP.

1925

Feb 21 — First issue of the *New Yorker* magazine published.

Oct 25 — First television broadcast of moving images by inventor John L. Baird.

Nov 26 — The first regular network broadcasts begin, featuring radio variety shows originating from station WEAF in New York and carried by 21 National Broadcasting Corporation (NBC) affiliates.

MEDIA IN THE 20th CENTURY

1926

Jan	1	New York and London celebrate New Year together over the radio.
Apr	30	Picture service via radio opened between London and *New York Times*.
Sep	18	*New York Times* newspaper celebrates 75 years of publication.

1927

Jan	5	First underwater color photographs published by *National Geographic* magazine.
Jan	5	Fox Studios exhibits Movietone, a new invention synchronizing sound and motion pictures.
Feb	23	The Federal Board of Radio Control (later the Federal Communications Commission) begins to regulate the networks of radio stations.
Apr	7	Television successfully tested in New York.
May	22	Front page headline in *Nebraska State Journal*: "Lindbergh Is Lone Eagle of Air."
Sep	8	Television inventor John Baird sends own image from Leeds to London.
◆		The National Broadcasting Company (NBC) begins two radio networks.

1928

Jan		Television broadcast to home receivers is demonstrated by General Electric.
Feb	8	John Baird makes first overseas television broadcast from London to New York.
May	11	Schenectady, New York, station WGY offers the first scheduled television broadcasts on Tuesday, Thursdays and Fridays from 1:30 to 2:30 p.m.
July	3	Television set sells for $75.
◆		The Columbia Broadcasting System (CBS) network is founded by William S. Paley.

1929

June		Color television set demonstrated by Bell Labs.
Aug	22	WGY in Schenectady, New York, begins the first televised news broadcast.
Sep	2	Radio service opens between New York and Costa Rica.

1930-1939

1930

- ◆ Golden Age of Radio begins in U.S.
- ◆ AT&T commences the process toward the invention of the picture telephone.
- ◆ WZXBS, the CBS experimental TV station, begins operation with the first telecast of Felix the Cat.

CHRONOLOGY

1931

Feb 26 *New York World* newspaper sold to Scripps-Howard newspaper chain.

May 8 London transmits first overseas television broadcast.

1932

Mar 1 Charles A. Lindbergh Jr., the son of famous transatlantic aviator Charles Lindbergh, who made the first solo flight across the English Channel, is kidnapped. Media attention is rampant.

May 12 Charles Lindbergh Jr. found dead. This became one of the most famous cases of the era, sparking a number of "copycat" abductions; the intense media scrutiny prompted by Lindbergh's celebrity is blamed.

Aug 13 Wireless inventor Guglielmo Marconi successfully tests first short-wave radio in Rome.

Dec Popular newspaper columnist Walter Winchell moves his gossip column to the airwaves.

1933

Feb 17 *News-Week* magazine begins publication; name is later changed to *Newsweek*.

May 19 Exchange of correspondence in the pages of the *New York Times* between industrialist John D. Rockefeller Jr. and artist Diego Rivera, over a large mural Rockefeller had commissioned for the RCA Building.

Nov 1 Nazi party of Germany takes over Ulstein press, largest publishers in the German Republic.

◆ American inventor Edwin Armstrong invents FM (frequency modulation) radio, but its real future is 20 years away.

1934

◆ Associated Press, a universal news wire service, starts a photo wire service as well.

◆ Communications Act of 1934 creates Federal Communications Commission (FCC). The FCC regulates radio and television broadcasting in the United States.

1935

Dec 30 First Lady Eleanor Roosevelt begins syndicated column titled "My Day," for publication in newspapers six days a week.

◆ New York's WNEW is first music and radio news station.

◆ *Triumph of the Will*, the most controversial documentary ever made, features quick editing, camera movement, and a stirring film score to promote German leader Adolf Hitler.

MEDIA IN THE 20th CENTURY

1936

Dec 10   The *Washington Star* headline reads: "York to Become King as Edward Quits," with huge photo of George VI on front page."

Dec   Radio broadcast of abdication speech by King Edward VIII from the English crown, in order to marry American divorcee Wallis Simpson.

- *Life* magazine, featuring stunning photography, begins publication in U.S.
- Britain's government-run BBC becomes the second provider of regularly scheduled television programming.

1937

May 6   The explosion of the German zeppelin *Hindenburg* as it attempts to land in New Jersey is broadcast live over coast-to-coast radio.

1938

May 17   "Information Please" becomes the first panel quiz show on radio.

May 31   In London, England the BBC broadcasts "Spelling Bee," the first televised game show.

Oct 30   Orson Welles' radio version of the H.G. Wells story, *War of the Worlds*, terrifies listeners into believing that Martians are invading the United States, spreading panic in many areas.

- Television pioneer, inventor John Baird, demonstrates live TV in color.
- Edward R. Murrow of CBS World News begins his famous nightly news broadcasts, "This Is London," during World War II, broadcasting from the roof of the BBC London headquarters.

1939

Apr 30   Shortly before the world turns to war, the 1939 World's Fair, "Building the World of Tomorrow," opens in New York. Displays of technology include television.

Dec   President Franklin D. Roosevelt gives speech over nationwide radio decrying the Neutrality Act just passed by Congress, and the ban is soon lifted, allowing the U.S. to ship war supplies to the Allies.

- *Reader's Digest* magazine circulation reaches 8 million.
- Regular TV broadcasts begin in U.S., with 22 private, experimental stations providing programming.
- NBC's experimental television station in New York airs television's first commercial: sportscaster Red Barber pitched Proctor & Gamble soap and Wheaties cereal during a baseball game.
- To protest the Daughters of the American Revolution denial of African American Marian Anderson's access to Constitution Hall, Washington, Eleanor Roosevelt announces her resignation from the DAR in her syndicated newspaper column.

CHRONOLOGY

1940-1949

1940

Jan 5 — Demonstration of FM (frequency modulation) radio by Edwin H. Armstrong on station WIMOJ in Worcester, Massachusetts.

Mar 20 — RCA initiates a publicity campaign for television technology, which it hopes to implement by September.

Sep 4 — CBS (Columbia Broadcasting System) demonstrates the transmission of color television over station W2XAB in New York City, New York.

♦ Seeking to head off RCA's (Radio Corporation of America) attempts to force its specifications on the infant television industry, the FCC delays commercial broadcasts until all broadcasters reach agreement on U.S. television standards: 30 frames and 525 lines of resolution per second. FCC begins to develop television regulations.

1941

Jan 16 — FCC ruled that "the broadcaster cannot be an advocate," to prevent political bias by radio and television announcers in news reporting.

May 1 — Orson Welles stars in the title role of the classic movie *Citizen Kane*, loosely based on the life of newspaper publisher William Randolph Hearst. Welles demonstrated how idealism is corrupted by power. Offended, Hearst unsuccessfully attempted to prevent the movie's showing and refused to print reviews or advertisements for the film in any of his papers.

May 2 — An FCC study, "Report on Chain Broadcasting," addressed the problem of monopolies in radio station and network ownership.

May 3 — FCC establishes television standards for manufacturing and broadcasting.

May 5 — Pulitzer Prize given to *New York Times* newspaper for war reporting.

July 1 — Both CBS and NBC start transmitting commercial television programming, consisting of 15 hours per week of cartoons, sports, and news from New York City.

Dec 7 — Japan attacks Pearl Harbor, Hawaii, and radio is the first to announce the news, followed by the famous "a day that will live in infamy" radio speech by President Franklin Delano Roosevelt.

1942

Jan 15 — National Association of Broadcasters (NAB) distributes guidelines for reporting war news and information in its Code of Wartime Practices for American Broadcasters.

Feb 23 — FCC announces freeze on new radio and television licenses during the war to allow for the diversion of construction and electronic equipment to the military for the war effort.

♦ "Voice of America," radio program disseminating news around the world, begins broadcasting. Its purpose is to relay information overseas.

MEDIA IN THE 20th CENTURY

1943

May 10 — U.S. Supreme Court upholds the FCC's right to regulate broadcasting in *NBC v. the United States.*

◆ — Publication of several World War II journalists' accounts of the war, including Richard Tregaskis' *Guadalcanal Diary* and Ernie Pyle's *Here Is Your War.*

1944

June 6 — At 6:33 a.m. European Time, Berlin radio announces "bombardment in the port of Le Havre, France....The invasion has begun." Four minutes later, the Associated Press put the Berlin radio announcement on the wire.

June 6 — At 12:37 a.m. Eastern Standard Time, the Associated Press teletype bells go off throughout New York. At CBS radio, newscaster Ned Calmer announces, "We are interrupting this program to bring you a special bulletin.... the invasion of Western Europe has begun." At 11:15 p.m. EST, George Hicks' recording of live invasion footage is broadcast on the Blue Network (the future ABC) television station.

◆ — NBC presents first U.S. network nightly newscast.

1945

Apr 12 — President Franklin D. Roosevelt dies while in office; Vice President Harry S. Truman is sworn in. Roosevelt, the first U.S. president to use radio broadcasts extensively during his lifetime, received similar broadcast coverage of his death.

Oct — The U.S. government lifted its wartime ban on the manufacturing of new TV sets and the establishment of television stations.

◆ — The FCC allots 13 channels for television broadcasting.

◆ — NBC Blue officially becomes ABC network after the FCC's ruling requires NBC to divest one of the two networks.

1946

Mar 7 — The FCC defines appropriate public conduct for broadcasters, specifically limiting advertising obligations to any party or organization and political objectivity in its report entitled "Public Service Responsibility of Broadcast Licensees."

Apr 16 — The Lea Act is signed by President Harry Truman, restricting the legal control of the broadcast industry by the labor unions.

May 24 — Covering a major national railroad strike, the *New York Times* runs headlines: "Strike Halts Railroads, Paralyzes Nation, and Truman Calls Men to Return at Once, Will Use Army to Run Trains if They Do Not."

Aug 31 — *New Yorker* magazine publishes John Hersey's "Hiroshima."

1947

Nov 20 — NBC debuts "Meet the Press," a made-for-TV news conference. It will become the longest-running series of its type on network TV.

CHRONOLOGY

- The House Un-American Activities Committee (HUAC) charges the Hollywood Ten with contempt; portions of the hearings are televised.

1948

Apr 19 — Associated Press, worldwide news gathering agency, celebrates its 100th anniversary.

July — FCC freeze granting new television broadcast licenses due to mounting problems with interference among existing television stations. The hold on licenses will last almost four years.

Nov 2 — President Harry Truman surprisingly defeats Republican Thomas A. Dewey; *Chicago Daily Tribune* goes to press before all the results are in and puts out headline, "DEWEY DEFEATS TRUMAN."

- CBS begins nightly TV newscast.

1949

Jan 20 — First telecast of a presidential inauguration, as Harry S. Truman is sworn in as the 33rd president.

June 1 — The FCC issues the Fairness Doctrine, making broadcasters responsible for seeking out and presenting "all reasonable viewpoints" prior to editorializing, again addressing the concerns over bias or perceived bias in news presentation.

- Radio Free Europe begins broadcasting to East Germany, behind the Iron Curtain.
- Community Antenna Television, forerunner to cable, begins broadcasting.

1950-1959

1950

Apr 13 — FCC again warns radio broadcasters to present all sides of an issue prior to stating editorial positions; they have a "duty to seek out, aid and encourage the broadcast of opposing views."

Oct 11 — FCC approves color television broadcasting for CBS.

Nov 20 — CBS begins color television broadcasting.

Dec 12 — As the perceived threat of communism grows, CBS requests 2,400 employees to sign loyalty oaths to the United States.

- 101 television stations operating as the decade begins; estimated number of television sets worldwide is 3.1 million.
- Senator Joseph McCarthy warns of communists in the State Department and begins committee hearings, which are televised in part.

1951

May 1 — In Munich, Germany, the U.S. begins broadcasting Radio Free Europe, a neutral news broadcasting station, in the Eastern bloc.

Media in the 20th Century

May	2	The Radio Corporation of America (RCA) broadcasts color TV programs from the Empire State Building in New York.
May	28	U.S. Supreme Court supports CBS method for transmitting TV in full color.
June	3	RCA hands over tricolor TV technology to CBS.
June	25	Although the majority of black and white television sets cannot receive the CBS color broadcasts, CBS starts broadcasting commercial programming in color.
Oct	16	RCA demonstrates large-screen color TV.
Oct	31	British Princess Elizabeth and her husband, the Duke of Edinburgh, make an appearance on NBC television, in the first international telecast ever.
Nov	18	First transcontinental television premier of Edward R. Murrow's "See It Now."

1952

Jan		NBC introduces "The Today Show" to television viewers; it is the first and longest-running early-morning network show.
Apr	13	FCC lifts three-year ban on new TV stations, assigning 2,000 new licenses.
Apr	22	Millions view Nevada A-bomb blast on TV.
Sep	24	Over 55 million people watch Republican vice presidential nominee Richard M. Nixon deliver his famous "Checkers" speech on television.
◆		National Association of Radio and Television Broadcasters ratifies new Television Code, establishing guidelines of content. Nearly half the code is devoted to advertising.
◆		In response to protests about program content, a House subcommittee investigates "offensive" and "immoral" TV programs and touches on such topics as beer ads and dramas depicting suicides.

1953

Sep	27	AT&T has 41 new TV stations in 35 cities.
Nov	8	A photoengravers' 11-day strike in New York City shuts down newspaper production. It is the first time since 1778 the city has gone without a daily paper.
Nov	27	FCC rules that the maximum number of television stations one person or firm may have a financial interest in is five.
Dec	18	FCC rules that color TV can go on the air.

1954

Feb	6	U.S. TV stations total 360, with 231 opened in 1953.
Mar	25	RCA starts mass production of color TV with 12-inch screens for under $1000.
Apr	1	First H-bomb blast shown on TV.
Apr	22	Senator Joseph McCarthy, in televised hearings, seeks to prove Communist infiltration of the U.S. military; his conduct during the Army-McCarthy Hearings was later condemned by the Senate.

CHRONOLOGY

1955

Jan	19	President Dwight D. Eisenhower holds the first televised press conference and U.S. cabinet meeting.
Feb	22	*Kansas City Star* publishers are found guilty of attempting to monopolize advertising and press coverage in the Kansas City, Kansas, area and are convicted in a federal court.
Apr	6	After CBS radio prevents Zenith Radio Corporation from airing a Phonevision commercial (a subscription television service the networks oppose), Zenith withdraws its sponsorship of the "Omnibus" program and publicly rebukes CBS for unwarranted censorship.

1956

June	20	All of MGM (Metro-Goldwyn-Mayer) pre-1949 movies are released for television broadcast with one exception: *Gone With the Wind*.
Oct		NBC inaugurates a new era in TV journalism when Chet Huntley and David Brinkley co-anchor the "Huntley-Brinkley Report," a 15-minute news broadcast (later expanded to half hour). The pair soon became TV's first superstar newsmen.
Nov		Television broadcasts the first commercial videotape on "Douglas Edwards with the News" on CBS.
♦		First transatlantic telephone cable links Oban, Scotland with Sydney Mines, Nova Scotia.

1957

Jan	4	The ethical-production code of the National Association of Radio and Television Broadcasters is adopted by the Alliance of Television Film Producers.
May	19	CBS airs documentary on Cuban revolution with interview of President Fidel Castro.
May		*Variety* magazine reports that during a typical week viewers encounter 420 commercials totaling 5 hours 8 minutes.
♦		Arkansas Governor Orval Faubus calls up the National Guard to keep black students out of Central High in Little Rock; President Eisenhower sends in federal troops to enforce desegregation. Televised accounts of the event are given.

1958

Jan	13	The *Daily Worker*, a Communist paper published in the U.S., shuts down.
Mar	3	FCC scandal: member Richard Mack resigns after admitting he received loans and gifts of stock from a friend who hoped to be awarded a valuable Miami television channel.
May	24	United Press merges with International News Service to form United Press International (UPI).
Oct	11	FCC gives new interpretation to "equal time" provision: radio and television must now include all legally qualified political candidates.

Media in the 20th Century

Oct 16   The NBC quiz show "Twenty-One" comes under grand jury investigation for manipulating contest results, and advertisers remove their sponsorship of the program.

◆   Edward R. Murrow writes in *TV Guide* that viewers must recognize "television is being used to distract, delude, amuse and insulate us."

1959

July 28   Addressing the new FCC guideline regarding equal air time for all political candidates, the Senate passes a bill exempting radio and television news shows from the FCC requirement if any one of them are included in a broadcast.

Oct 6   Investigation of television quiz shows begins under the auspices of the Special House Subcommittee on Legislative Oversight.

Nov 3   Latin bandleader Xavier Cugat testifies under oath that while a contestant on CBS's "$64,000 Question" quiz show, he received the questions and answers prior to filming the program.

◆   *Explorer VI*, a U.S. satellite, transmits the first TV pictures of Earth from space.

1960-1969

1960

Sep 26   The first of four presidential debates between candidates Senator John F. Kennedy (Democrat) and current Vice President Richard M. Nixon (Republican) are broadcast on national TV, watched by the largest audience yet measured. Television viewers believed Kennedy won the debates, yet radio listeners largely believed Nixon won.

◆   Federal law prohibiting quiz-show rigging passed.

1961

Jan 10   New FCC chairman Newton N. Minow is appointed.

Jan 25   Presidential press conference televised live for first time.

Mar 9   *Newsweek* magazine is purchased by the Washington Post Company.

May 9   FCC Chairman Newton N. Minow delivers a speech in which he denounces U.S. TV as a "vast wasteland," calling for heightened federal regulation. The same day, politician Hubert H. Humphrey calls U.S. TV the "greatest single achievement in communication that anybody or any area of the world has ever known."

◆   FCC approves FM stereo broadcasting, spurs FM radio development.

1962

Jan 5   The newspapers *Los Angeles Daily Mirror* and *Los Angeles Examiner* fold.

Feb 14   First Lady Jackie Kennedy leads a CBS-televised tour of the recently renovated White House.

CHRONOLOGY

Feb	20	Anchor Walter Cronkite of CBS leads the news coverage of American astronaut John Glenn making the first Earth orbit.
Apr	16	Walter Cronkite first appears as the television anchor of CBS "Evening News" a position he held until 1980, emerging as the most influential television news caster of his time.
May	1	Public TV receives $32 million federal funding.
July	1	Communications satellite *Telstar I* is launched successfully and passes its first communications test: a broadcast between the U.S. and Europe.
July	11	*Telstar I* sends the first worldwide television program.
◆		WBAI is the first television station to publicly broadcast former FBI agent Jack Levin's expose of J. Edgar Hoover and the FBI. The program is followed by threats of arrests and bombings as well as pressure from the FBI, the Justice Department and major broadcast networks.
◆		The "Tonight Show," a nightly entertainment news talk show with host Johnny Carson premiers.

1963

June	26	"Ich bin ein Berliner," speech by President John F. Kennedy in West Berlin is televised, with Kennedy pledging American support in defending the city from communism while aiding in the reunification of Germany and Europe.
Mar	31	New York City papers resume printing after a 114-day strike. It was estimated that the economic losses in circulation and advertising totaled between $190 million and $250 million.
Aug	28	Millions watch the peaceful civil rights demonstration march upon Washington, D.C. led by the Reverend Martin Luther King Jr. He gives his famous speech "I Have a Dream" to the 200,000 people gathered there.
Sep	2	CBS and NBC television newscasts expand from 15 to 30 minutes, in color.
Oct	16	The newspaper *New York Mirror* folds.
Nov	22	The assassination of President John F. Kennedy. Television showed the president slumping in his convertible Lincoln Continental. Lee Harvey Oswald is arrested 80 minutes later and charged with killing patrolman J.D. Tippit. Total print and broadcast media blanket the country with coverage and commentary on the assassination and funeral for four days. The shared assassination experience by a nation marks the dominance of television as the preferred media for news information.
Nov	24	Millions of television viewers watch in shock as alleged assassin of President Kennedy, Lee Harvey Oswald, is shot to death by Dallas, Texas, nightclub owner Jack Ruby as Oswald is transported from the Dallas jail to safer quarters.
Dec		TV surpasses newspapers as an information source for first time: a November Roper Poll indicates 36% of Americans find TV a more reliable news source, compared with 24% who favor print.
◆		First transatlantic telephone cable links Tuckerton, New Jersey and Cornwall, England.

Media in the 20th Century

1964

Feb 9 — Appearance of the Beatles musical group on the nightly television "Ed Sullivan Show" (the beginning of the British music invasion); 73 million viewers tune in.

Mar 9 — In *New York Times v. Sullivan*, the U.S. Supreme Court rules that a public official alleging libel by a newspaper must prove that the libelous statements were made with "actual malice," not merely that the statements were false, overturning a previous ruling. This extended the guaranteed protection and freedom of the press under the First Amendment, preventing libel suits caused by honest errors. The Court defined malice as "with knowledge that (the defamatory statement) was false or with reckless disregard of whether it was false or not."

Aug 7 — Congress authorizes presidential action in Vietnam by passing the Tonkin Gulf Resolution; soon after, President Johnson orders the bombing of North Vietnam. The first anti-war demonstrations begin. After U.S. ground troops land in Vietnam in 1965, the first "televised" war coverage will also cover anti-war demonstrations, continuing the Fairness Doctrine policy of equal time for opposing political groups.

Sep — The first network station to broadcast over 50% of its programming in color is NBC.

1965

Feb 1 — Peter Jennings debuts as anchor for ABC's evening news program.

Apr 6 — World's first working commercial communications satellite, the *Early Bird*, orbits above the Atlantic. The planet's first commercial satellite, *Early Bird* relays telephone messages and television programs between Europe and the United States, beginning a new era of global space communications.

Oct 24 — The first network to offer a consistent 30-minute newscast every evening is NBC.

◆ — International Telephone and Telegraph (ITT) acquires the American Broadcasting Company (ABC), in major communications merger.

1966

Jan 1 — Changes at NBC: president Robert Kinter steps down, David Sarnoff relinquishes daily management of RCA, and later this year NBC leads the switch to full color television programming, marketing itself as "The Full Color Network."

Aug 15 — The *New York Herald Tribune* newspaper ceases publication.

1967

Jan 9 — ABC finally transitions to a 30-minute news program, becoming the last major network to do so.

Jan — The first coast-to-coast educational programming is broadcast from National Educational Television station.

CHRONOLOGY

May 5   The *New York World Journal Tribune* ceases publication, leaving New York with just three regular dailies, the *Times, Daily News*, and *Post*. Management claims the shutdown is due to union pressure to maintain 500 unnecessary employees.

Nov   U.S. Congress establishes the Corporation for Public Broadcasting (CPB) to provide financial support for educational and noncommercial television and radio broadcasting. The Public Broadcasting System is established as well.

1968

Apr 4   Escaped convict James Earl Ray arrested for assassinating civil rights leader and non-violence advocate Reverend Martin Luther King, Jr. in Memphis, Tennessee; race riots break out in over 100 cities. Chicago's Mayor Daley authorizes police to "shoot to kill." The results are: 46 deaths, 55,000 federal troops and National Guardsmen mobilized, and 21,270 arrests made in the post-assassination fallout. The events are televised.

Apr 25   A militant group of Columbia University students seize five university buildings to protest and halt the construction of a new gymnasium in an area they feel is better served by low-cost housing. The students' demands are televised. After five days of the sit-in and random property destruction, police swarm in on April 30, arresting 628.

Sep 14   The weekly news program "60 Minutes," featuring Dan Rather, Harry Reasoner, Morley Safer, and Mike Wallace, begins on CBS.

Oct 13   First live space broadcast is from *Apollo VII*.

◆   Anti-war protesters clash with Chicago police in televised demonstrations during the Democratic National Convention.

◆   Feminists crash the televised Miss America Pageant, tossing bras and stenography pads into freedom trash cans and proclaiming Women's Liberation.

1969

Jan 10   The *Saturday Evening Post* suspends publication.

July 20   American Astronaut Neil Armstrong becomes the first man to walk on the Moon; 100 million viewers worldwide watch live TV broadcast from the Moon; Astronauts also send back live photographs. Armstrong's famous first words were actually, "That's one small step for a man, one giant leap for mankind." The July 21, 1969 *New York Times* newspaper quoted Armstrong as "one small step for man, one giant leap for mankind."

Apr   U.S. forces in Vietnam peak at 543,000; My Lai incident raises the issue of American atrocities. Nightly broadcasts of war scenes, including the carrying of body bags, are largely viewed as helping the anti-war movement.

◆   Public Broadcasting begins in November and launches the children's educational program "Sesame Street."

◆   Pacifica is the only news organization willing to break *New York Times* story by reporter Seymour Hersh of the My Lai massacre in Vietnam.

MEDIA IN THE 20th CENTURY

1970-1979

1970

Jan 26 — Ted Turner purchases his first independent television station, WTCG, which will later be named after its owner, WTBS (Turner Broadcasting System). By 1978, WTBS will be a superstation valued at over $40 million.

Feb — The Chicago 7 are found not guilty of rioting at the televised 1968 Democratic National Convention.

Mar — The FCC forbids one entity from owning both radio and television stations in the same market.

May 2 — The state of Mississippi's educational television stations ban the children's program "Sesame Street" due to its racial content.

May 4 — The National Guard, called out to quell student demonstrations, panic and open fire, killing four anti-war protesters at Kent State University in Ohio. The event is headlined in newspapers around the country.

Aug 14 — FCC orders prime time television coverage to be allotted to critics of the Vietnam War.

Oct 5 — PBS (Public Broadcasting System) supersedes the older NET (National Education Television).

♦ — FCC enacts the Financial Interest and Syndication Rules prohibiting the three major networks from owning and controlling the rebroadcast of prime time shows.

♦ — NBC's "Huntley-Brinkley Report," an American institution in news and rivaled only by CBS's "Evening News" with Walter Cronkite, goes off the air after 14 years.

1971

Jan 2 — Cigarettes can no longer be advertised on radio or television as the 1969 Public Health Cigarettes Smoking Act is enforced.

June 6 — After 23 years, the "Ed Sullivan Show," a entertainment talk show program (originally "Toast of the Town"), is canceled.

June 15 — The *New York Times* publishes a series on the "Pentagon Papers," classified documents outlining the history of U.S. involvement in Southeast Asia from World War II to 1969. A court injunction was immediately filed by the Justice Department citing concerns over national security.

June 30 — The Supreme Court ruled that the Freedom of the Press was more important than government embarrassment and permission to continue publishing the "Pentagon Papers" series was granted.

1972

Feb — New FCC rules require community and public access channels in the 100+ existing cable markets.

May 1 — *New York Times* wins Pulitzer Prize for publishing the "Pentagon Papers."

CHRONOLOGY

July		*Ms.* magazine is founded; investigative journalist and feminist Gloria Steinem is editor and former *Look* editor Patricia Carbine is publisher.
Sep		Reporters of the *Washington Post* Bob Woodward and Carl Bernstein write that CREEP aides control a secret fund, showing withdrawls by Jeb Magruder and Herbert L. Porter and that Attorney General John Mitchell controls the fund.
Oct	10	*Washington Post* Watergate story opens with: "F.B.I. agents have established that the Watergate bugging incident stemmed from a massive campaign of political spying and sabotage conducted on behalf of President Nixon's reelection and directed by officials of the White House and the Committee for the Re-Election of the President."
Nov	8	HBO (Home Box Office) starts pay TV service for cable, with 365 Pennsylvanian subscribers.
♦		Under Open Skies treaty, any U.S. firm can have communication satellites.
♦		President Nixon goes to China; historic meeting which results in normalization of U.S. and China relations is televised.

1973

May	7	*Washington Post* honored for its controversial and ground-breaking coverage of the Watergate scandal.
May	17	The Senate Watergate Hearings begin. Together, ABC, NBC, and CBS offer almost 300 hours of rotating coverage, estimated to have cost a combined total of $10 million in lost ad revenues and air time.
Oct	20	President Nixon discharged Special Prosecutor Archibald Cox when he asked for the tapes of conversations between Nixon and his aides. (Some tapes are claimed "missing" and others have large gaps of blank recording space.)

1974

Mar	4	*People* magazine, focusing on the lives of celebrities, is first published.
Mar	4	The Supreme Court rules that cable television providers may legally pick up long-distance television signals and offer them to paid customers, without fear of violating copyright law.
Mar	16	American daily newspapers increased total circulation by 600,000 during 1973, according to *Editor and Publisher* magazine.
Aug	6	The *Philadelphia Enquirer* headline reads: "Nixon Admits Serious Omission in Withholding Key Evidence," while the *Chicago Daily News* headlines are: "I won't quit, Nixon vows. Let impeachment process continue."
Aug	8	The *Chicago Daily News* reports in huge headline: "Nixon to Quit!" and in smaller type: "President Goes on TV at 8 p.m."
Aug	8	The U.S. House Judiciary Committee votes to impeach President Richard Nixon, who then resigns publicly over television.
Aug	9	The *Washington Post* headline reads simply, "Nixon Resigns," in large banner type; The *Washington Star News* headline states: "Nixon Bids Tearful Farewell to White House; Ford Becomes President."

Media in the 20th Century

Sep	9	The *Atlantic City Press* features the following headline in huge letters: "Nixon Pardoned," with accompanying article, "Nixon Admits He Was Wrong."
Nov	30	Ridder Publications and Knight Newspapers merge, creating a 36-newspaper chain covering sixteen states.
♦		*Washington Post* reporters Carl Bernstein and Bob Woodward publish *All the President's Men*, an account of the Watergate scandal that was covered in depth by the journalists.

1975

Apr	9	Family viewing time is incorporated into National Association of Broadcasters (NAB) TV code. It was decided that the time before 9:00 p.m. was supposed to be devoted to all members of the household.
♦		Comedian George Carlin's "seven dirty words you can't say on television" routine broadcast by WBAI in New York leads to several First Amendment litigation and a hearing by the U.S. Supreme Court. The Carlin case sets the limit of broadcasting for over a decade.

1976

Jan	5	PBS offers a new in-depth news program called "The Robert MacNeil Report," which will become "The MacNeil-Lehrer Report" later the same year.
July	10	Showtime, another cable network, debuts.
Nov	3	Americans watch the first "Good Morning America" program, a daily morning news talk show on ABC.
♦		Ted Turner, owner of the Cable News Network, CNN, a 24 hour news television station delivers programming nationwide by satellite.
♦		Barbara Walters becomes first U.S. woman news anchor for major network in $1-million deal.

1977

Feb	7	FCC forbids the direct marketing of Spiderman vitamins to children via television advertising.
Feb		A Mississippi minister, Rev. Donald Wildmon, and his grass-roots protest group, American Family Association, organized a national Turn Off TV Week.
Mar	5	President Jimmy Carter tries to reach the American people by hosting a national call-in interview show on radio.
Apr		Debut of the Christian Broadcasting Network (CBN).
Sep		Cable television debuts another new station: USA Network.

1978

Jan	1	The Copyright Act of 1976 takes effect, which means programs may now be copyrighted and Cable TV may purchase secondary rights for programs they send to subscribers.

CHRONOLOGY

Mar	6	During an obscenity trial for material in his brazenly pornographic magazine, *Hustler*, Larry Flynt is shot in Lawrenceville, Georgia. Flynt will be permanently paralyzed as a result of the shooting.
July	3	Continuing the legal saga of the public radio broadcast of comedian George Carlin's "Seven dirty words you can never say on television," the U.S. Supreme Court rules that the FCC can ban or censor language that is not legally obscene.
Sep	25	U.S. District Court Judge Constance Baker Motley rules that baseball teams cannot legally bar a female sportswriter from the locker room, bringing resolution to the suit filed by *Sports Illustrated* reporter Melissa Ludtke.
Nov	1	National Public Radio introduces "Morning Edition" with Bob Edwards as host. PBS goes to satellite for delivery, abandoning telephone lines.

1979

Mar		C-SPAN (Cable Satellite Public Affairs Network) is established by the U.S. House of Representatives, and televises actual sessions in chambers.
Apr		Nickelodean, a network featuring children's programming, begins broadcasting on cable television.
Sep	25	ABC wins the network bidding war to broadcast the 1984 Summer Olympics at a cost of $225 million.
♦		ESPN, a total sports network, makes its debut on cable.
♦		Pacific League of Women Voters and Congressman Henry Waxman challenge the constitutionality of prohibiting the editorializing of news by noncommercial broadcasters.

1980-1989

1980

June	1	Ted Turner's Cable News Network (CNN), the first U.S. 24-hour news channel, begins broadcasting with TV's two major sponsors: Proctor & Gamble and General Foods.
July	2	The U.S. Supreme Court rules that both the media and public may attend criminal trials in *Richmond Newspapers vs. Virginia*.
Aug	1	MTV makes its cable debut in August, featuring blocks of 1 to 2 hours of rock and roll music videos, repeated throughout the day.
Oct	14	A new law was signed by President Jimmy Carter, making unannounced searches of newsrooms illegal, with exceptions for special circumstances.

MEDIA IN THE 20th CENTURY

1981

Jan 20 — Hours after President Ronald Reagan's inauguration, the 52 remaining diplomats held hostage are released by Iran after 444 days, at a cost of $8 billion in Iranian assets. The events of the kidnapping and the release of the hostages were continuously televised and thought to have prevented the reelection of President Jimmy Carter.

Mar 6 — CBS news anchor Walter Cronkite retires after 19 years; Dan Rather replaces him.

Apr 15 — *Washington Post* acknowledges story about eight-year-old heroin addict that won Pulitzer Prize was faked by reporter Janet Cooke.

1982

Aug 16 — The *Saturday Review* (critiquing art and literature) ceases to exist.

Sep 15 — Gannett's national daily newspaper, *USA Today*, debuts. Featuring shorter articles and high graphics content, including weather maps and charts, other newspapers will eventually adopt some of its style. Type is set in regional plants by satellite command.

Sep — General William C. Westmoreland sues CBS for $120 million for libeling him in a documentary on the Vietnam War.

Nov 20 — ABC broadcasts "The Day After," a two-hour made-for-TV film about the after-effects of a nuclear war between U.S. and Russia.

1983

Dec — Chicago residents can now talk in their automobiles using cellular phones for a cost of $3,000 for the unit, plus $150 per month.

◆ *Time* magazine names the personal computer as Man of the Year.

◆ Journalist Seymour Hersh publishes *The Price of Power: Kissinger in the Nixon White House*.

◆ Tom Brokaw named news anchor at NBC; Peter Jennings takes a position as a news anchor at ABC.

1984

Jan 17 — The U.S. Supreme Court rules that home videotaping of movies is not an infringement of copyright law; VCR makers rejoice and film makers despair.

Jan 24 — Apple Computer introduces the Macintosh computer with a 60-second commercial based on the novel *1984* by George Orwell created by Chiat/Day advertising agency beginning an era of advertising as news.

1985

Feb — General Westmoreland drops his libel lawsuit against CBS.

Mar 18 — Capital Cities buys ABC for $3.5 billion.

Mar — Newhouse Publications purchases the *New Yorker* magazine for $142 million.

CHRONOLOGY

July	19	The FCC's "must carry" clause, which requires cable systems to carry community broadcasting, are ruled a violation of the First Amendment by the U.S. Court of Appeals.
Dec		RCA and NBC are acquired by General Electric at a cost of $6.3 billion.
◆		U.S. TV networks begin satellite distribution to affiliates.
◆		Capital Cities acquires ABC network for $3.43 billion.
◆		Australian entrepreneur Rupert Murdoch buys seven TV stations and 20th Century Fox movie studio; plans to start Fox network.

1986

May	8	Oliver North, former official of the National Security Office, testifies before congressional committee investigating the Iran-Contra scandal. Ollie is a hit on television, and receives thousands of letters and telegrams of support, even though North admitted lying to Congress.
Sep	29	The Soviet Union released Nicholas Daniloff, an American journalist held for a month on spying charges.
◆		A fourth major television network in the U.S., Fox Network, begins telecasts.

1987

Mar	13	A $2 million libel judgment against the *Washington Post* newspaper is reversed upon appeal.
Sep	24	A.C. Nielsen Company updates its methods for recording viewer habits: push-button "people meters" replace the decades-old diary system.
◆		Jim Baker's TV ministry is brought down after sexual and financial scandals come to light.

1988

Feb	24	The U.S. Supreme Court rules that pornographic magazine *Hustler's* satirical portrayals of the Reverend Jerry Falwell fall under protection of freedom of speech, per the First Amendment.
Apr	13	French publisher S.A. Hachette's purchases Diamantis Communications, Inc., and becomes the largest magazine publisher on the planet, with 75 periodicals in 10 countries.
May	17	The first American company to purchase advertising air time in Russia is Pepsico.
Aug	7	Triangle Publications, which includes *Seventeen* magazine and *TV Guide*, is sold to Rupert Murdoch for $3 billion.

1989

June	6	Chinese students' month-long demonstrations against the Communist government end in bloodshed when Deng Xiaoping deploys soldiers who fire AK-47 assault rifles into the crowds, killing hundreds. China can no longer hide from the power of TV media to inform the world.

Media in the 20th Century

Nov 2 — After 86 years, the *Los Angeles Herald Examiner* stops publication.

♦ Time-Life, Inc. and Warner Communications merge in $11.7 billion deal, making Time Warner the largest communications company in the U.S.

1990 - 1999

1990

Feb 12 — *Entertainment Weekly* is launched by Time Warner who spend $150 million to ensure the publication's success.

Feb 24 — The Cable News Network, CNN, dominates news coverage worldwide during the Persian Gulf War. The high-tech war known as Operation Desert Storm is followed by millions on television.

♦ The Children's Television Act takes effect limiting the amount of commercials in children's TV programming.

♦ U.S. spacecraft *Voyager I* sent back the first photographs of the entire solar system. *Voyager II* flew by Saturn, sending back pictures of its rings.

1991

Mar 6 — Amateur videotape of motorist Rodney King being beaten by Los Angeles police officers was aired repeatedly worldwide, increasing awareness of racial problems in large urban areas.

June 21 — The U.S. Supreme Court rules 5-4 that communities may prohibit totally nude dancing without violating the First Amendment by enacting laws requiring dancers to at least wear G- strings.

Aug — Collapse of Russian anti-Gorbachev plot, to rid the country of its president, is aided by distribution of information through global computer system called the Internet.

Sep 16 — Lieutenant Colonel Oliver North is acquitted of any wrongdoing in the Iran-Contra affair.

Oct 11-12 — Televised Senate hearings to confirm Clarence Thomas' nomination to the Supreme Court include testimony from Professor Anita Hill that Thomas sexually harassed her eight years ago, while he was her boss at the EEOC.

1992

Apr 17 — After four Los Angeles police officers are acquitted of all charges but one in the videotaped beating of black motorist Rodney King, massive rioting breaks out all over the city. Televised coverage of looting show lack of police response in the early hours of the riot.

Aug 4 — Sgt. Stacey Koon and Officer Laurence Powell were convicted and sentenced to 2 years in prison for their roles in the Rodney King beating. No riots result.

♦ Cable TV revenues reach $22 billion annually.

CHRONOLOGY

1993

Feb 28 — Four federal agents are killed and more than a dozen injured in a raid on religious cult compound in Waco, Texas. The televised 51-day standoff ends when the compound burns to the ground, killing more than 80 cult members. Media coverage on television is dramatic.

Sep 30 — According to the 1994 *Editor & Publisher International Yearbook*, the top three newspapers in the country are: the *Wall Street Journal* (New York, NY) with a circulation of 1,818,562; *USA Today* (Arlington, VA), daily circulation, 1,494,929; and the *New York Times* (New York, NY), with a total circulation of 1,141,366.

Oct 1 — For a price of $1.1 billion, the *New York Times* purchased the *Boston Globe* newspaper.

◆ Consumer demand begins for V chip to block out violent programming.

1994

May — According to Nielsen Media Research, 98% of all American households own at least one TV (approximately 94.2 million homes). Of those households, 99% are color sets, 38% own two or more sets; 28% have three or more sets; 63% received at least basic cable, 28% received pay cable and 79% owned VCRs.

June 17 — Football legend, actor and broadcaster O.J. Simpson is arrested as the primary suspect in the brutal murders of his ex-wife Nicole Brown and her friend Ronald Goldman. The incident throws media coverage into overdrive, as 95 million viewers watch at least some of the televised 90-minute slow-speed freeway chase. The televised criminal trial during 1995 was a much-watched event.

July — Disney announces plan to purchase Capital Cities and ABC; Westinghouse Electric Corporation states its intention to purchase CBS.

◆ After 25 years, U.S. government privatizes Internet management.

1995

Sep 22 — Time Warner and Turner Broadcasting announce their plans to merge. Plans to create the world's largest media company will have to first prove the merger will not constitute a monopoly.

◆ Two major U.S. dailies now offer online newspapers via the Internet, namely *USA Today* and the *Wall Street Journal*.

◆ Republican Lamar Alexander chooses the Internet to announce presidential candidacy.

1996

Oct — Presidential candidate Bob Dole encourages voters to access his Web site at the close of the televised presidential debates by giving out the Web site address to viewers.

Dec — The Distilled Spirits Council of the United States announces it will lift the voluntary ban on radio and television liquor advertising in order to compete with wine- and beer-makers.

Media in the 20th Century

◆ All major, and even some minor, candidates for U.S. president publish home pages on the World Wide Web, in a continuing attempt to sidestep mainstream media and deliver information directly to the public.

1997

Jan 27 "Fear and Favor in the Newsroom" airs on public television channel 54, KTEH San Jose, California, after being rejected by other major PBS (Public Broadcasting System) channels. The documentary covers the influence of conglomerates and large corporations in media and advertising.

Jan 31 *USA Today* publishes its survey results of 534 sixth through 12th grade students: while the majority recognized and liked several image advertising campaigns, their feelings did not automatically result in brand usage.

Jan Major network and cable channels introduce a seven-tiered self-labeled rating system. Noted non-participants are BET (Black Entertainment Network), which waits for a better system, and HBO (Home Box Office), which elects to maintain its current 10-label system, which is based on content, not an overall "grade."

Feb 4 O.J. Simpson is found liable for the deaths of his ex-wife Nicole Brown Simpson and her friend Ronald Goldman in a non-televised civil trial. Media coverage after the verdict was announced was extensive.

Apr 30 The television show "Ellen" aired starring Ellen DeGeneres, the first openly gay lead character.

May 1 Television anchor Carol Marin resigns from her position at WMAQ, criticizing the station for hiring talk show host Jerry Springer to do daily commentaries.

May 12 Jerry Springer resigns from his position as daily commentator at WMAQ-TV.

July 4 Live pictures from Mars are televised from Pathfinder Mission.

July 10 Rating System for TV shows proposed to provide more information to parents on contents of programs. All networks and cable, with the exception of NBC, agree to comply.

MEDIA
chapter 1
1900-1909
Sensationalism, Muckraking & Social Reform

New York Journal cover featuring the Yellow Kid

Media in the 20th Century

As the new century dawned, the media consisted primarily of newspapers and various periodicals. The newspaper industry packaged news, entertainment, and advertising into one paper, not divided into special sections like it is today. Newspaper and magazine reporters were limited to covering local and regional news. At that time there were no extensive communication systems like we have today. Special-interest stories, such as the outbreak and progress of a war or exposés on government and business, were usually assigned to in-house reporters who would be sent on location to conduct research and interviews. They would either telegraph pieces of the story to their home office where the stories were fully written and printed, or wait until their return to write a full account themselves.

Reporters were sometimes assigned not only to report the news, but to create news. In 1889, *New York World* reporter Elizabeth Cochrane (pen name Nellie Bly) was assigned to meet or beat the fictional record of Phileas Fogg in Jules Verne's book *Around the World in 80 Days*. Starting and ending in New Jersey, she achieved her goal in 72 days, 6 hours and 11 minutes via train, rickshaw, sampan and steamship. She wrote about her adventures in her column at the *World*. In 1896, William Randolph Hearst, early in his publishing career, dispatched a group of reporters and artists on his personal yacht, the *Buccaneer*, to Cuba to report on the landing of Spain's troops there. Inconclusive reports which prematurely laid blame on Spain for the sinking of the American ship *USS Maine*, were telegraphed to New York and printed. The story supposedly contributed to the outbreak of the Spanish American War in 1898.

Media in the first decade of the 20th century became a big business in America, as did other industries such as coal, oil, steel and railroads. The jobs created by these growing industries brought in millions of new immigrants, many of whom spoke little or no English, and depended on the daily penny papers to learn the language, customs and important issues pertaining to their new homes. Cities such as New York, Chicago and Philadelphia rushed to accommodate the 9 million new immigrants who arrived between 1900 and 1910. They hastily erected cold-water temporary tenements to house the new working class. In 1900 the second largest city in the world was New York City, with 3.5 million people. London, England, was the largest with 4,537,000 people.

The *New York Journal*

1900-1909

Publishers saw the opportunity to profit with the sale of newspapers and magazines to the new population. As a big business, their goal was profit. The news they provided was secondary. Emphasis was placed on the stories that would sell papers. The newspapers available at the time, like the *New York World* published by Joseph Pulitzer, were largely dependent on sales to maintain the business. Newspapers were comprised of only one section with an average of twelve pages. The pages were visually crowded with a variety of stories written in simple language, usually pertaining to local government and business issues. Simple line drawings illustrated major stories, usually on the front page. Exciting headlines were usually centered above the story, with one sentence immediately below that explained the headline. For example, a *New York World* front-page story on January 1, 1900, stated, "Pink Bows Shocked Old Union Leaguers," which was followed by the explanation "Violet Dale Wore 'em and She Sang a Song That Startled Staid Brooklyn Clubmen" at the annual vaudeville show.

Magazine and newspaper publishers derived most of their profits from two sources: newspaper sales and advertising. Advertisers had the power to influence the extent of information printed about products that may have been the topic of controversy. Similarly, the style and content of articles printed influenced the ways advertisers marketed their products.

Like other industries such as coal and steel, the newspaper business attracted self-educated youth from poor families. During the first decade of the 20th century, printing and reporting was considered a grubby, dead-end job.

PULITZER PRIZES

Pulitzer Prizes in journalism are awarded annually to American reporters, cartoonists and photographers and news organizations by the president of Columbia University, New York. The Pulitzer Prize Board makes recommendations for all categories of work done during the preceding year. Categories are: Meritorious Public Service, Reporting, Criticism or Commentary, National Reporting, International Reporting, Correspondence, Editorial Writing, Editorial Cartooning, Spot News Photography, Feature Photography, Special Citation, Feature Writing, Explanatory Journalism and Specialized Reporting. When first issued in 1917, prizes were $500, increasing to $3,000 by 1996.

Immigrants awaiting examination, Ellis Island

MEDIA IN THE 20th CENTURY

In 1903, Joseph Pulitzer, publisher of the *New York World*, helped improve life for the reporters he referred to as "ink-stained wretches" when he agreed to endow Columbia University in New York with $2 million to found a school of journalism. Founded in 1912, after Pulitzer's death, the school offered a high quality of training similar to other professions, such as law and medicine. The first school of journalism was founded in 1908 at the University of Missouri.

The competition for readership among newspapers and magazines led to a bidding war for new talent, and reporters began to gain prestige in society. Ambitious middle-to-upper-class young men, and even a few women, were now drawn to the newspaper business. With a spirit of adventure and disenchantment with yellow journalism, many of this new breed of writers and reporters set out to investigate news stories like never before. Going to great lengths, many set out to uncover serious news by gathering hard facts. They solved murders, cracked burglary rings or went undercover to investigate various forms of corruption and injustice. Advances in technology occurred in the decade that allowed media to expand its coverage of a story. Linotype machines provided for more column space and the expansion of stories. The invention of offset printing, also known as lithography, in 1904, gave printers the ability to make changes and corrections to individual characters in one line of text instead of re-setting the entire page. The introduction of photography induced the public to give more credibility to the content of a story. The beginning of experiments with wireless radio would lead to the increase of dissemination of news across the globe.

MAKING HEADLINES

"Extra! Extra! Read all about it!" barked the newsboys as more people of all ages, races and classes bought and read daily newspapers. In the 1890s, sensational, colorful and sometimes suspicious "**yellow journalism**," referring to a type of reporting that was often speculative and half truth, dominated the press. It later evolved into the investigative, in-depth exposés of "**muckraking journalism**" in the early 1900s.

The term "yellow journalism" originated from an enormously popular comic strip, **Hogan's Alley**. The strip

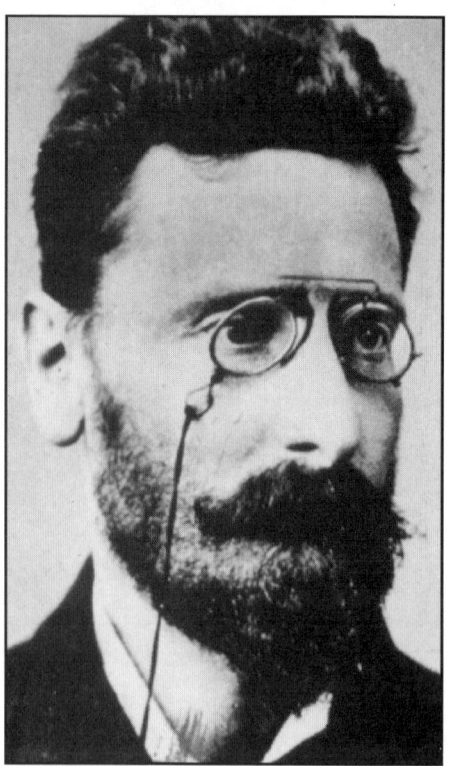

Joseph Pulitzer

first appeared in the *New York World* as a supplement to attract readers. Its main character was an odd tenement district street urchin with a single tooth and perpetually grinning smirk, known as the **Yellow Kid**. He irreverently poked fun at a variety of upper-class fads, from motorcars to golf to Madison Square Garden dog shows. Noticing the popularity the cartoon had with the public, **William Randolph Hearst**, who had recently purchased the *New York Journal* newspaper to compete with the *New York World*, induced the creator and cartoonist, **Richard F. Outcault**, to work for him. The term "yellow journalism" was then equated to using any means necessary to uncover or create a news event.

> "Journalism is popular, but it is popular mainly as fiction. Life is one world, and life seen in the newspapers another."
>
> G.K. Chesterton, British author. *All Things Considered* 1908.

Many new immigrants from Europe, as well as second-and third-generation Americans, saw themselves in the comic strip, as they laughed and sympathized with the Yellow Kid of Hogan's Alley. This new working class who came to America found it hard to adjust to a new society. They faced difficult living conditions, prejudice, grueling labor, and the stories classified as "yellow journalism" spoke to these immigrants in a way in which they could understand and relate to. Yellow journalism also exposed the people and political figures who the media judged to be responsible for these conditions. **Joseph Pulitzer** insisted a newspaper could not survive if it underestimated the intelligence of the people and appealed only to base and vulgar instincts. However, he believed in the use of colorful devices, such as photographs and startling headlines to entice the masses to buy newspapers. In fact Pulitzer's *New York World* gained a wide and diverse readership by emphasizing scandals or the unusual, and treating it as major news. Yellow journalism helped Pulitzer to increase circulation of the *World* from 15,770 copies in 1883 to 153,312 copies in 1885, only two years after he bought the newspaper from its previous owner, Jay Gould. The success of Pulitzer's *World* caught the attention of William Randolph Hearst, a wealthy entrepreneur and publisher of the *San Francisco Examiner* newspaper in California. Hearst had learned the ropes of running a newspaper by working as a reporter for the *New York World* in 1886.

The Yellow Kid

Media in the 20th Century

Although Hearst never met Pulitzer, while he was employed at the paper, he learned Pulitzer's technique of writing and editing for the masses. Hearst purchased the *New York Journal* on October 7, 1895, expanded boldly on the sensational stories and editorials found in the *World* and added color printing to his press to compete with Pulitzer for the growing immigrant market. Using color photography to add credibility or tell a story without words, Hearst expanded the market by appealing to a semi-literate public. Hearst relocated to New York and then deliberately recruited the best of Pulitzer's staff, including the creator of Hogan's Alley, Richard F. Outcault. In retaliation, Pulitzer hired **George B. Luks** to keep the original strip going, while Hearst resorted to naming his new strip the **Yellow Feller**. A fierce competition escalated all over the New York City, with billboards promoting each of the papers' own yellow character.

Typical of yellow journalism, and considered major news were stories of notable characters such as actress Anna Held, who was sued by her milkman for not paying her bill. Ms. Held defended her case by stating that the milk delivered to her was too rich and completely unsuitable for her milk beauty baths. Readers could also follow the saga of British actress Lillie Langtry, who was filing for divorce from her husband to pursue her affair with the Prince of Wales.

Along with these sensationalized stories, the newspapers did present credible news, stories that reflected the opinions and concerns of the publisher. For example, Joseph Pulitzer was sympathetic to the Democratic party and defended its political philosophy, yet not its affiliated party leaders. During the 1896 election, he and most of the other Eastern newspaper publishers abandoned the Democratic party to back Republican candidate **William McKinley** and supported the gold standard in their editorials. In contrast, Hearst in his editorials and political cartoons, remained faithful to the Democratic party and supported **William Jennings Bryan** and free silver— a belief in a money system based on both gold and silver and unlimited coinage of silver. Although labeled a socialist, anarchist and worse, Hearst succeeded in his mission: to make a name for the *Journal*. Bryan lost the election of 1896, but Hearst won the war; the *Journal's* Election Day paper sold an unprecedented number of copies.

William Randolph Hearst

1900-1909

As the competition continued, Hearst invested in the latest printing equipment, acquired a superb staff (many recruited from the *World*) and created an energetic style of reporting – one that hunted down the news, then printed it boldly and dramatically. By maintaining a one cent price, circulation of the *Journal* increased from 30,000 to nearly 400,000 that first year. With *World* daily circulation at 500,000, Pulitzer was forced to remain competitive by cutting the price back from two cents to one cent.

Early in the year, Hearst ran a poem written by reporter and author **Ambrose Bierce** that read:

The bullet that pierced Goebel's breast
Can Not be found in all the West;
Good Reason, it is speeding here
To stretch McKinley on his bier.

Goebel was a governor of Kentucky who was the victim of an assassin. In April 1901, Hearst ran an editorial attacking the McKinley presidency with the words, "If bad institutions and bad men can be got rid of only by killing, then the killing must be done." President McKinley was shot on September 6, 1901 by an anarchist named Leon Czolgosz, and died eight days later. The article later damaged Hearst when he sought the governorship of New York state in 1906, and his prior assaults on President McKinley resurfaced.

At that time newspapers and magazines played a major role in shaping public opinion. With that power the publishers, who had total control over their media empires, had the opportunity to interject personal views and create public interest in matters of their own concern.

America was throwing its political and economic weight around at the turn

President William McKinley

of the century. Trade concessions and political influence was sought with Asia, Africa, and South America. Many economists of the time subscribed to the expansionist view that breaking into new markets abroad would benefit American businesses. Cuban rebels were fighting a war against Spain for independence in 1898. Cuba was a high priority on the list of American expansionist interests because of American investments and its strategic importance to the projected building of the Panama Canal. Unlike the expansionists, Pulitzer believed that the United States should remove itself from its former colonizing principles and promote democracy and union among its states. His editorials reflected his views, condemning the administration of then President Grover Cleveland, for meddling in disputes that were "none of our business." Pulitzer warned the public

Media in the 20th Century

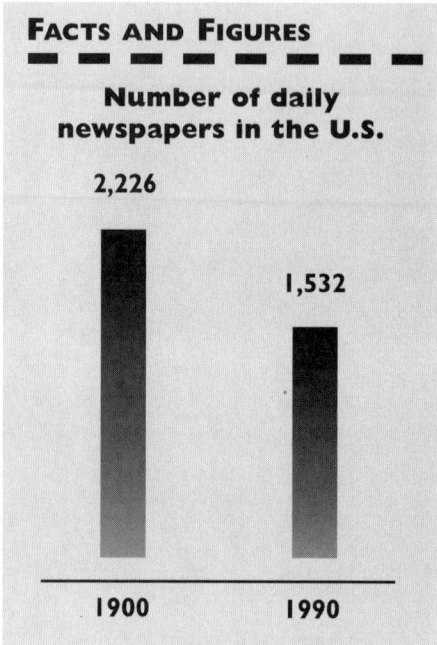

Facts and Figures

Number of daily newspapers in the U.S.

2,226 — 1900
1,532 — 1990

that the president was manipulating them through scare tactics of economic depression. In efforts to enlist support of his views, Pulitzer telegraphed messages to the Prince of Wales and Lord Salisbury, inviting them to submit messages of peace for the newspaper. Featuring their portraits and messages under the headline "Peace and Good Will," the impact of the issue dampened the war spirit. Secretary of State Richard Olney threatened to have Pulitzer prosecuted on grounds of violating the law against conducting "intercourse with any foreign government, with intent to influence their conduct in retaliation to any controversy with the United States."

William Randolph Hearst believed in the expansionist theory, and it is presumed that his paper the *New York Journal* had a hand in promoting the **Spanish-American War** of 1898. He initially dispatched the reporter **Richard Harding Davis** and the artist **Frederic Remington** to Cuba in 1896 to report on the rebellion, but they found nothing and telegraphed Hearst with the notice that there was no indication of unrest or revolution. Hearst is said to have sent the following message: "Please remain. You furnish the pictures and I'll furnish the war," although Hearst denied ever having sent a message. Nonetheless, the *Journal* was unrelenting in creating public sentiment for war. People depended on the available press to inform them of events. As Cuba was thought to be another world, people were inclined to believe what they read, especially if pictures accompanied the story. Drawings and photographs captured public attention and were a strong tool for selling newspapers and for generating the belief that the news was accurate. Throughout the war competition between the two papers was fierce.

On February 15, 1898, the battleship *USS Maine*, docked at Havana, Cuba, went down in a series of explosions. **Frances Scovel**, war correspondent for the *New York World*, immediately reviewed the scene and wired a report stating, "There is some doubt as to whether the explosion took place on the *Maine*." Scovel had previously obtained a blank cable with a censor's seal of approval from a Cuban sympathizer, although the editors at the office in the United States were not aware of his acquisition. On night duty at the *New York World*, **Ernest Chamberlin** assumed the cable had been worded to pass through censors. The next day, the morning headline read, "It is Not Known Whether the Explosion Occurred On or Under the Maine."

Publisher Hearst was informed of the incident by phone and devoted the entire front page to the story, stating

1900-1909

that "Until further facts are known, we are bound to accept the accident theory." The "accident theory" referred to spontaneous explosions common to coal-powered Navy warships, caused by combustion fires in the coal bunkers, which were located near the ship's weapon supply. The World and the rival Journal each hired a team of divers for first-hand information on the cause of the explosion. Although they were not permitted to inspect the ship themselves, they kept a close watch on the Spanish and American Navy diving teams, and learned of the discovery of a hole eight inches in diameter in the vicinity of the forward compartment of the deck. Just 24 hours after supporting the accident theory, a Hearst reporter, concluded that the mystery of the Maine was solved and wrote, "The Maine was destroyed by a torpedo...the whole city knows it and is waiting almost with bated breath for what must follow" under the headline:

"WAR! SURE! MAINE DESTROYED BY SPANISH ...THIS PROVED ABSOLUTELY BY DISCOVERY OF THE TORPEDO HOLE!"

The unexamined and unsubstantiated proof of an eight-inch-diameter hole became the basis for the war campaign in America. Within three days of the sinking of the USS Maine, the Journal's headline read:

"THE WHOLE COUNTRY THRILLS WITH WAR FEVER."

A persistent conspiracy theory still exists which claims that Hearst instigated the war in response to Spain's seizure of his private yacht. Joseph Pulitzer and the New York World were more subdued in their exposés, and tried to sway the public against a war. For example, the World featured maps of the location of Spain's ship The Vizcaya, docked off New York Harbor, along with information about the ship's firing-range capabilities.

Hearst's Journal declared war on Spain three months prior to when Congress officially did. When the victorious American fleet returned in August from what Hearst called "our war," it was the Journal that granted New York City a holiday, informing all major retailers and advertisers to close and join the paper in a celebration. The Journal's circulation, divided into morning and evening editions, reached a peak of 1,250,000. Upon his retirement from publishing in 1907, Pulitzer shared his policy for the New York World: "... always fight for progress and reform, never tolerate injustice and corruption, always fight demagogues of all articles, never belong to any party, always oppose privileged classes and public plunderers, never lack sympathy with the poor, always remain devoted to the public welfare, never be satisfied with merely printing news; always be drastically independent, never be afraid to attack wrong, whether by predatory plutocracy or predatory poverty."

The USS Maine in Havana Harbor

Media in the 20th Century

INVESTIGATIVE REPORTING

Admirers of yellow journalism felt the press supported the poor and under represented classes, while those opposed felt it did not do enough to present accurate and unbiased information.

After the Spanish American War, yellow journalism evolved into a type of reporting known as **muckraking**, which pervaded the daily press and magazines. Characterized by investigative reporting concerned with the implementation of social reforms, media took on a new role of exposing corrupt government and business practices. The beginning of education for journalists and the growing rise in their status coincided with the progressive movement occurring at the turn of the 20th century. The first real investigative reporters of the century worked diligently to uncover serious problems such as injustice, investment scams and fraud on behalf of the immigrant poor and others who did not have a forum to voice their opinions.

President **Theodore Roosevelt** coined the term "muckraking" on April 14, 1906, in an address to the Gridiron Club in Washington, D.C., to describe reporters, digging to discovering the muck (dirt or mud), and raking it (exposing the problem in such a way that it could no longer be ignored). The term came from an allegory out of **John Bunyan's** timeless classic, *Pilgrim's Progress*. Roosevelt compared the reporters to the "man with the muck-rake," a character so busy examining the dirt at his feet that he forgets to look up and notice the good in the world. Muckraking, the forerunner of **investigative journalism**, was often well rooted in fact, hard-hitting in tone and sometimes vindictively brutal in its exposure of corruption and other ills in society's institutions and businesses.

President Theodore Roosevelt

1900-1909

While yellow journalism is characterized by brief stories based on speculation, muckraking provided more in-depth coverage of events and was specifically born out of the various reform movements to improve the condition of the United States. Unlike yellow journalism, the main purpose of muckraking was not entirely profit-motivated. Intent on affecting change in politics, business, work, government and social institutions, muckraking journalists were inspired by a sense of social responsibility, and saw themselves as educators to the masses.

The Cosmopolitan, February, 1906

Attempting to attract a mass audience with an affordable 15 cent price, **S.S. McClure** began publishing **McClure's**, one of the most popular nationally circulated monthly magazines, in 1893. Recognizing the appeal of muckraking, *McClure's* articles focused on critical social, economic and political issues, emphasizing accurate information, verifiable sources and direct language. Reporters uncovered shocking truths about monopolies in industry, municipal corruption, patent-medicine abuses, insurance manipulations and other social ills of that time.

Reporters such as **Ida Tarbell** and **Lincoln Steffens** of *McClure's* rose to prominence, writing scathing exposés on big business and government, which revealed the unethical practices of corporations to the general public. Reporters prided themselves on being thorough investigators, unrelenting in their pursuit to effect change in society. The public devoured their work and clamored for more. Many exposés inspired the public to organize and petition for change. Journalism evolved into a respectable profession as the public became dependent on reporters to responsibly uncover otherwise hidden or privileged information about public officials and private industries.

In 1900, many senators were wealthy and the Senate became referred to as the **Millionaires' Club**. Primarily elected by state legislatures who were dominated by big business, they often paid little attention to their supposed constituents. In *Cosmopolitan* magazine, reporter **David G. Phillips** shocked the nation with his series "**The Treason of the Senate**" in 1906. He charged that 83 percent of the current senators (75 out of 90) actually represented the railroads and trusts and not the people. Supported by financial figures and donation records, this aggressive article impressed President Roosevelt. After multiple verifications of the links between greedy corporations and the Senate, the state legislatures decided to listen to the voice of the people. In 1913, the **17th Amendment** to the Constitution was approved. It established the direct election of senators by the public. Several other major rights were won for the American voting public. The **ballot initiative** that allowed voters to directly propose legislation without going through the bureaucracy of state legislature, was won. **Referendums**, which placed laws on the ballot for final approval by the people, was passed. Finally, the **recall** empowered voters to remove corrupt or faithless elected officials they could no longer tolerate. At its best, media became a "government watchdog," alerting the public to real or potential danger through its written and verbal warnings.

"**The Oil War of 1872**," by Ida Tarbell, was published in *McClure's* in 1902. Consisting of three essays on the history of Standard Oil, owned by John D. Rockefeller, the article focused on the bitter conflict between Pennsylvania oil producers and Standard Oil. Rockefeller bribed the railroad owners to set favorable shipping rates for his large refineries at the expense of the independent oil producers. The result was a furious battle in the oil regions for control of the industry. As a child, Tarbell witnessed the resentment of her neighbors and her own father, who had been bought out of their businesses by Rockefeller. Through two years of intensive research, she exposed Rockefeller's pattern of undercutting oil companies in order to buy them out. She revealed how Rockefeller spied on his competitors, forced them out of business, and then raised his prices. After her exposé, Congress launched an investigation and prosecuted Standard Oil under the Sherman Antitrust Act. Ida Tarbell left *McClure's* in 1906 and joined the staff of the ***American Magazine***, where other muckrakers assembled to continue to write stories concerning the social wrongs of the world.

Lincoln Steffens was managing editor of *McClure's* between 1902 and 1906. His landmark article, published in six installments in 1902, was entitled, "**The Shame of Minneapolis: The Rescue and Redemption of a City that was Sold Out**." Exposing urban corruption between deceitful politicians, crooked police and businessmen, a sensation was created upon its publication. To protect against lawsuits, *McClure's* spent up to $3,000 per article to verify the accuracy of its exposés.

President Theodore Roosevelt embodied the social activism and quest for truth of the muckraking journalists. As the reporters uncovered fraud, corruption and festering social ills, Roosevelt diligently worked to correct the problems. After big businesses were exposed for creating monopolies and demolishing their competition, Roosevelt employed the Sherman Antitrust Act which forbade businesses from restricting competition, and broke the growing power of the industrialists. When Roosevelt targeted the Northern Securities Company, he fought against four wealthy men (J.P. Morgan, James J. Hill, E.H. Harriman and John D. Rockefeller). Referred to as the "banker's banker," J.P. Morgan immediately rushed to Washington upon receiving the shocking indictment, and said, "If we have done anything wrong, send your man to my man and they can fix it up." When the president refused, Attorney General Philander C. Knox elaborated, "We don't want to fix it up; we want to stop it." After successfully breaking Northern Securities, Roosevelt attacked the Chicago meat packers, American Tobacco, Du Pont, and over 40 other major monopolies.

A generation of authors had begun to write about the abundant abuses that plagued American businesses and politics as well. On assignment from a socialist weekly magazine, journalist **Upton Sinclair's** fact-based novel, *The Jungle*, which was first released as a series of magazine articles, graphically exposed American meat packers disregard for the health of the consumer. Eight pages describing typical meat packing, based on Sinclair's own work experience, turned Americans' stomachs. "I aimed at the

1900-1909

public's heart, and by accident I hit it in the stomach," stated Sinclair. He described how sausage contained rats killed by poisoned bread, lamb and mutton was often really goat meat, deviled ham was just red-dyed minced tripe, and lard sometimes contained the remains of humans who accidentally fell into the boiling vats. Many converted to vegetarianism after reading about the unsanitary practices rampant in the industry. Due to a drop in product demand and bad public relations, U.S. meat packers cleaned up their act. Coupled with disclosures outlining the dangerous and false "medical products" often advertised in respectable publications, the **Pure Food and Drug Act** of 1906 was passed. Later the government established the Food and Drug Administration to determine guidelines and monitor compliance for consumer safety.

Another development of the decade included the commercial consolidation of newspapers into chains. Newspaper chains gave advertisers the opportunity to promote products throughout the nation through one source. The chains had the advantage over smaller independents by providing wider coverage at less cost. **Edward W. Scripps** began the first newspaper chain. The success of Scripps' chains could be summarized in his instructions to young editors: "Serve that class of people and only that class of people from whom you cannot even hope to derive any other income than the one cent a day for your paper." In other words, Scripps catered the paper to the public and not big business.

In 1902 Scripps founded the first independent news syndicate, the **Newspaper Enterprise Association (NEA)**, which supplied feature stories, illustrations, and cartoons to a variety of newspapers. Scripps owned several franchises of the **Associated Press (AP)** wire service, before he relinquished his interests to begin his own news syndicate. He realized that independent newspapers were dependent on AP and that AP was selective as to which newspapers received their service. Scripps then bought the **Publisher's Press** in 1906. In 1907 he merged **Scripps-MacRae Press Association** with Publisher's Press to create the news service **United Press (UP)**. The United Press became the **United Press International (UPI)** in 1958, after merging with the **International News Service (INS)**, which was started in 1909 by William Randolph Hearst.

> **"People accuse journalism of being too personal; but to me it has always seemed far too impersonal. It is charged with tearing away the veils from private life; but it seems to me to be always dropping diaphanous but blinding veils between men and men. The Yellow Press is abused for exposing facts which are private; I wish the Yellow Press did anything so valuable. It is exactly the decisive individual touches that it never gives; and a proof of this is that after one has met a man a million times in the newspapers it is always a complete shock and reversal to meet him in real life."**
>
> G. K. Chesterton, British author. *Tremendous Trifles*, 1909

Media in the 20th Century

Edward Willis Scripps

Scripps was a proponent of journalistic independence and the free flow of information. His vision allowed a nation of people from all corners of the world to receive news and information.

ADVERTISING

In the first decade of the 20th century radio or television was not commercially available, and product awareness was communicated through print advertising, primarily in newspapers and periodicals. Advertisements were used primarily by shop owners to communicate commercial information. As industrialism and mass production of consumer goods grew, the field of advertising began developing. The newspaper chains were well positioned to accommodate these large advertisers in need of wide market exposure. A mutually beneficial relationship between the two ensued.

The advertisements of 1900 to 1910 primarily sold unregulated "cures" and "tonics," along with the more standard household products. Many of these advertisements tried to create a sense of urgency and danger of what might happen if you didn't purchase the product. One of the mildest was Centliver Tonic, which claimed it "Builds up the system, Gives strength and Enjoyment to Life!" Snake oil claimed to simultaneously cure warts, baldness and stomach ache, among other miracles. Dr. Pierce's Pleasant Pellets for the Liver supposedly "Makes Weak Women Strong, Sick Women Well" by giving "Strength to the Stomach, Purity to the Blood and Life to the Lungs." The sensational stories

NEWS ORGANIZATIONS

Major news service organizations of the 20th century include: United Press International (UPI), which includes the former NEA and covers United States news stories; Associated Press (AP), which reports on American news stories; Reuters, which covers British and European news, and Kyoto's, covering news from Japan and Asia.

1900-1909

Kodak Brownie camera ad

Far-thinking Italian physicist **Gugliel-mo Marconi** patented an invention that allowed wireless telegraph stations to operate on different wavelengths without interference. On December 12, 1901, Marconi sent and received the first wireless transmissions across the Atlantic Ocean. On February 22, 1903, he helped publish the first newspaper at sea, on the Cunard ocean liner *Etruria*, featuring news accounts transmitted from Britain to the middle of the Atlantic Ocean by wireless telegraphy. When the passengers awoke in the morning, they were presented with a newspaper containing brief accounts of a coal shortage in New York and the dispatch of an American warship to Honduras, among other events. Marconi later founded the **American Marconi Company** (AMC), later to become the **Radio Corporation of America** (RCA). The speed, range and quantity of information of these small, short-range transmissions would continually increase in the coming decades, forming the basis of radio and television "news flashes."

appearing in the media during the heyday of yellow journalism, directly influenced the way advertisers portrayed their products and the techniques they used to gain public attention.

AUDIO MEDIA

While journalism was primarily a print medium for the first three decades of the 20th century, new ways of communicating were constantly under development, lending media the power to reach more people around the world at a faster pace. American electrical engineer **Reginald A. Fessenden** transmitted the first human voice by **radio** to a receiver one mile away in 1900, initiating radio into the 20th century.

Early advertisement

Media in the 20th Century

KCBS building and tower, San Jose, California

In 1901 German physicist **Karl F. Braun** introduced crystal detectors that generated, detected and amplified radio signals used in "**crystal sets**," the harbingers of radios. While developments in radio technology were exciting, a more practical first came with the broadcast from "the oldest radio station in the world," **KCBS** in San Jose, California, in 1909. Dr. **Charles Herrold** began regular programming on a 15-watt station, identifying himself only as "This is San Jose calling" because the station did not yet have call letters. Later, Dr. Herrold used several call letters to ensure that his listeners would be able to discern his station from others trying out radio as a new hobby around the city. When broadcast licenses were issued in 1921, he was assigned the call letters **KQW**. The primary programming was music, but newscasts were heard as well, as he and his assistant **Ray Newby** read the newspaper over the air and gave their own personal editorial opinions. The station would develop into the origination point for hundreds of network news reports and handled all-short wave transmissions for the Pacific war region during World War II. It was this station that intercepted the first news reports from the Japanese Domei News Agency on the surrender of Japan in 1945. The station kept the KQW call letters until CBS purchased it in 1949 and moved to San Francisco. KCBS became the first "all-news talk station" in the Sixties, and in 1968 pioneered the "all-news station" format for radio.

By the end of the first decade of the century, it seemed the world was becoming smaller as news traveled wider and faster. With the advent of new technologies such as wireless telegraphy and radio transmissions, the ability to report and obtain news, information and entertainment was at an exciting threshold.

MEDIA
chapter 2
1910-1919
Tabloids, Radio and Global Politics

WWI Recruiting Poster

Media in the 20th Century

While the muckraking journalists achieved broad social awareness of government and business fraud and corruption in the first decade, the majority of legislative changes designed to correct those problems occurred between 1910 and 1920. President Woodrow Wilson, whose two terms spanned from 1913 to 1921, furthered the goals of the progressives by keeping a close watch on big business and tried to maintain a policy of isolation for America. Newspapers and magazines dominated media and the dissemination of news in the second decade of the 20th century. They were under the constant scrutiny by the public who was looking for news they could trust. As a result of World War I (WWI) the majority of newspapers followed trends in the style and content of news, and were often faulted for not taking a position in their reporting.

In America, the press is free from government control. In non-democratic nations, media are often controlled by the prevailing government, and used as an organ for spreading the ideals and doctrines of the ruling political power. In Russia, Vladimir Lenin, founder of the Russian Communist Party, known as the Bolsheviks, successfully launched a revolution using an illegally produced newspaper, *Pravda* to incite change. The paper was a tool of the Communist Party, and was used to criticize the czarist regime of Nicholas II, who had involved Russia in a bloody war with Germany. One of the goals of communism is to allow people the opportunity to reach their full potential by abolishing capitalistic economic structures. *Pravda's* principles—to serve and obey the sole need of the Communist Party—were discredited by the Western press for its censorship of views opposed to those supported by the party. *Pravda* defended itself in its definition of news policy: "News is agitation through facts. News must be didactic and instructive." *Pravda* did not seek to entertain readers to earn sales, as was characteristic of the American press. Although *Pravda* initially functioned illegally, the issues of censorship were brought to the democratic United States during World War I under the authority of President Woodrow Wilson.

World War I changed the relationship between the press, the public, and the government. Some censorship of the news was considered necessary for national security. News correspondents were therefore required to submit their stories to military censors for approval. Some people accused the press of concealing factual accounts of the war, and the nation was forced to examine the ability and responsibility of the press to inform the public. As the owners and distributors of information, media have the capability to shape the ideas of the public. In their evolution, media must continuously

Banner of the Communist party newspaper

1910-1919

establish their purpose and acknowledge their role to the people and the nation during times of crisis.

After the war, tabloid or "jazz journalism" and radio furthered the spread of media in America. Jazz journalism was defined by its sensationalistic approach to news, emphasizing scandal to attract attention, alleviate the stress of war, and sell newspapers. Tabloid journalism created stories often unsubstantiated by valid proof, and employed the extensive use of photographs, some of them faked or misrepresented. Tabloid journalism provided a source of escapism from the bleak news of everyday life, by presenting news in a sensational light to detract from the grim reality of the situation. The sensationalism of tabloid newspapers would spread to other publications and characterize media in the 1920s.

Radio, first considered merely a public-relations or minor advertising tool, began to demonstrate its potential to deliver news faster than newspapers and to influence ideas and opinions through the power of voice. Radio allowed people to share the intrinsic drama of news events. People felt involved as they listened to news broadcast over the airwaves, more than they did reading the facts in the paper. The decade dominated by war saw many changes in the way the media presented news and influenced its readers and listeners.

POLITICS, CENSORSHIP AND REVOLT

Media and government share a mutually necessary but adversarial relationship. In the United States, government depends on the media to deliver to the public accurate information about policy enactment, proposed laws and domestic and international affairs. Through the First Amendment, the government guarantees the freedom to distribute information, ideas, and opinions, however unpopular, through the media. As servants of the public, the media must disclose corruption in government practices and provide a forum for public response. Media outlets are caught between two extremes. They can be overzealous in their pursuit of stories, and perhaps exaggerate issues and accuse innocent people of wrongdoing. Or they can be to conservative, desensitizing news and events by failing to disclose facts or properly address all the issues. In America, "freedom of the press" implies that media has the right to print news necessary to the public welfare, without restrictions by government institutions. The public fails to consider that media are still representatives of the nation and that the state, in protecting the well-being of the nation as a whole, has the right to intervene upon the freedom of the press if the press is perceived to be acting against the security of the nation.

In non-democratic countries, media are blatantly controlled by the forces of government and do not have the liberty to print news that allegedly defames the state. Media are regulated in some nations because they have the power to incite revolutions, change governments, and create or abolish social classes. In Russia, the overthrowing of czar **Nicholas II**, the supreme ruler of the nation, and the establishment of fundamental obedience to the **Communist Party** was aided by the illegal publication of the government-banned newspaper *Pravda*.

Media in the 20th Century

Lenin addressing a Moscow crowd

Throughout its history, *Pravda* was the newspaper and propaganda organ of the Communist Party. Communism is a theory that professes that the wealth of the nation should be equally distributed among the citizens for the common interest of the state. The principles stem from the doctrines of the German theorist **Karl Marx** and German political writer **Friedrich Engels**. Known as **Marxism**, its claim is that all history is the history of class struggles and that the bourgeoisie (middle class or owners of the means of production) are due to be replaced by the proletariat, or working class, just as the bourgeoisie had replaced the feudal aristocracy.

The first *Pravda* was produced in Vienna, Austria, in 1908 by author **Leon Trotsky** as an organ of the **Menshevik Party**, also referred to as the minority Communist Party. It criticized **Vladimir Lenin's Bolshevik Party**, known as the majority Communist Party. Lenin was a follower of Marx, and believed that a small group of professional revolutionaries should establish a dictatorship of the working class. Members of the Menshevik Party supported the communist ideal, but believed that Lenin would create a dictatorship *over* the people rather than *of* the people. Sharing in the belief that a revolution was necessary, the two groups formed the main branch of the **Russian Socialist Party** from 1903 to 1918. The two became partners and the Bolsheviks assisted with the funding of *Pravda*. Lenin used his friendship with Russian author **Maxim Gorky** to persuade the writer to submit articles to *Pravda*. He organized a section called "**Peasant Life**" to widen the paper's appeal beyond the urban proletariat. Workers were also encouraged to submit articles about their concerns to the paper.

Of the 645 issues of *Pravda* produced under the monarchy of Nicholas II almost one-third were confiscated or fined by the czar. *Pravda* itself was barely legal, as the Bolshevik Party was banned in Russia. Code names, referring to the Bolsheviks as "consistent and staunch labor democrats," were used within the publication to describe key members. Due to state pressure, *Pravda* was relaunched eight times, each with slightly different names, such as *Put Pravda* (Path of Truth) and *Rabochaya Pravda* (Worker's Truth). *Pravda* reported on the persecution of trade unions, gaining access to political rallies under the pretense of recording the speeches of the czar's agents. After a wave of strikes by the citizens of Russia in 1912, Nicholas II finally allowed the publication of opposition papers. Although Lenin was in exile in Cracow, Poland, then part of Austria,

1910-1919

he grasped the opportunity to continue the paper, stole the name *Pravda*, and on May 5, 1912, the official Bolshevik *Pravda* was launched.

The establishment of its new offices in St. Petersburg (soon to become Leningrad) in 1912 also served as the illegal headquarters of the Bolshevik Party. The history of the Communist Party claims that *Pravda* inspired a generation of revolutionary workers that forced the abdication of Nicholas II in 1917. Lenin sent articles and gave direction on running the paper from his residence in Cracow. As *Pravda* was party-sponsored, it did not depend on, nor answer to, advertisers in the articles it printed.

After the February Revolution in 1917, a temporary government was erected. Both the Menshevik and Bolshevik parties vied for control of *Pravda*. *Pravda's* columns showed the conflict between the ideals of the two parties. Lenin returned to Russia from exile to share in the governing of the nation and closed all opposition papers except *Pravda*. A civil war ensued in Russia between the Menshevik and Bolshevik parties, and *Pravda* became the propaganda organ for the Bolsheviks, distributed free around the country to win support. Articles had such headlines as "Workers, if you do not destroy the bourgeoisie, it will destroy you," printed in *Pravda* on August 31, 1918.

The Bolsheviks won the war and Lenin created the **Central Committee** in 1921 to structure the guidelines of all the press in the nation. The committee established standards on the amount of space allotted to foreign news, industrial news, the arts, and so on. The design created total party control of the press.

Pravda was the Communist Party's

> "... **Freedom of the press is freedom for the political organizations of the bourgeoisie. To give these people such a weapon as the press is to help our enemy ... in the capitalist world, freedom of the press represents the freedom to buy, corrupt, and mold public opinion in the interests of the bourgeoisie.**"
>
> Vladimir Lenin (1870-1924), leader of the Bolshevik Party in Russia. *Pravda*, September 12, 1918.

propaganda machine for decades and controlled the information available in the country. After democracy took hold in Russia in the late Eighties, the press gained much greater freedom and both the Communist Party and *Pravda* fell into disfavor. *Pravda's* readership shrank, and the paper closed temporarily in 1992. It continues to be published today.

WAR AND CENSORSHIP IN THE PRESS

By 1910, the forces that created the modern newspapers for the masses— industrialization, mechanization and urbanization— led to the creation of a more standardized product that focused less on individual style. Newspapers were continuously consolidated into chains, sharing news stories between them. Muckraking continued as a prominent force in journalism, yet there were few foreign correspondents—at least

Media in the 20th Century

Official U.S. Army photographer of World War I

literacy levels were high, most people and publishers were focusing on events in or close to America's borders. Most people wanted to avoid participating in a war they did not understand. Censorship agreements between government and the press began in the United States as fears for national security grew. Media were torn between providing reliable news and their responsibility to follow the restrictions of the government. After witnessing the power of the press to instigate the overthrow of the government in Russia, President **Woodrow Wilson** was not going to risk dissension in America.

President Wilson was reluctant to enter the war. Yet after a German U-boat sank the British passenger ship *Lusitania* on May 7, 1915, carrying 124 Americans, Wilson could no longer avoid committing America to the war. Once President Wilson declared war, he focused on stimulating public morale, preparing people for the difficult days ahead, and uniting the country in the war effort. He brilliantly united isolationist and crusading Americans with his publicized statements in the press of "a war to end war" with the purpose "to make the world safe for democracy."

Wilson created the **Committee on Public Information** one week after the declaration of war. Its job was to convey facts about the war to the press and coordinate the propaganda effort to promote the war. Propaganda is defined as "the systematic propagation of a doctrine or cause or of information reflecting the views and interests of those people advocating such a doctrine or cause; material disseminated by the advocates of a doctrine or cause; the selected truths, exaggerations, and lies of wartime." Wilson appointed a young, outspoken and somewhat tactless muck-

ones who could discern government or ideological propaganda from the facts. Publishers continued to compete with each other, especially in their editorials about European events. The assassination of the **Archduke Francis Ferdinand**, heir to Austria-Hungary's throne, by a Serbian patriot in 1914 is considered by most historians to have been the trigger that sparked **World War I**. Without a clear understanding of the existing political regime of each nation, class hierarchy and emerging ideological groups, the explosive aftermath of war was difficult for Americans to comprehend. Although

1910-1919

raking editor, **George Creel**, to run the new committee. The organization employed journalists to write, collect and distribute information favorable to the American war effort and serve as the government's liaison with newspapers. Creel's job was "to sell America on the war ... and sell the world on Wilson's war goals." With imagination and enthusiasm, Creel's organization grew to 150,000 employees in America and Europe. His "**four-minute men**," so called for their four-minute "patriotic pep" speeches delivered to the press and public, numbered 75,000. Millions of red, white and blue pamphlets, billboards and posters colored with the strongest "Wilsonisms" were splashed everywhere. The Committee published roughly 6,000 press releases and even enrolled the Boy Scouts to deliver door-to-door copies of Wilson's addresses. Wilson and the media, used censorship, to shield America from the harshest realities of war and to promote America's involvement in the conflict.

Many of the investigative reporters found it difficult to discern the facts amid the wartime propaganda. A high percentage of stories reported were inspired by press agents who provided journalists with the "official story."

As Creel himself explained, "It was a plain publicity proposition, a vast enterprise in salesmanship, the world's greatest adventure in advertising." The Committee on Public Information found itself "mobilizing the mind of the world." Creel called in skilled painters, sculptors, illustrators, cartoonists, photographers, advertising men, writers and movie stars—anyone whose skills could possibly contribute to military enlistment. In addition to massive public relations, Wilson also suppressed media considered to be disloyal to the American war cause.

LITERACY

By 1910, the US illiteracy rate was at a low of 7.7 percent, meaning 84,916,000 Americans could read. The population of the United States at the time was 91,972,266.

The **Espionage Act** of June 15, 1917 was a landmark of press censorship. It was enacted to prevent false information with the intent to interfere with the success of military operations or to obstruct recruitment propaganda from being printed. In conjunction with the act was the **Trading with the Enemy Act** of October 1917, which authorized

President Wilson and his wife Edith

Media in the 20th Century

Albert Sterner painting WWI posters

attacked by other media and boycotted. The *New York Tribune*, although a critic of the manner in which the Wilson administration was conducting the war, ran a cartoon showing a snake coiled in the American flag, with the snake's body spelling out "Hears-ss-ss-t."

The power of government to control the expression of opinion was strengthened by passage of the **Sedition Act** in 1918, which made it a crime to write or publish "any disloyal, profane, scurrilous or abusive language about the form of government of the United States or the Constitution, military or naval forces, flag or the uniform." It also forbade use of language intended to bring these ideas and institutions "into contempt, scorn, contumely, or disrepute."

Concerned with the media's control of public opinion, President Wilson established the **Censorship Board** in October 1917 to control outgoing communication about the war and still provide media with the sense of liberty to observe and report the news. American war correspondents were given more freedom to observe military actions. Under the guidance of General John J. Pershing, reporters were allowed to travel unescorted to the front line, follow the fighting advances or roam in the rear areas, living wherever they chose. These correspondents covered "war news" of general engagements, troop identifications and casualties suffered.

censorship of all communication into and out of the United States. Under the act 75 papers, most of which were socialist publications, German-American newspapers, or anti-Allied, lost mailing privileges. Foreign-language publications were required to have an English translation available for review prior to mailing by the Postal Service. Whether media agreed with the war effort or not, they were prohibited from exercising the right to print any opinions that would promote disloyalty to the war, punishable by heavy fines and imprisonment under the Espionage Act. Many newspapers that did not wholeheartedly support the war felt the power of public opinion, influenced by Creel and the Committee on Public Information. The newspapers of publisher **William Randolph Hearst**, which included the *San Francisco Examiner* and the *New York Journal*, supported the American war effort, but were opposed to American entry into the war. Hearst was denounced as disloyal to America, and his papers were widely

1910-1919

TABLOIDS AND JAZZ JOURNALISM POSTWAR

Supplanting the muckraking journalism of the first decade of the 20th century was **tabloid journalism**, also known as **jazz journalism**. It began as a reaction to the war and tried to alleviate the pressure and stress placed on the public. Newspapers were still time-consuming and difficult to produce, and in order to increase sales the press was forced to adopt newer technology as well as change its style to follow trends.

The postwar period, with its cynical disillusionment, its interest in sports and heroics, and its desire for excitement, provided a fertile ground for the lurid display of human drama presented in the tabloids. Tabloids were known for their human interest stories and blurbs, plus an extensive use of sensational photography to attract an audience, following many of the same techniques of yellow journalism. These publications targeted a reading public who, according to circulation surveys, previously had not read newspapers. A focus on sex, crime and entertainment fit the atmosphere of the beginning of the Roaring Twenties.

The tabloids' financial success, can be attributed to their smaller, more convenient size, condensed accounts and emphasis on the drama of life. The tabloid halved the size of the newspaper page, which allowed easier handling by the reader. It was a innovation of publisher **Alfred Harmsworth** of Great Britain, and the first widely circulated tabloid was his *Daily Mirror* of London, which began in 1903. Originally a newspaper for women, the publication transformed into a tabloid of amusing stories, illustrated with photographs, offered at an affordable halfpenny price, which helped it achieve a circulation of one million by 1909. In 1919, **Robert R. McCormick** and **Joseph M. Patterson** had successfully launched a similar publication with the *Illustrated Daily News* in New York City. Its first editorial stated: "We shall give you every day the best and newest pictures of the interesting things that are happening in the world. Nothing that is not interesting is news. The story that is told by a picture can be grasped instantly." Focusing on sensationalism, sin, heroics and scandal, the picture was often not an accurate one. A method of pasting faces over an existing photograph, then re-photographing the image into a "**composograph**," was employed by some tabloids, depicting such images as the King of England scrubbing his back in the privacy of his royal bath, in efforts to gain readership as other papers spread across the country and acquired unprecedented following.

In efforts to compete, publishers invested in improved printing technology. Although new composing machines, which had the ability to combine letters onto one metal "slug," were developed in 1880, the cost of building them hindered their introduction until the period 1890 through 1920. The **Hattersley** and **Kastenbein** composing machines, which were common in the newspaper industry before then, required workers to adjust the type in the presses letter by letter. Type distribution was time-consuming and expensive, so that it could be economically lucrative only if done by inexpensive child labor.

Monotype and **Linotype** machines revolutionized the newspaper industry in the 1910s by solving the problems of automatic line justification and type distribution (a visually balanced centering of both characters and spaces to completely and equally fill the line space). Nearly every newspaper in the world was composed on Linotype or similar machines until the advent of filmsetting in the late 1950s and 1960s.

American **Tolbert Lanston**, inventor of the Monotype, based his creation on a similar principle as the Linotype, with one advantage. Each letter is cast separately instead of in a compact line, making correction easy. A skilled compositor could compose about 2,000 letters per hour on a Hattersley composing machine; on a Linotype or Monotype, the same compositor could compose at least 6,000 letters in the same amount of time.

ADVERTISING

Advertising sets the stage for how people "should" act and live, and the products they should purchase. The content of a publication influences the type of advertising included, and simultaneously, media will delete or edit articles so as not to offend advertisers. Advertisers often seek to reach a mass audience, so they promote their products in magazines and newspapers with the largest circulation. As chains of newspapers and magazines grew, advertisers frequently preferred to purchase space in one metropolitan daily with a wide readership over several small publications with overlapping or specialized readership bases. Conflicts arose when the principles of the publications did not comply with the product being advertised, but the media was dependent on advertising to support their publications. Publications were increasingly supported by advertising, more so than by circulation. Publishers were forced to consider the effects stories would have on their advertisers. They were obligated to notify an advertiser if a story would bring bad publicity to the product marketed. The concept of "consideration" developed to balance the publication's responsibility to present informative and necessary news accounts while still maintaining the interest of the advertiser. Consideration took the form of arranging layouts to detract from possible connection of a story to a product, or even postponing a story to a later date to avoid conflict of interests.

> **"You can tell the ideals of a nation by its advertisements."**
>
> Norman Douglas, British author. *South Wind*, 1917.

The **Federal Trade Commission** (FTC), an independent U.S. agency established in 1914, was created to keep business competition free and fair. Its duties included enforcing the antitrust laws, preventing the dissemination of false and deceptive advertising, regulating the labeling and packaging of commodities, and gathering data concerning business conditions and making it available to Congress, the president, and the public. It was empowered to require corporations to submit information about their business practices if there was substantial evidence of wrongdoing. The FTC could also issue mandatory cease-and-desist orders and could pursue violators in court.

The Federal Trade Commission was especially interested in enforcing truth in advertising. Whereas unscrupulous businesses could pay to advertise their dubi-

1910-1919

ous products even in reputable publications, there was often no recourse for consumers who were deceived, injured or even killed by unsafe products. The FTC would help substantiate the case for requiring warnings on products such as cigarettes and alcohol later in the 20th century.

RADIO

During World War I all use of wireless communication was placed under government control. The need to reduce interference of voice transmission between airplanes and ground stations provided an impetus for further research into the development of **radio**. The vacuum tube proved to be the best means of upgrading the radio receiver.

Lee De Forest's triode tube, invented in 1906, improved voice broadcasting over radio. He put the great tenor Enrico Caruso on the air in 1910 to broadcast from the stage of the Metropolitan Opera in New York. Unfortunately, most of the reporters heard static instead of music, and the resulting media coverage was disparaging. De Forest conducted the first news cast in the United States from an experimental station in the Bronx, New York, when he announced the presidential election results between Woodrow Wilson and Charles Evans Hughes in 1916. In 1919, De Forest helped President Wilson coordinate broadcasting the results of the Paris Peace Conference; unfortunately, only ships at sea heard the broadcast.

David Sarnoff and the **American Marconi Co.** (AMC) radio music box made the radio a "household utility" just like the piano or phonograph. By 1910, amateur radio clubs were popular among enthusiasts who mail-ordered parts from small manufacturers and crudely assembled the primitive crystal sets that could pick up radio transmissions.

The power of radio to relay information across the airwaves at incomparable speed was realized by accident. While working as a operator for Marconi Wireless Company in 1912, Sarnoff picked up what he understood to be distress signals from the S.S. Titanic. Marconi immediately relayed the unbelievable story of the sinking vessel to the newspapers.

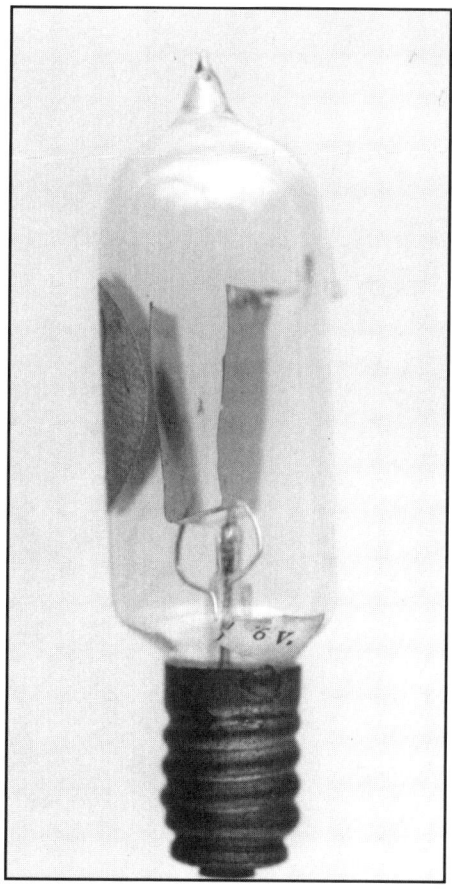

Lee De Forest's Audion

Without waiting for the usual verification, major papers carried the story, based solely on Marconi's transmission.

Marconi's quick action in communicating the devastating accident accomplished two things: knowing about the accident and its location aided the rescue effort in responding quickly, most probably increasing the number of survivors, and it dramatically decreased the story's usual "lag time," the time it took for the report of an incident to reach the press.

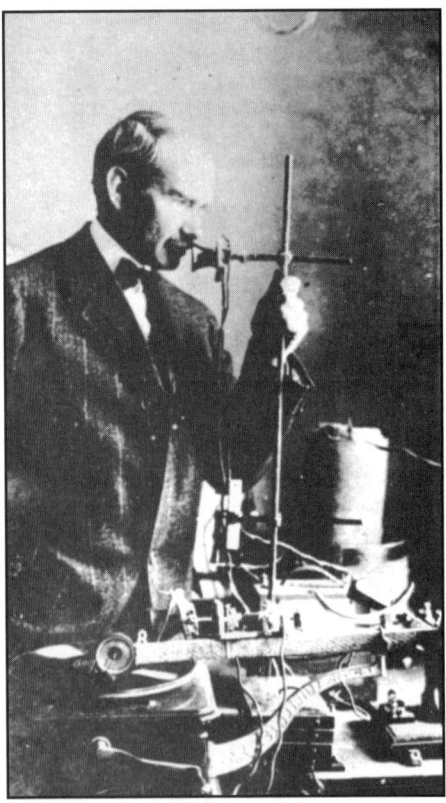

De Forest conducting daily broadcast

"I have in mind a plan of development which would make radio a household utility...The idea is to bring music into the home by wireless. The receiver can be designed in the form of a simple "Radio Music Box" and arranged for several different wavelengths, which can be changeable with the throwing of a single switch or the pressing of a single button...The same principle can be extended to numerous other fields, as for example receiving lectures at home, which could be perfectly audible; and events of national importance which can be simultaneously announced and received. Baseball scores can be transmitted in the air...This proposition would be especially interesting to farmers and others living in outlying districts."

David Sarnoff, American Marconi Company telegrapher, 1916. Sarnoff later became president of RCA, the Radio Corporation of America.

After the war, radio would emerge as the news medium of choice for the public. Radio would be the new competition in media for public attention. The growth of broadcasting would lead to battle for advertising dollars with the print media. Radio would shape the public's perception of news as people became conditioned to the voice and reports of the broadcaster. The Roaring Twenties would demonstrate the glamour of radio and the disparity of news reports as the development of radio conflicted with the interests of other media.

MEDIA
chapter 3
1920-1929
Jazz Journalism, Radio & The News

Early Westinghouse receiver

Media in the 20th Century

In the Twenties, radio dominated American culture. Roughly 5,000 Americans owned radio receivers in 1920, and most of them were primitive "cat's-whisker" crystal sets. Crystal-set receivers contained a fragment of germanium crystal, coiled copper wire and headphones. By 1923, three million people in the United States owned radios, but most listeners still used crystal sets with earphones to receive news and bulletins, advertising and music from the existing stations. Radio speakers became available allowing groups of people to listen together. Radio established itself as a new competitor in the mass media market. The appeal of the spoken word attracted audiences and advertisers, and print journalism was forced to change its image to retain a profit.

Television, a machine capable of wireless transmission of moving images, pioneered by Scottish inventor John L. Baird and publicly demonstrated for the first time in 1926, combined sound and pictures to deliver news as a rival to radio. Television had the ability to project viewers to the scene of a news event visually and audible, creating a dramatic appeal and lending the illusion of credibility to the report made by the broadcaster. What remains an issue is that television ultimately decides what stories to project, like any other media. The audience is told that they have the power to form personal opinions on the news accounts displayed on television, told on the radio, or printed in the press, yet those opinions are based on what the media choose to present to the public. Television revolutionized the perception of media as a mechanism for manipulating the public to accept the news as relevant and as truth.

Muckraking journalism from the first decade of the century was resurrected in the 1920s in the form of tabloids, characterized by a preoccupation with scandal, crime, and the sordid lives of the rich and famous. Also labeled "jazz journalism," this style of media reflected the decadent life and adventurous spirit of the time. Film celebrities, war heroes, and criminal proceedings dominated the popular news.

The press clamored to gain the exclusive on the first person to fly solo in an airplane across the Atlantic Ocean, Charles A. Lindbergh. Completing the flight from New York to Paris on May 20, 1927, a total of 3,610 miles in 33 $^1/_2$ hours, was an act of daring and skill, indicative of a world that wanted to be

Charles Lindbergh

1920-1929

FACTS AND FIGURES OF THE 1920s

Daily paper:	2¢
Sunday paper:	5¢
Paperback novel:	$1.75
Biography:	$4.00

free of the burdens of World War I. The press labeled Lindbergh "Lucky Lindy" and glorified him as an international hero. His success inspired the media companies to use air travel to deploy reporters to a scene to obtain first-hand accounts of domestic and international affairs away from their home bases. Regular air mail was initiated as a result of these air feats, allowing readers in rural areas to receive timely news through subscriptions to national papers and magazines.

It was an era where anyone who appeared in the press was an automatic celebrity. In politics, jazz journalism flourished during the scandalous government of President Warren G. Harding. Americans elected the jovial and personable Harding to the presidency in 1920, based on his campaign to "return to normalcy." As the owner/publisher of the *Marion Star* newspaper in Ohio, Harding was aware of the power of the press to uncover fraud in politics and shape public opinion toward the support or denouncement of a candidate. Unashamedly pro-business, the Republican Harding was quiet, virtuous, honest and deeply loyal, but refused to face responsibility. A skillful mediator, he became known as the "Great Handshaker." Unfortunately, Harding proved the old saying "loyal to a fault."

Although loved by the American people, his loyalty to corrupt cronies destroyed the growing trust in government built during the previous two decades. The Teapot Dome scandal ruined Harding and most of his administration. The tabloids played up the scandal of Teapot Dome, in which two federal oil reserves, one at Teapot Dome in Wyoming, were turned over to the secretary of the interior, Albert B. Fall, who sold drilling contracts to developers for personal gain. The exposés of government corruption were valued and given priority by the press above the economic problems in the world. Fraud, theft,

President Warren Harding and "Laddie" play for the camera

Media in the 20th Century

and political scandal were profitable exposés for tabloids, and the Teapot Dome scandal met all the criteria. The tabloids initiated the participation of the more reputable newspapers in their scrutiny of Harding on the front page. The papers uncovered corruption in government due to the president's delegation of responsibility to subordinates without lending attention to their actions. The media did not support his belief in cutting taxes for the wealthy as a means to stimulate the economy. Harding suffered a heart attack in August 1923 and died before he could rectify the tarnish upon his character and his administration.

JAZZ JOURNALISM

"Jazz journalism" defined the decade known as the **Roaring Twenties**. The press was often preoccupied with entertainment, rather than taking on a leadership role of displaying significant news stories or interpreting news events. Typical stories passed as news glorified celebrities and built up sordid events, such as murder trials, into national sensations.

Throughout his career as a journalist and "critic of ideas" **Henry Louis Mencken** crusaded on the behalf of the "civilized minority" against the tyranny of the majority. He began a newspaper career as a reporter at age 16 in Baltimore, Maryland, where he acquired fame for his satiric wit and campaign against the mindless acts of Americans in the *Baltimore Sun* newspaper. In his observations of the American scene, he wrote about the best and worst of the people, commenting that "No one ever went broke underestimating the intelligence of the American people."

H. L. Mencken's *American Mercury* magazine, which he and **George Jean Nathan** founded in 1924, continued much of the "jazz journalism" style which he had used during the last decade at the *Baltimore Sun* newspaper. Mencken's rapier wit left few survivors without memorable wounds. A

H.L. Mencken

1920-1929

friend of author **F. Scott Fitzgerald**, who was famous at the time for his writing on the excesses of the 1920s in novels such as *The Great Gatsby* and *This Side of Paradise*, Mencken relentlessly printed his opinions about society. The "**Bad Boy of Baltimore**" wielded his pen like a sword. He disparaged the middle class as the "booboosie" (instead of bourgeoisie), dismissed the backwardness of the South as "the Sahara of the Bozart" (a play on the phrase *beaux arts*, which is French for "fine arts"), and attacked the progressives as "do-gooders" and "Puritans" who lived with "the haunting fear that someone, somewhere, might be happy." Although Mencken focused on ridiculing American values, other tabloids exploited them through the sensational style of presenting news.

1925 Daily Press, Utica NY

DAILY NEWSPAPERS

Year	Number	Circulation (in millions)
1920	2,042	27,791
1930	1,942	39,589
1940	1,878	41,137
1950	1,772	51,829
1960	1,763	58,882
1970	1,748	62,108

New York's ***Illustrated Daily News***, begun in 1919 by **Joseph M. Patterson** and **Robert R. McCormick**, was a strong tabloid in the 1920s. Continuing to employ photographs as a technique to sell papers, the publication also offered lotteries, coupon prizes, and other similar inducements to attract an audience. In 1924 the *Daily News* became the most widely circulated paper in America. As in any industry, competition surfaces. That same year the paper was confronted by direct competition from other tabloids such as the ***Daily Mirror***, published by **William Randolph Hearst**, and the *Daily Graphic*, published by the team of **Bernarr Macfadden** and **Emile Gauvreau**.

The *Daily Mirror* challenged the coverage of events provided by the *Daily News* with a higher level of journalistic integrity. It did not seek to make the news content as lurid as possible to attract readers, but did use similar techniques, such as: bold headlines and photographs to appeal to audiences. The strategy failed and in 1926 the *Daily Mirror* became desperate in its competition with the *Daily News* and the *Daily Graphic*. To increase sales, the *Daily Mirror* resurrected a four-year-old murder case from 1922 in New Brunswick, New Jersey. The case involved the mysterious death of a clergyman, Edward Hall, and his mistress, a choir singer, Eleanor Mills. The *Mirror* printed excerpts of the case and succeeded in bringing the minister's widow, Mrs. Hall, to trial. For months New Brunswick became the center of attention for press associations and large newspapers in America. Tabloids began to set the precedent for what was considered news. Legitimate and reputable news organizations were forced to cover sensational news stories created by tabloids, due to the mass public demand. The papers were confronted with the challenges of catering to public demands for accurate information, while presenting the news that the public found important and relevant. Mrs. Hall sued the paper for libel after she was acquitted of the murder charges.

> **"Journalism over here is not only an obsession but a drawback that cannot be overrated. Politicians are frightened of the press, and in the same way as bullfighting has a brutalizing effect upon Spain (of which she is unconscious), headlines of murder, rape, and rubbish excite and demoralizes the American public."**
>
> Margot Asquith, British socialite. *My Impressions of America*, 1922

Pressing on with the news that tantalized the American public, a second sordid murder case became a national sensation. In 1927 a corset salesman, Judd Gray, had collaborated with his girlfriend, Mrs. Ruth Snyder, to dispose of Mr. Snyder. The case was brought to trial and Ruth Snyder was convicted of murder and sentenced to execution by the electric chair at Sing Sing prison in New York. The *Daily Graphic*, which became the most notorious of tabloids, blasted its headlines to readers with direct language. The headline read: "Don't fail to read tomorrow's *Daily Graphic*. An installment that thrills and stuns! A story that fairly pierces the heart and reveals Ruth Snyder's last thought on earth; that pulses the blood as it discloses her final letters. Think of it! A woman's final thoughts just before she is clutched in the deadly snare that sears and burns and FRIES AND KILLS! Her very last words! Exclusively in tomorrow's *Graphic*!"

The *Daily Graphic* aimed to obtain a confession and bring the reader into the mind of the convicted murderess. The *Daily News* would bring the terror of Mrs. Snyder to the people. Priding itself as a photographic news source, the *Daily News* was determined to bring the reader into the execution chamber to experience the momentous occasion. **Tom Howard**, a reporter for the *Daily News*, concealed a camera on his ankle and took a picture just after the current was turned on. The *Daily News* put a touched-up picture on the front page the next day and sold 450,000 papers, later selling an additional 750,000.

The *Daily News* sought to find hidden or unique angles to stories. Upon hearing about the sinking of the British steamer *Vestris* in 1928 off the Virginia coast, in which 110 people lost their lives, the *Daily News* dispatched all of its reporters to interview the survivors on the chance that one might have taken a picture. For the huge sum of $1,200 the *Daily News* bought an action photo depicting the ship sinking and the desperate expressions of the passengers.

1920-1929

The tabloids thrived on controversy, and became the subject of debate from social commentators on their content and from other newspapers concerned about the competition. To denounce

NEW PUBLICATIONS

The Twenties saw a variety of new publications emerge as the tabloids lent themselves to the development of interpretive reporting. The *New Yorker* is often considered the best general magazine in America, especially for those who appreciate sophisticated humor and style. It is world-renowned for its marvelous cartoons. The first issue came out on February 21, 1925. *Time* magazine debuted in March 1923, published by **Briton Hadden** and **Henry R. Luce**, as the first condensed weekly news magazine, offering comprehensive national and world news with in-depth commentary and photos. News was organized and divided into departments by its editors, whose slogan was "*Time* is written as if by one man for one man." *Time* covered national affairs, foreign news, science, religion, business, education, and other subjects, written for the "busy man" who had little knowledge of the various areas. *Time* developed an extensive research staff to supplement its stories received from press associations and incorporate as much fact as possible in a story. With the advent of *Time*, the question of "why" a story held importance replaced the traditional "who did what."

First issue of *The Reader's Digest*

tabloids and gain readership, respectable papers would print opinions such as: "Tabloids are converting readers into witless gossips, gutter vamps and backyard sheiks." Notices similar to these were printed to embarrass the tabloid audience and influence its purchase of other papers. In April 1927 the magazine *Forum* headlined an article "**Are Tabloid Newspapers a Menace?**"

To keep pace with the fast times and maximize personal efficiency, this decade saw the birth of new "condensed" publications. **DeWitt** and **Lila Wallace** pioneered the combination of news and entertainment articles, taken from other magazines and reprinted in their magazine *Reader's Digest*, which began on February 5, 1922. With a borrowed $5,000, Wallace and his wife began publishing the *Reader's Digest* in a Greenwich Village basement in New York City.

Media in the 20th Century

Based on articles printed whole or edited from other publications, *Reader's Digest*, a pocket-sized magazine, delivered a wide range of general information topics for people who didn't have time to read multiple periodicals. DeWitt Wallace was an avid reader who kept a file of magazine articles that interested him, and deleted the unnecessary information and words. The aim was to "inform, entertain, inspire and guide people in their daily lives" by providing practical advice and anecdotes. The title of one article printed in the first edition, a page and a half in length, was "**How to Keep Young Mentally**," and it was indicative of the type of stories featured. The first issue also contained reprinted articles from the magazines **House Beautiful**, **Scientific American**, and **McClure's**. By balancing national politics, health, social and business articles with seasonings of humor, family life, profiles and occasional international topics, the magazine provided news for a diverse audience. Within a decade, its circulation reached 500,000. According to the company, by 1996 *Reader's Digest* was "the world's most widely read magazine...over 27 million copies in 19 languages bought monthly."

RADIO NEWS

Entering into the year 1920, people thought of radio as an art that could be understood by only the expert or the electronic whiz. Radio in the 1920s began being used for the promotion of newspapers, with the news being read from papers that sponsored time on the radio. In the mid-Twenties a significant percentage of radio stations were operated by non-profit organizations, and in particular, college and universities. For-profit private broadcasters such as newspapers, department stores, power companies, and automobile dealerships also emerged to generate favorable publicity for their enterprises.

One of the first newspapers to capitalize on the radio craze was the **Detroit News** in Michigan. On August 20, 1920, the paper debuted its first broadcast news programs, obtaining its full commercial license in October 1921 under the call letters **WWJ**. WWJ sporadically aired election results, occasional music programs, talks and shows. WWJ was merely a vehicle for self-promotion, public relations and community goodwill for the *Detroit News*. WWJ and other radio stations were money-makers, not for

Early amateur radio station

1920-1929

themselves, but for the newspapers or sponsors until the power of radio advertising revealed its potential as a revenue source. As interest in radio grew, publications such as the *New York Times* began carrying radio programming information.

The first *scheduled* broadcast of a *commercial* radio station was **Westinghouse Corporation's KDKA**, Pittsburgh, Pennsylvania, airing on November 2, 1920, with reports on the Harding-Cox presidential election returns. Scores of telephone calls from listeners came through the Westinghouse switchboard the next day, confirming the success of the first radio broadcast to appeal to a mass audience. In those days the air waves were uncluttered, and weather permitting, the signal from Pittsburgh could be picked up in Washington, D.C., or as far as Illinois. Westinghouse, as a manufacturer of radios, had the added incentive of making radio a viable medium. By 1922, there were 30 stations nationwide, growing to more than 550 stations by 1923. Most of the stations were owned by corporations such as the **American Telephone & Telegraph Company** and by newspapers who sought to promote publications. All 550 stations broadcast over the same two frequencies. Due to their transmitters' low wattage and the large distance between stations, interference and static was minimal.

Early in 1921 **Harold W. Arlin** was hired at KDKA as its first announcer.

KDKA, Pittsburgh, the first commercial radio station

When his voice began giving out, he began playing phonograph records. People excitedly called in and requested their favorites, and soon he'd exhausted his personal music supply. A local music store offered to let him borrow phonograph records to play on the air in return for announcing their store as his music source. Thus the first "sponsored" radio program was born. In addition to playing music, the announcer read news headlines and community bulletins. During this beginning phase, the medium still appealed to only a narrow audience. In the fall of 1921, **David Sarnoff**, president of the **Radio Corporation of America** (RCA), found a way to gain widespread public attention by broadcasting the heavyweight boxing championship fight between Jack Dempsey and Georges Carpentier, gaining an audience of 300,000 listeners, including some as far away as Florida.

Media in the 20th Century

In addition to music and news, radio programming expanded into stock market reports, weather reports, comedy and major sporting events, such as the 1921 World Series. The first newscaster to become an on-air celebrity was **Graham McNamee**. He was first introduced to the public by the Radio Corporation of America and received 50,000 fan letters a year. The machine-gun delivery of **Floyd Gibbons** made the 217-words-per-minute newscaster a celebrity too. Radio personalized politicians by bringing them into people's homes, and many politicians went to school to learn effective public speaking for radio. Radio could reach millions more easily than print publications. People were susceptible to voices, and more easily convinced of a political stance based on the tone of the voice, more than by the actual words spoken. One of the first experiences of radio's power to link people around the globe occurred on March 7, 1924. Speeches made at a New York City dinner were simultaneously transmitted over a loosely formed six-station **network**. The signals sped from WJZ in

Zenith's first commercially produced radio to run on AC household current

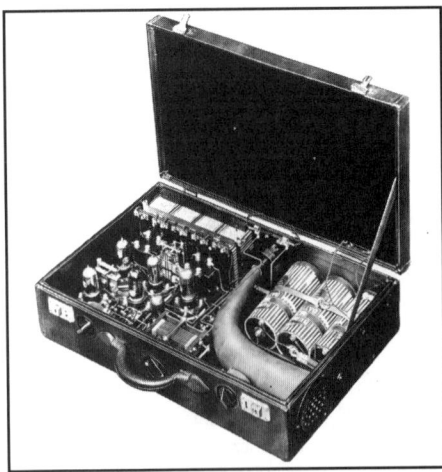

The first portable radio from Zenith cost $200

New York across the entire United States, to San Francisco. They also reached across the ocean to a radio station in Manchester, England.

Secretary of Commerce **Herbert Hoover** assumed the regulation of broadcasting under the **Radio Act** of 1927, which established a five-person **Federal Radio Commission** to issue broadcast licenses and assign frequency wavelengths to applicants. Licenses were granted to radio stations on the basis of "public interest, convenience or necessity to provide fair, efficient and equitable service throughout the country."

The first national radio network, the **National Broadcasting Company** (NBC), was established in late 1926 by RCA when it purchased American Telegraph & Telephone's (AT&T) broadcast-

1920-1929

ing properties. Its first competitor was the **Columbia Broadcasting System** (CBS), created in 1927. These two networks and their associate stations across the country were the dynamic component of American broadcasting. One of the major reasons for the formation of networks was convenience to advertisers, similar to the newspapers in the forming of chains.

Aware of the power of radio as an advertising medium, **William S. Paley** invested in CBS in 1927, became its president on September 26, 1928, and quickly signed 49 affiliated stations. With financial assistance from his father, a wealthy cigar manufacturer, he intended to stay in New York for only a few months to put the network in shape and then return to the cigar business. The months turned into years and he remained at the forefront of CBS until 1990.

Paley quickly established CBS as a leader over NBC through his innovations in station relations. NBC charged affiliate stations for broadcasting programs that were not sponsored and reimbursed them for airing sponsored programs. Paley offered the entire CBS program schedule free to affiliate stations with one stipulation. Paley could sell guaranteed coast-to-coast air time to a network sponsor and give affiliates two weeks' notice to clear their programming schedule for that time slot. This practice is sometimes called **preempting**. This was an unexpected financial gain to many struggling stations, as it eliminated bookkeeping, advertising sales and time-consuming negotiation. CBS grew rapidly on the strength of this strategy.

The Roaring Twenties also brought talking movies, or "talkies" that destroyed the careers of some successful silent stars. As with politicians, thousands of actors and actresses went back to school or sought special voice coaches and training in order to improve their speech, projection, presentation and vocal skills.

ADVERTISING

The rising success of radio as a tool of mass communication attracted advertisers to market their wares to a large and growing audience. The prospects of selling to huge audiences at low cost enamored many advertisers of this fledgling new medium. After all, for the same $100 cost of one magazine ad to reach 50,000 readers, an advertiser could

WEAF, NYC radio station

MEDIA IN THE 20th CENTURY

Helen Hann, WEAF's first studio hostess and announcer

potentially reach a million listeners. Plus, there was the advantage of the audience's perception of radio as advanced and futuristic. Everyone wanted to be associated with radio's success at all levels.

When AT&T's station **WEAF** went on the air in August 1922, it also featured the first paid advertisement. For $100, the Queensboro Corporation purchased a ten-minute commercial for its new real estate development, Hawthorne Court. Tirelessly, Queensboro's representative, Mr. Blackwell, droned relentlessly on and on about "The Hawthorne Court system of high-grade dwelling apartments ... the home removed from the congested part of the city, right at the boundaries of God's great outdoors ... offering a chance to unfold, more opportunity to get near Mother Earth, to play, to romp, to plant and to dig."

Although literacy levels were still high, radio was perceived as a more effective communications tool compared to print. Even people who couldn't read (or read very well) could grasp the spoken word. And as commercials were repeated verbatim, any words not understood the first time around were likely to be understood by the tenth or twentieth: many non-English speaking immigrants listened to the radio to become familiar with the language and customs of their new country.

In 1922 Commerce Secretary Herbert Hoover, in charge of regulating broadcasting, worried that radio could "be drowned in advertising chatter." That "advertising chatter" translated into ringing cash registers for many of the forward-thinking companies such as the American Tobacco Company (the makers of Lucky Strike cigarettes) and the A & P grocery stores, which successfully advertised their products on the radio. In addition, broadcasting companies such as AT&T, Westinghouse, and General Electric also benefitted by the popularity of radio and by promoting their own products on the air. Widespread public attention was fueled through broadcasts of prizefights and major league baseball games, along with political speeches and newscasts.

Print advertising changed during this

time as well. Replacing the softly illustrated family look were realistic photographs and bold, striking graphics of children looking directly at the consumer. Many timeless product images were created during this era, such as the Morton's Salt girl, with the slogan "When it rains, it pours," and the Cracker Jack boy. In keeping with the tabloid journalism of the time, advertisements were presented to a consuming public with false promises. A mouthwash claimed the approval of 45,512 doctors, none of whom were named. Another phenomenon used in advertisements of this decade was the celebrity testimonial endorsements of products. The dominating trend of advertising in this decade was the use of psychology to induce people to buy. Advertising quickly learned to play upon people's fears and desires. Self-improvement ads, suggesting that a product would drastically improve lives, or ads promoting the need for a product merely because it was fashionable among people of wealth and high position, were effective tactics. The use of vulgar language in poetic story format, combined with pictures to create illusions of glamour, adventure, and freedom, was typical of ads hawking everything from automobiles to facial soap. Everywhere people of the Twenties were confronted by images of beautiful people with expensive toys having more fun. With its sensational promises, advertising in the Twenties was certainly the offspring of tabloid journalism. Great advertising had the power to bring instant success to a business or to salvage a discredited product, just as news had the power to incite feeling or interest in the sordid and astonishing.

TELEVISION

As early as 1907, *Scientific American* magazine used the word **television** to describe the transmission of pictures. In 1910, the *Kansas City Times* told its readers that "television is on the way." Television, the newspaper said, induced a viewer into the action through moving pictures and sound, and would become the most successful competitor to newspapers and radio.

Then Secretary of Commerce, Herbert Hoover demonstrates early television, 1927

MEDIA IN THE 20th CENTURY

The first telecast of an object in motion was achieved by Scottish inventor **John L. Baird** in England in 1926. On May 11, 1928, General Electric began the first regularly scheduled television broadcast, over station **WGY** in Schenectady, New York. These media milestones broke ground for the coming television revolution. Due to the high cost of the technology in the experimental phase of its development, the medium wouldn't dominate American culture until the Fifties.

The Twenties was a time of frivolity in media. Much of what was printed and aired on the radio was trivial, as editors and broadcasters feared that serious or difficult material would antagonize the readers or listeners they depended on for their livelihood. Instead, popular culture dominated media in the decade labeled as the Roaring Twenties and established media as a powerful tool for influencing the ideas and opinions and buying habits of a mass audience.

Vladimir Zworykin, left

MEDIA
chapter 4
1930-1939
The Great Depression, Scrutiny of the Press, Radio's Dominance and World War II

Rita Hayworth with a 1936 Zenith radio

Media in the 20th Century

With the collapse of the American stock market in 1929, America's Great Depression, which would last most of the decade, caused worldwide economic insecurity.

At the lowest point of the Depression in 1933, 16 million people, or one-third of the United States labor force, were unemployed. Some 1,616 U.S. banks failed and nearly 20,000 business firms went bankrupt. The world's population reached almost two billion in 1930, with much of it caught in the stranglehold of economic depression. Despite, and in part, due to the grave economic conditions radio remained strong. The sale of radio sets increased to 13.5 million in 1930 in the United States, up from 75,000 in 1921. Advertisers spent $60 million on radio commercials, using money previously allotted to print advertising.

Publishers who invested in expensive new presses and photographic equipment became economically squeezed as their circulation and advertising revenues decreased. Even the *New York Times* experienced a 20 percent decline in ad dollars in the first year of the Great Depression. Periodicals such as *Time* and *Reader's Digest* captured more market share, as people saw the increased value in purchasing one or two condensed magazines filled with the most important news gathered from multiple publications. With few job prospects and less money, people were more selective about the newspapers they chose to read. Without jobs, people had time to debate issues including newspapers' coverage, style, slant and editorials.

Herbert Hoover, the 31st president of the United States, believed the economy would regenerate spontaneously, and was reluctant to extend federal aid. The Democratic-controlled Congress defied him, and passed the Emergency Relief Act and created the federal home loan banks. In 1931 Hoover proposed a one-year suspension on reimbursements and war debts to ease Europe's troubled financial situation. In 1932 some 15,000 veterans, known as Bonus Marchers, marched on Washington, demanding immediate payment of their World War I bonus certificates. Hoover ordered federal troops to remove them from government property. Hoover finally initiated a large public works program and the Reconstruction Finance Corporation in 1932 to relieve the stress of the Depression. His delays in working for public relief cost him the election, and Franklin Delano Roosevelt became the 32nd president.

Number of Radio Stations on Air

Year	AM	FM
1930	612	
1935	605	
1940	814	
1945	943	53

During the months prior to the presidential nominations of 1932, the major publishers promoted their favored candidates in their papers. In the *San Francisco Examiner* and his other papers, William Randolph Hearst, previously a Herbert Hoover supporter, changed his allegiance to Franklin D. Roosevelt and helped him obtain the nomination for the presidency. Robert R. McCormick and his papers, especially his flagship *Chicago Tribune*, represented the conservative right wing and

1930-1939

constantly opposed Roosevelt and his "New Deal." With Roosevelt's election, many publishers became even more politically involved through their editorials, especially targeting the New Deal programs. The New Deal was a plan designed to preserve the capitalist system by managing the economy and undertaking relief programs to increase consumer spending.

The growth of radio, President Roosevelt's (FDR's) New Deal and rumblings of concern in Europe created a new mood. Although poor and afraid, people discovered a new pride and unity in their identity as Americans. FDR's radio "Fireside Chats" were weekly speeches that brought messages of inspiration and relief to millions. His bold economic plans and his ability to address, relate to, and encourage the public inspired hope for American economic recovery.

Radio infiltrated all aspects of American life, filling it with music, news and advertisements. Among the existing mass media during the depression, radio received the majority of advertising revenue. As the depression progressed, newspapers were resentful about supplying news to radio stations, as competition saw many newspapers go out of business. The development of widespread network broadcasting and regulation of the airwaves by the Federal Communications Commission brought radio to the media forefront. In 1932 the Associated Press, a news wire service, began selling news accounts of the presidential election coverage to radio networks. People were able to receive immediate bulletins of events around the world and were given the opinion of the broadcaster, before the news was printed. The newspapers and the American Newspaper Publishers Association board of directors instigated a two-year battle to eliminate

W2DKJ demonstrates mobile communications at the 1939 World's Fair

radio news competition. The board members implored press associations to refrain from selling news to radio stations in advance of the publication of the story in the press. The broadcasting of news, they felt, should be limited to brief bulletins that would encourage newspaper sales. The Associated Press agreed not to furnish news to radio networks, and the radio industry was forced to take on the responsibility of news gathering for itself.

The Columbia Broadcasting System established news service bureaus in New York, Washington, D.C., Chicago, Los Angeles, and London and built an extensive system of correspondents. It also imported reports from the British Exchange Telegraph service for daily newscasts. The National Broadcasting Corporation established a similar bureau to obtain news. Local radio stations used

Media in the 20th Century

First "Fireside Chat" by FDR, March 12, 1935

early-edition newspapers to broadcast news to their audience. The networks discovered that gathering news was an expensive, yet effective method to stay competitive with the newspapers.

Radio brought events live to the American public from faraway places like London, England. Presidential campaigns and nominations were presented as they happened, and King Edward VIII of England abdicated his throne before an audience of radio listeners. Through the expansion of its technical facilities, radio began to establish a position of importance in keeping the public informed on a timely basis.

POLITICS OF THE PRESS

With the depressed economy, advertising and consumer budgets decreased. While some publications went under, many others consolidated. The two major American publishers, **William Randolph Hearst** (*San Francisco Examiner* and *New York Journal*) and **Robert R. McCormick** (*Chicago Tribune*) found themselves targets of their audience. People without jobs had more time to read and criticize the newspapers and the information they printed. Consumers became aware of media group consolidation, which sometimes resulted in one publisher owning all the publications in a given market. People objected to the standardization of news, the lack of true exchange of ideas and the emphasis on sensational and trivial "distractions" over in-depth coverage of real issues. People looked to their paper to provide answers to the uncertainty of the economy and guide them in choosing a leader who would best govern their interests. However, newspapers were prone to be biased and tried to influence public opinion to support their ideas.

People purchased and perused the papers diligently for several reasons: (1) to find a job opening listed in the want ads; (2) to discover a story about a promising company where they could apply for a job; and (3) an inexpensive form of entertainment. Debating issues, including which newspaper offered the most value, best coverage, variety of opinions and comics, was a way to pass the time and discuss the nation's options.

1930-1939

During the hopelessness and uncertainty of the Thirties, America engaged in a re-examination of all its social, political and economic institutions. The press as an institution was challenged more directly than at any time since the Federalists (a party of land owners and merchants) attacked press freedom in the 18th century. As a liberal resurgence began to take place, caustic surveys of the American press and their unquestionable political power became the subject of several books, which enjoyed wide circulation and success. Criticism of the press emerged as political tension grew and the press failed to provide objective articles analyzing the character of potential political candidates. Books such as *Lords of the Press* by George Seldes (1938) and *America's House of Lords* by Harold Ickes (1939) were accounts of a press controlled by its business offices and advertisers. These books and others made many people suspicious about their sources of news. For the first time, the "press lords" were the subjects of investigative reporting by critics who felt the press was acting irresponsibly in doing its job to educate the public about national and international issues.

William Randolph Hearst

> **"These unhappy times call for the building of plans...that build from the bottom up and not the top down, that put their faith once more in the forgotten man at the bottom of the economic pyramid."**
>
> President Franklin D. Roosevelt

Hearst and McCormick were the prominent publishers who were at the center of scrutiny during this period. Critics complained about the effects of media group ownership and the shrinking number of cities that had more than one publisher. The constant change in the political beliefs of the various papers and the information they printed confused the public. Much of the press changed its stance from liberal to conservative, which angered the public, who supported President **Franklin D. Roosevelt's** liberal New Deal plans.

Although the papers were guilty of some of the accusations, what had really changed were the readers. People were

Media in the 20th Century

Growth of U.S. Newspapers

Year	1920	1930
Cities with daily paper	1,295	1,402
Cities with one-daily paper	716	1,002
Cities with competing daily papers	552	288

presented editorials and feature stories that focused intensely on the governing of the nation. President **Herbert Hoover**, who held office from 1929 to 1933, was deeply distressed by the widespread misery the nation was experiencing. He had great faith in the efficiency of industry and free enterprise and shrank from the idea of government hand-outs. Despite optimistic statements of prosperity around the corner, conditions continually worsened. Publishers Hearst and McCormick were on opposite sides in their support of presidential candidates. Hearst was a strong supporter of Franklin Roosevelt, a position that would later change after Roosevelt was elected and began to enact reforms. McCormick believed in the policies of Herbert Hoover and felt that America would restructure itself and did not need government assistance.

hungry and out of work. They wanted answers to the dismal conditions they were collectively facing. Consumers expected journalists to return to the ethics of the investigative reporters and deliver real news stories, as opposed to the tabloid stories of the previous decade.

While the press faced scrutiny from the public and authors, the publishers

Interestingly, William Randolph Hearst, who built what was then the world's largest publishing empire, was hurt badly by the Depression. In the early 1930s his newspapers publicized and sold a $50 million stock issue just to keep themselves afloat. Hearst continued to pour money from personal profits from his silver mines, ranch land

IBM electric typewriter, 1935

and other business operations into his vast newspaper chain. Prior to the stock market crash, Hearst had spent freely with an estimated $40 million on art treasures and oddities, untold millions for his personal life, and more than $50 million of real estate, which during the Depression became an enormous liability. Still, in 1935 he owned 26 daily papers and 17 Sunday editions in 19 cities. He also controlled the King Features Syndicate and the International News Service, along with 13 magazines, such as *Harper's Bazaar* and *Cosmopolitan*, eight radio stations, and two-motion picture companies. Although Hearst had supported Herbert Hoover in the previous election, he switched his allegiance to Franklin Roosevelt in 1932. Using articles and cartoons to present Roosevelt as a savior to America and to depict the failures of Hoover, Hearst helped obtain Roosevelt's nomination for the presidency.

Roosevelt's **New Deal** programs aimed at three R's: **Relief, Recovery** and **Reform**. Within his first 100 days of office, Congress passed many essential programs of the New Deal. FDR created a revolution for America. Roosevelt's method was "Take a method and try it. If it fails, try another." Among the many programs he created was the **Agricultural Adjustment Administration (AAA)** to raise farm prices by paying farmers to take land out of production. The plan failed, as people were outraged by the destruction of crops to raise prices while people were starving. He created the **National Recovery Administration (NRA)**, a program meant to increase employment and regulate the prices of goods. Consumers were advised to shop at locations that displayed the NRA symbol. But prices were fixed at high amounts and production was limited, so the opposite effect occurred. Roosevelt also created the **Works Progress Administration (WPA)** to place people in jobs that equated to their experience, although that was not always the case.

Of the major initiatives proposed by Roosevelt, in New Deal measures, the Supreme Court rejected eleven of them. The conservative Supreme Court was a block to progress, and Roosevelt wanted to "pack" it with judges who would be sympathetic to the New Deal legislation. Six of the nine judges serving at the time were over 70 years of age, and they strongly felt it was their patriotic duty to curb the socialistic tendencies of the man in the White House. Roosevelt bluntly asked Congress for legislation that would permit him to add a new justice for every member over the age of 70 who would not retire. Democrats and Republicans alike savagely condemned Roosevelt for attempting to break the delicate checks and balances among the three branches of government. The Supreme Court later became more friendly toward Roosevelt's reforms. By the end of his term, he was able to make nine new appointments through the death and resignation of judges, the most by any president since Washington.

While Hearst supported Roosevelt in the first election and stressed that in his editorials, the other great "press lord" of the Thirties, Robert R. McCormick became a principal spokesman for the ultraconservative right wing in American politics. McCormick's editorial columns in his *Chicago Tribune* were bitter personal warning stating that America would succumb to communism under the regulatory programs instituted by Roosevelt. His ultraconservative newspaper had a nationalistic and isolationist point of view that kept it from printing all sides

Media in the 20th Century

Gallup Poll

In 1935 an American social researcher from Iowa, George H. Gallup, founded the American Institute of Public Opinion, commonly referred to as the Gallup Poll. The poll was the first to utilize scientific techniques to assess public opinion through the use of sample surveys. In October 1935, sponsored weekly reports on the state of public opinion on national issues in the U.S. began to appear in newspapers. Gallup demonstrated that an accurate account of attitudes and opinions of the national population could be achieved by interviewing a small representative group. The poll changed election forecasting and made government more aware of the weight of public opinion.

about an issue, thus making the paper unreliable and unfair. Its aim was to keep America from participating in foreign cooperative affairs, and its prejudices extended into the presentation of news. McCormick opposed Roosevelt and the domestic policies of the New Deal with every resource he had at his disposal. When World War II began, the *Tribune* denounced Roosevelt for lending assistance to Great Britain. Roosevelt, with the support of Congress, passed the Lend-Lease bill, granting unprecedented powers to aid any country whose own defense was vital to the defense of the United States. A typical eight-column banner headline in the *Tribune* read "HOUSE PASSES DICTATOR BILL" in reference to America's assistance. The paper's activities would serve as an embarrassment to America for its elitist, isolationist views and its failure to maintain objectivity in reporting.

By 1935 William Randolph Hearst had changed his tune, calling Roosevelt's "New Deal" a "Raw Deal" and his National Recovery Administration the "National Run Around" and "No Recovery Allowed," feeling that the NRA was "creeping socialism." Hearst feared communism and believed Roosevelt's radical changes in domestic government would turn America into a communistic regime. As a well known and outspoken Democrat, Hearst criticized the Democratic president and shook the public's trust in its leaders. Hearst installed a special squad of newsmen in Washington, called the "**smear bureau**," whose duty was to unearth anti-New Deal stories for the chain's papers to run. Over the Supreme Court incident, Hearst's editorials said Roosevelt was on his way toward establishing a "personal dictatorship." The great publisher of yellow journalism who always believed that he understood the common people and was understood by them, printed extensive front-page coverage of Roosevelt's WPA program. One of Hearst's headlines regarding the WPA activities ran: "Taxpayers Feed 20,000 Reds on N.Y. Relief Rolls" and Hearst continually called Roosevelt's programs Communist schemes, and labeled him "**Rooseveltski**." The truth was something different. Roosevelt's policies were slowly but surely turning the economy around, and the WPA and other programs were helping millions of Americans.

The print media attempted to bend people's trust in President Roosevelt and his reforms to revitalize the economy. Many papers became so conventional,

1930-1939

conservative in tone, and interested in their own gains that they could not provide objective coverage on the progress of New Deal measures. The press attempted to separate America from the world by reopening the wounds of World War I, and ultimately painting Roosevelt as an advocate of war. The press weathered public attacks on its character, and with the progress of radio it was forced to provide objective international news in order to compete for audience appeal.

ON THE AIR

While the print media continued to exert influence and shape public opinion either for or against Roosevelt, radio made it possible for him to go beyond the opinions of individual publishers and speak directly to the masses. Beginning with his presidential inauguration on March 4, 1933, his booming voice was broadcast nationally, inspiring the American people with inspiration and new hope. Roosevelt was a master showman, and he used radio to speak to the people personally in broadcasts that were called "**fireside chats**," so named to evoke a cozy and intimate feeling amongst listeners. Despite what one read in print, Americans could now draw their own conclusions through these personal encounters over the radio. Roosevelt's first fireside chat was delivered to some 35 million listeners on March 12, 1935. In a calming voice he personally gave his assurance that it was safe to keep money in the banks. Confidence returned, and the banks began to unlock the doors. Receiving information directly from an authoritative voice added credibility to the content of the report. Listeners appreciated Roosevelt and his informal approach, believing he was speaking to them personally, in contrast to newspapers' anonymous address to the public.

The new marvel of radio posed an interesting challenge to the politicians who had to adjust their speaking techniques to this new medium, where millions, rather than thousands, heard their promises. The literate and illiterate, the intellectual and the working person, the rich and the poor, every race, nationality or creed was now one audience instead of separate and individual audiences that the print media had maintained. The immediacy of radio made the vast listening masses a participant in world-shaking events as they were breaking, knitting the country and the world closer together.

In the Thirties, radio became a thriving industry. Despite the Depression, more than 50 million sets were in use, and 700 stations operated nationwide by the close of the decade. Radio revenue from advertising doubled during the Depression years, while newspapers' revenue fell 45 percent and magazine income was cut in half. Radio could provide more for the advertising dollar with its ability to reach a vast national audience, more effectively than through the newspaper chains. Radio continued to focus on entertainment first and news second, until World War II gave radio newsmen the opportunity to expand newscasts and establish a prominent position for the news on the radio.

Germany, under its leader **Adolf Hitler**, suddenly invaded Austria on March 13, 1938. The democratic powers of the world hoped that this would be Hitler's only conquest. Intoxicated by his easy victory, Hitler then began making demands for the German-inhabited

Media in the 20th Century

William Shirer

democracies, unprepared for another war, allowed Germany to take the Sudetenland. The surrender only made Hitler bolder. Six months later Hitler invaded the remains of Czechoslovakia. The democratic world was stunned and anxious.

The Munich crisis of 1938 and the outbreak of war in 1939 gave radio newsmen an opportunity they fully embraced. The networks expanded their news reporting and technical facilities on a large scale. At the station level, newscasts became the prime importance and focus.

In 1937, **CBS** sent the then unknown correspondent **Edward R. Murrow** to London as the European news chief. As his assistant, Murrow hired **William L. Shirer**, formerly a reporter with Hearst's Universal Service. Prior to Hitler's invasion of Austria, radio networks in Europe broadcast cultural programs and human-interest stories for short-wave broadcasts to America which were then re-broadcast by U.S. stations. After Hitler's invasion, Murrow went directly to Austria and on March 12, 1938, improvised the first coordinated broadcast from multiple locations. Shirer

Sudetenland of his neighbor, Czechoslovakia. The leaders of Britain, Prime Minister **Neville Chamberlain**, and France, Prime Minister **Edouard Daladier**, were eager to appease Hitler and frantically tried to bring the dispute to the conference table. President Roosevelt, also deeply alarmed, sent personal messages to Hitler, strongly urging for a peaceful settlement. A conference was held in Munich, Germany, on September 30, 1938. The Western European

1930-1939

reported from London and Murrow from Vienna, Austria, and three newspapermen CBS had hired sent radio news reports from Berlin, Paris and Rome. This set the pattern for radio coverage of the 20 days of crisis in September, beginning with Hitler's demand that the Czechs give him the Sudetenland and ending with the signing of the Munich Pact.

America heard live broadcasts from 14 European cities during the 20-day Munich crisis period. The voices of Hitler, Czech President Benes, British Prime Minister Chamberlain, and Italian dictator Benito Mussolini was heard firsthand. In CBS's "Studio Nine" in New York City, commentator **H.V. Kaltenborn** spent the three weeks of the crisis analyzing the news reports with hours of commentary. Kaltenborn translated Hitler's fiery oratory for the listeners of America and predicted the diplomatic steps would lead to war. Kaltenborn was heard 85 times during these three weeks, as CBS devoted 471 broadcasts to the crisis, nearly 48 hours of air time, of which 135 were bulletin interruptions, including 98 from European correspondents. **NBC's** two networks logged 443 programs. CBS had the most prominent and colorful lineup of correspondents who were later to leave their mark on network television news. The radio coverage of the Munich crisis confirmed the power of radio to inform and influence the minds of its audience. The reality of events brought into the lives of people isolated from the war made radio a symbol of truth.

Radio was relatively new and often presented entertainment in the form of regular comedy programs or music shows. The radio play "Invasion from

Edward R. Murrow

Mars," based on the book ***The War of the Worlds*** by H. G. Wells, was broadcast by CBS on October 30, 1938. The host was **Orson Welles**, known to the radio public as the voice of **The Shadow**. In a commanding and monotone voice, Welles told the American public that Earth was being invaded by Martians. One can only speculate why Americans were so easily persuaded to believe the story especially since Welles announced several times that it was just a story adapted from a famous novel. It may have been that the urgent "news flash" used as a lead in helped listeners to believe the actuality of the event. The public was nervous about the events in Europe and an atmosphere of tension was present. In addition, the public believed and relied on what they heard on the radio as "news" and the context of Welles' performance was more like news than entertainment. People across the nation ran out into the streets with wet towels over their faces to protect themselves from the Martians' poison gas, called the police, and caused traffic jams. Informed of the national panic, CBS reassured the audience about the Halloween prank by closing the show with the line, "If your doorbell rings and nobody's there, that was no Martian . . . it's Halloween."

Orson Welles broadcasting "The War of the Worlds"

ADVERTISING

Radio advertising matured and became more sophisticated in its ability to lure the consumer. Auto manufacturer Henry Ford described the atmosphere of the Thirties in the quote "These are really good times but only a few know it," and only a few could actually afford the products that advertising promoted. Despite this fact, radio advertising blossomed. By 1935, CBS had 97 stations. To attract the attention of advertisers, CBS created reports on the power radio and its ability to influence

1930-1939

the public, for distribution to potential advertisers. **Paul Keston** of CBS churned out volumes of promotional pamphlets and brochures that became conversation pieces and guides for radio advertisers.

> "We grew up founding our dreams on the infinite promise of American advertising. I still believe that one can learn to play the piano by mail and that mud will give you a perfect complexion."
>
> Zelda Fitzgerald, U.S. writer. *Save Me the Waltz*, 1932

A Keston instruction booklet for advertisers from 1935 titled, "You Do What You're Told," caused a stir in the advertising industry because of its strong theme, which implied that people do as they are told without thinking. Using simple examples from everyday life, he proposed questions such as: When the dentist says, "Open your mouth," you open your mouth, don't you? When the Western Union messenger says, "Sign here," you sign, don't you? So too with "have a cigarette," "listen to this," "don't go yet," or "shake hands with so and so," and of course, "come right in." The point, stated the booklet, was that voices of affection and authority were involved in each of these cases, and that those voices could be projected out on radio with profound impact, something that advertisers were unable to do using print media. With such voices involved, the booklet said the basic rule is "seven times, eight times, nine times out of ten, people do what they're told." Scores of advertisers wanted to try it. Buick defined the intelligent family with "Today the discriminating family finds it absolutely necessary to own two or more motor cars." Keston's brilliant message confirmed what propagandists have always known: People accept as true those ideas that are repeated to them most often. Advertising shapes our opinions, and yet we seem oddly unaware of how much what we believe to be true derives from these ideas we hear repeatedly. Radio began to refine the enormous power of mass communications to tell the public how to live, what to be afraid of, what to be proud of or how to be successful.

As radio established itself as a business, its needs and interests became directed toward increasing profits, and not necessarily toward promoting the collective welfare of society. Regardless of the economic climate of the Thirties, by the end of the decade 85 percent of American households owned a radio.

Radio had become the fourth largest industry in the nation and the most pervasive medium of communication in the 1930s. Business executives in radio and advertising joined the high-income ranks, and their view of the world supported, justified and glamorized the values within their circle. Radio became the most innovative and effective way for advertisers to bring a product directly into the home. The fact that it used the spoken word created new strategies. The singing commercial, known as the **jingle**, became an American phenomenon by capturing the attention and retention of the audience.

The social messages of radio advertising were closely linked to the social messages of mass magazine advertising in that advertisers paid less attention to the special qualities and advantages of their products and more to the study of what people desired, feared or aspired to. Advertisers claimed that their products could help people feel young and desirable, rich, or envied. Magazines of this era were running endless messages warning of body odor, "pink toothbrush," and bad complexions. Listerine (the mouthwash) presented weekly full-page stories of lives forever ruined because of bad breath.

Those who had built the radio industry did not intend broadcasting to become a commercial vehicle. In the early days of radio, everyone from Secretary of Commerce Herbert Hoover to broadcasters such as RCA executive David Sarnoff were opposed to paid commercial messages. In 1933, U.S. Senators **Robert Wagner** of New York and **Henry Hatfield** of West Virginia proposed the cancellation and redistribution of all radio licenses, to counteract commercial domination of the medium.

The move failed, and broadcasting became a medium run by private corporations, financed by the dollars of other private corporations through advertising revenue. Further, the **Federal Communication Act** of 1934 promised a "hands-off" attitude on the part of government toward broadcast program content, leaving the industry free to determine what type of programming was best for the public. Part of the act states: "Nothing in this Act shall be understood or construed to give the Commission the power of censorship over radio communication or signals transmitted by any radio station and no regulation or condition shall be promulgated or fixed by the Commission which shall interfere with the right of free speech."

The advertising community quickly discovered radio to be a much stronger selling force than it had ever known. It could not rest with the limited right to just have a sponsor's name mentioned as the patron of a program. Under the leadership of such advertising giants as **Albert Lasker** of the Lord & Thomas agency, sponsors won the right to broadcast commercial messages in return for sponsoring programs. By the Thirties, sponsors actually bought blocks of time on a network. For instance, Pepsodent (the toothpaste) brought listeners "**Amos 'n' Andy**" on weeknights at 7 o'clock, and on Sunday nights Jell-O presented "**Jack Benny**." Sponsors were clearly identified with specific programs in the hopes of earning the gratitude of the listeners.

Not all sponsors were appreciated by the public. In the early 1930s CBS was under attack for its many laxative commercials. In 1935 **William Paley**, president of CBS, announced that laxatives and other products involving "questions of taste" would be banned, and his policy was to take effect when the laxative company's contract had expired. The timing of the laxative incident was near June, when many sponsors left the air for a "summer hiatus" because fewer people listened to the radio during the summer months. Paley's announcement to honor existing contracts meant that a laxative manufacturer could remain as a sponsor by extending their contract into summer, which was separate from the normal agreement. If the sponsors left for the summer, the tenure would end. That year CBS received an "avalanche of praise" for its good taste by banning laxatives. But it also turned out to be the best year for laxative ad sales. Despite the criticisms, the laxative ban was eventually forgotten. The public evidently became used to "bad taste" and the networks continued to make phenomenal profits from unsavory advertising.

1930-1939

OPINIONS ON FILM

While radio was booming and television was still in the developmental stages, theatrical **newsreels** were a predominant form of entertainment and information, and were considered the forerunner of television news. In the hopelessness and harsh economic climate of the Thirties, feature films provided an element of escape, and for just 15 cents one could be transported by hours of romance, adventure, glamour and humor. By the end of the decade, Americans were buying 80 million movie tickets annually. Each showing included a newsreel, a cartoon, a short subject, previews of coming attractions, and a double feature. The newsreel presented the lives of public figures on the screen, and also brought the events of the nation and the world to the mass public. Newsreels could also sway public opinion. In 1934 socialist writer **Upton Sinclair** ran for governor of California on the Democratic ticket and was initially dismissed as an idealistic fringe candidate. Astounding everyone, Sinclair won the primary election with a majority vote, receiving more votes than all the other candidates combined. Republican businessmen collected the unheard of sum of $10 million to mount an advertising campaign against him, which included mass billboards all over the state, and a series of newsreel commercial messages that hinted that Sinclair was an agent of Russian communism. One of the newsreels showed a vagrant in torn and soiled clothes being interviewed by a roving reporter. When asked whom he was going to vote for, he replied in a thick Russian accent: "I am voting for Seen-clair. His system vorked vell in Russia, so vy can't it vork here?" Another depicted a scene of hoboes jumping off a freight train in California and joyfully celebrating. One of the bums stated: "Sinclair says he'll take the property of the working people and give

William Paley

it to us." Sinclair, whose candidacy seemed strong, was defeated by the combined power of advertising and corporate money.

Cartoons also carried political themes. A 1933 commercial for Franklin Roosevelt depicted Mickey Mouse racing down an endless tunnel crying in fear as visions of stock market panics and bank collapses filled his mind. Mickey rushes to the office of Dr. Pill, asking what will cure his horrible depression. The doctor points knowingly to a picture of FDR, and then breaks out into a little soft-shoe dance as music swells to a song with the theme of "Confidence." Most early political advertising relied on blatant undermining techniques such as bad mouthing the opposition, that left indelible impressions in the minds of viewers.

Throughout the 1930s David Sarnoff, president of the Radio Corporation of America, started the drive to develop television technology. Television, many people predicted, would write radio's obituary as they saw 17 experimental television stations emerge in 1937. Television had its public debut at the 1939 World's Fair in New York. NBC broadcast the opening ceremonies on April 30, with a speech by President Roosevelt received by over 100 experimental receivers set up in the metropolitan area. The phenomenon of television bringing the news using both pictures and sound to an audience would supplant the position of the print and radio media. However, World War II suspended the development of television until the 1950s, allowing radio news to thrive in the Thirties and Forties.

By the end of the 1930s media had made conquests in their ability to present news. Regulations were challenged, and the media continued to assert and test their freedom in the content and style of news stories printed or aired. Radio made people more trusting of media by using live and unfiltered sound, as would television through the use of images. The responsibility to keep people informed with accurate and objective accounts of world, national and local events was placed on media with few checks and balances. After the 1938 hoax by Orson Welles, people were startled into questioning their sources of information and scrutinizing the opinions and material written in the press and spoken over the airwaves.

At the end of the Thirties, Americans found themselves on the verge of war. Media's power to communicate brought pleasure in the form of entertainment, power in its ability to relay information quickly and pain in the realities it displayed. Surviving the Great Depression, and perhaps having become better people for it, the United States reluctantly prepared for war.

MEDIA
chapter 5
1940-1949
The War Ends: Radio Wins, Newspapers Lose

Iva Toguri, "Tokyo Rose"

Media in the 20th Century

Radio became the dominant form of media during and after World War II. As broadcasting technology improved, people soon learned that radio could provide war information faster than newspapers. Newspapers still supplied daily information and advertising, as well as late editions and special runs on extraordinary occasions. Economy was a factor in the popularity of radio. With a one-time investment in a radio, consumers received a continual source of news and entertainment in the comfort of their homes. Continued newspaper consolidation caused consumers to question whether the press barons, such as William Randolph Hearst, were profiting at public expense while offering a more standardized product. Despite the pubic concern, large media conglomerates would continue to grow throughout the Forties.

War news dominated the first five years of the Forties, and the threat of war with Russia, known as the Cold War, began after World War II and continued throughout most of the rest of the century. Radio thrived during this decade, as it delivered timely news of the war. The radio coverage was riveting and compelling, beginning with Pearl Harbor on December 7, 1941, continuing with the war's turning point, D-day on June 6, 1944, and the dropping of atomic bombs on Hiroshima on August 6, 1945, and Nagasaki on August 9, 1945, the war finally concluded with Japan's surrender on August 14, 1945.

Radio news programming (usually one or two announcers reporting at a scheduled time) came of age during the war, as people desired current news of their loved ones fighting overseas. Both Elmer Davis, respected for his radio news analysis during and after World War II, and Edward R. Murrow, known for his factual reporting of events in London during World War II, came to represent the best in interpretive broadcasting, a presentation method in which the correspondents reported and commented upon the news at the same time. By 1944, NBC Radio devoted 26.4 percent of its program hours to news, up from 2.8 percent in 1937. Davis, a former staff member of the New York Times newspaper, served as news commentator at CBS Radio during the war. After the war he worked at ABC Radio, winning high praise for his clear-eyed reporting, his dry humor, and his ability to cut through conflicting news reports and statements to reveal the truth. Murrow later produced the popular television programs "See It Now" and "Person to Person."

Number of TV stations in U.S.

Year	TV Stations
1945	9
1950	97
1955	439

A Soldier's War

Radio brought the actual drama of war to America. Direct reports of battles, treaties, invasions, and the loss of lives were broadcast. During the glory days of radio news, a news print reporter, **Ernie Pyle**, captured the experiences of soldiers on the battlefield in World War II. Starting his coverage in 1940 during the **Battle of Britain**, he continued his press reports while living

1940-1949

with soldiers in North Africa, Sicily, Italy, France, and the Pacific. As a reporter for **E.W. Scripps** newspapers, Pyle provided more than a documentary account of the war. He allowed America to see through the eyes of the soldiers, letting people experience the boredom and fright they lived through, the conversion of boys into trained killers, and how they died in foreign lands. He observed the individual lives of these men and personalized the war for America by conveying the every day routine and feelings of these soldiers to a distant America.

Ernie Pyle was a true journalist, an idealist who believed that a journalist had the responsibility to be a champion for the victim. He entered into the throes of war like a soldier, following the battlefronts, to give a real-life account of the individual in the midst of fighting. His reports made it difficult for America to remain detached by removing the anonymity of war and writing about real people. He counseled the public to exercise patience and understanding, as these men had suffered trauma that was inconceivable to Americans at home. Pyle offered a different sort of news to the readers. His reports often voiced the beliefs and opinions of the soldier to the public. One of his reports stated: "The jump from camp life into front-line living is just as great as the original jump from civilian life into the Army. Only those who served in the last war can conceive of the makeshift, deadly urgent, always moving onward complexion of front-line existence. And existence is exactly the word: It is nothing more. From now on you sleep in bedrolls under little tents. You wash whenever and wherever you can. You carry your food on your back when you are fighting. You dig ditches for protection from bullets and from the chill."

Ernie Pyle, columnist for Scripps Howard

Ernie Pyle was killed by a sniper's bullet on April 18, 1945, two days after U.S. Marines landed on Ie Shima, an island west of Okinawa, Japan. He will always be remembered for dispelling the romantic notion of war and as a hero who used his writing to fight for the recognition of the unknown soldiers who were scared and were killed to protect democracy in America and abroad.

FACTS AND FIGURES OF THE 1940s

Radios produced: 30,600,000
AM radio stations: 814
Daily Newspaper: 3¢
Sunday paper: 10¢

MEDIA IN THE 20th CENTURY

WAR IN THE PRESS AND ON THE AIR

The early Forties were one of the darkest periods in modern history. The Axis alliance created on September 27, 1940, joined Germany, Italy, and Japan in a 10-year military and economic alliance. France, Belgium, the Netherlands, Luxembourg, Denmark, Norway, and Romania all fell to foreign governments. In Japan, a new militarist government ruled with despotic power. On December 7, 1941, after the Japanese launched a surprise air attack on the American naval base at **Pearl Harbor**, Hawaii, they mounted a massive invasion throughout Southeast Asia, including the Philippines. The "isolation" of America from European and Asian politics officially ended. Before the attack, the December 1, 1941, issue of Newsweek featured a story on Pacific tension, quoting from a November 27, 1941, United Press report from journalist **H.O. Thompson**:

UP182 BULLETIN:

1ST LEAD JAPAN —WASHINGTON, NOV. 27 — (UP)—AUTHORITATIVE SOURCES TODAY EXPRESSED FEAR THAT JAPAN'S ANSWER TO AMERICAN DEMANDS THAT SHE WITHDRAW FROM THE AXIS AND GET OUT OF CHINA MAY BE A JAPANESE ATTACK ON THAILAND WITHIN THE NEXT FEW DAYS.

Thompson and other American reporters with the same story were mostly ignored by the newspapers. The Sunday calm of December 7, 1941, was shattered for America's listening audience by radio bulletins announcing the bombing of Pearl Harbor at 8:10 a.m. Hawaii time (1:40 p.m. Eastern Standard Time). It was late morning on the West Coast and early afternoon on the East Coast. There were no Sunday afternoon papers, and radio was the first media source to deliver this devastating news to Americans. Over 1,500 American soldiers were killed and a similar number left wounded or missing after the initial attack.

In its issue of December 15, 1941, Newsweek gave this report on Pearl

One of FDR's 1944 "Fireside Chats"

1940-1949

Harbor: "The Japanese attack on the United States caught the nation's newspapers on a Sunday afternoon, when the presses were silent and cold." Although radio and cable communications to the East were partially blocked, the correspondents stationed in Hawaii, the Philippines, and other focal points sent eyewitness accounts to offices in San Francisco, California. The **International News Service (INS)** claimed a first with an on-the-scene account from Honolulu to San Francisco. At 2:22 p.m. EST, presidential press secretary, **Stephen Early**, telephoned the three primary wire services (the **New York Associated Press, United Press** and **International News Service**) with the horrifying announcement exclaiming, "The Japanese have attacked Pearl Harbor!" Soon, the *Los Angeles Times, San Francisco Chronicle,* and *San Francisco Examiner* were rolling out extras; the (Portland) *Oregon Journal* published five extras that day.

"We interrupt this program to bring you a special news bulletin. The Japanese have attacked Pearl Harbor, Hawaii, by air, President Roosevelt has just announced," read radio announcer **John Daly**. The shocked nation stayed glued to its radio sets to hear President Roosevelt's **"Day of Infamy"** address to Congress the next day. On December 9, a world audience of 90 million heard

Typesetters, 1949

FDR boldly proclaim: "We are going to win the war and ... the peace that follows."

While in prior years the country had floundered under Herbert Hoover, Franklin D. Roosevelt had made America's economy strong again, and his success had won him great popular support. Roosevelt's radical programs to help America out of the Great Depression offered editors, journalists and political cartoonists volumes of new material to lampoon (make fun of). Although Roosevelt's New Deal policies had been ridiculed in the press, he was the only U.S. President to be re-elected three times (1936, 1940, and 1944).

Roosevelt's mastery of radio would more than offset attacks in the print media during this time of crisis. He continued his famous "Fireside Chats" broadcasts and America loved it. Here was a president who finally understood and cared about "the forgotten man at the bottom of the economic ladder." With his friendly tone, he encouraged Americans by reminding them that: "We have nothing to fear but fear itself." His effective communication skills and use of modern technology gave people faith in their president, his programs and the country's ability to win the war. Radio helped to educate and unify the country during the Forties. More than any other president or politician before him, Roosevelt understood the power of media and used it to uplift the American people.

At the start of the war the overpowering challenge confronting America was to re-tool itself for all-out war production. Media support for the war effort came in a variety of forms. Newsreels shown at the movies, radio announcements and newspaper space given for government press releases all called for donations of metal and rubber and the purchase of War Bonds. Hollywood produced a flood of war movies that were greatly popular by an anxious public looking for reassurance. Phrases from Roosevelt's speeches, such as "We're all in this together" and "Don't you know there's a war going on?" became standard responses to individuals' complaints about discomfort.

What event indicated the power of radio to convince people that the news was real? It was Orson Welles' spoof "War of the Worlds" in 1938, which drove people into a panic, and hinted at the eventual power of mass communication via radio. In analyzing the event in his 1940 book, Dr. Hadley Cantril noted, "It (the radio audience) consists of thousands of small, congruent groups united in time and with a common stimulus, making possible the largest grouping of people ever known."

The turning point of the war was D-Day, June 6, 1944. That morning American and British troops landed at Normandy in France, beginning the liberation of Europe from the Axis. In his 1994 article in *American Scholar*, **"The Longest Night,"** marking the 50-year anniversary of D-Day, **John McDonough** examined the 36 hours of the invasion and what part media played in this world-changing event. The article noted that the actual news of the invasion arrived in three forms: (1) from New York announcers (farthest from the source), (2) pool correspondents who flew out to see the action, then returned to base studios of the British Ministry of Information, where they wrote their stories, and (3) direct war correspondents recording on-the-scene reports into military film or wire devices. All reports were first reviewed by the military **public relations officers** (PROs) for censoring prior to release, which was then sent over short-wave to America.

On D-Day at 5:50 a.m. Central European Time, Allied troops began storming the Normandy coast; by 6:33 a.m., Berlin radio announced "a bombardment in the port of Le Havre . . . The invasion has begun." Four minutes later, the Associated Press (AP) put the Berlin radio announcement on the wire. It was 12:37 a.m. in New York. At CBS Radio, newscaster **Ned Calmer** announced, "We are interrupting this program to bring you a special bulletin. A bulletin has just been received from the London Office of the Associated Press which quotes the **German Trans-Ocean** news agency as asserting that the invasion of Western Europe has begun." CBS then woke up another announcer, **Bob Trout**, whom they'd selected to broadcast the rest of

1940-1949

the story as it came in. As the wires were received, they were typed for distribution by a young United Press reporter, **Walter Cronkite**.

Since the first news received was from German radio, many did not trust or believe the reports until the **British Broadcasting Corporation (BBC)** confirmed them. At 2:00 a.m. (EST) CBS broadcaster Bob Trout went on the air to announce that the Germans were landing troops at the Seine River. By 3:00 a.m. a staff of thirty was on duty at CBS, and they read everything that was coming through the wire services. At 3:32 a.m. CBS broadcast the telephone call of military historian **Richard Dupuy** from a studio in the **Ministry of Information** in London. After his report, he then read the U.S. government official Communique Number 1: "Under the command of General Eisenhower, Allied naval forces, supported by strong air forces, began landing Allied armies this morning on the northern coast of France." Trout went back on the air and said, "This means invasion." At 3:44 a.m. the first eye witness account from Europe, written by war correspondent **Herbert Clark**, was read over the air. Clark's pre-recorded eyewitness account of the invasion was announced after Communique Number 1: "When you hear this you'll know that Allied forces have leaped the gap ... I am speaking to shore by the last available channel of communication ... " He then described the invasion. The same broadcasts were repeated at half hour intervals for the next two hours, because no new facts were available. By 4:17 a.m. America heard reports of combat sent in by reporter **Wright Bryan**. Reports came in continuously from London, and at 5:41 a.m. coverage shifted to Washington D.C., and by 6:00 a.m. Trout was recounting the event. The ratings for the next fourteen hours rose 82 percent above normal. At 9:58 a.m. Trout announced that regular broadcasting for CBS would resume, and news would be interjected if thought to be important. At 3:50 p.m. CBS aired the first report from a **Howard Marshall**, a correspondent for the BBC who had landed on the beach at Normandy, France. As coverage progressed, reports slowed down. At 10 p.m. President Roosevelt led the country in a six-minute prayer on all networks. Shortly after, Edward R. Murrow of CBS reminded listeners that "during the early phase of every operation, there is an absence of detailed information as both sides try to conceal their intentions."

DAILY NEWSPAPER CITIES

Year	1940	1945
Cities	1,426	1,396
Circulation (in millions)	41.1	45.9

The pre-recorded televised broadcast of D-Day came from the **Blue Network** (the future ABC). London news chief **George Hicks'** recorded coverage on a 75-pound Navy portable film camera from the ship S.S. *Ancon*, 8 miles off Omaha beach, was broadcast at 11:15 p.m. He began, "We're lying some few miles off the coast of France where the invasion of Europe has begun ..." He was speaking as the attack was occurring. The sound of German planes bombing Allied positions was captured on the tape. Before the D-Day invasion the networks had banned televised coverage of

MEDIA IN THE 20th CENTURY

the war because of the concern that the reports may be misleading and for security reasons. The *New York World Telegram* called it "the greatest recording yet to come out of the war." Hicks' broadcast was repeated at intervals during the next 72 hours, and was even made into a record. Hailed as a great technological and journalistic success, "live" pre-recorded films such as Hicks' would help media move closer to the age of television.

Newspapers and radio continued to motivate mass support for the war effort, reporting ceaselessly and daringly on the plight of soldiers all over the world. War correspondent Ernie Pyle wrote a widely read syndicated column documenting the war and how it affected "America's boys." As the war neared its end, it was radio that informed the nation of the shocking death of President Roosevelt in 1945 and the admission of **Harry S. Truman** as the new president, with solemn music in the background reflecting the sadness of the mourners. Truman continued to lead America in victory for the last six months of the war, literally bringing the world into the nuclear age by deciding to drop atomic bombs on the Japanese cities of **Hiroshima** (August 6, 1945) and **Nagasaki** (August 9, 1945). The war officially ended on August 14, 1945.

Truman holds newspaper with headline, "Dewey defeats Truman"

READING IS BELIEVING

Can You Really Believe Everything You Read in the Papers? The November 2, 1948, post-election-day *Chicago Daily Tribune* headline said "Dewey Defeats Truman." Although pollsters had predicted Truman's loss to Dewey (Dewey led in the polling in September), Truman's whirlwind 12-day train trip addressing country people with "plain speaking" won him the election. A 4:30 p.m. EST report by Dewey's campaign manager claimed Dewey's victory — yet by 6 a.m. EST Truman was ahead by two million votes, and gained the ultimate triumph of four more years in the White House.

POLITICS AND NEWS

Although the war was behind America, the memories of volatile changes in governmental systems were not. In 1945, everyone born since early 1918 had now lived through two world wars, and

1940-1949

Americans wanted to avoid further conflicts. In response to the Cold War with the U.S.S.R., America continued to develop atomic and nuclear weapons as a deterrent against the possibility of military conflict and another World War.

America feared Communist Russia and its expansionist activities after the war ended. President Truman launched a massive "loyalty" program. Nervous citizens feared communist spies were posing as Americans to undermine the government and treacherously misdirect foreign policy. A booklet put out by a conservative think tank contained advice on **"How to Spot a Communist in Your Own Business."** Loyalty oaths became common in all industries. Failure to comply would result in termination, as 20 professors at UCLA were quick to find out. Libraries were purged of suspicious and obvious communist media sources, such as the communist paper the *Daily Worker*. Even mainstream publications such as *National Geographic* were considered suspect.

To offset communism's influence, Congress continued to fund the **Voice of America** (VOA) to provide radio broadcasts to foreign countries as part of an overseas information program. The Voice of America was first launched in 1942 to counter Nazi propaganda as part of the Office of War Information. The Voice of America is responsible for delivering news, editorials, and music to people around the world in order to balance the propaganda issued by opposing governments of the United States. Since 1953 the Voice of America became part of the U.S. Information Agency and today broadcasts in over 50 languages around the world. In 1950 **Radio Free Europe** began beaming reports from a variety of sources on world news to listeners behind the Iron Curtain. During the

Whittaker Chambers

Cold War, Radio Free Europe provided daily uncensored programs to the peoples of Poland, the Czech Republic, Slovakia, Romania, Bulgaria, the Baltic states, and the former Yugoslav republics in their own languages. Its broadcasts included news and political commentaries, music, sports, and other entertainment. In 1976 Radio Free Europe was merged with **Radio Liberty**, founded in 1952, which broadcast to the former republics of the USSR.

The **House Committee on Un-American Activities (HUAC)** proved the noisiest and most persistent body to investigate alleged foreign subversion. HUAC targeted Hollywood, ensuring widespread national attention. During the war, several studios had made pro-Soviet films, and after the war a series of labor strikes hit the film industry, instigated, some studio executives claimed,

MEDIA IN THE 20th CENTURY

"Meet the Press," Spivak and Hoover

by communists. In 1947 the committee held two weeks of hearings to expose the supposed communist infiltration. Calling in everyone from Walt Disney to Jack Warner, plus scores of actors such as Robert Taylor, Gary Cooper, George Murphy and Ronald Reagan, the committee had members of the film industry stand trial for communist activity. Some decried communist infiltration of the **Screen Writers Guild** and other unions. Refusing to answer the obligatory question under the protection of the First Amendment, "Are you now or have you ever been a member of the Communist Party?" meant jail sentences for many. Roughly 500 writers, directors and actors were suspended from work and their names were added to the "**blacklist**" that was distributed throughout the film industry. Those listed were denied employment and denounced to such an extent that they were forced to live as virtual outcasts. Others feared involvement with anyone "blacklisted," aware that they could then be accused of being a communist, ending up with the same grim fate.

The following year, in 1948, the State Department came under scrutiny of the HUAC. **Whittaker Chambers**, a *Time* magazine editor, accused of receiving documents for transmission for a spy ring from State Department official **Alger Hiss**. Chambers was described by one reporter as "a fat, sad-looking man in a baggy blue suit." Chambers joined the Communist Party in the 1920s, but in 1938 underwent a patriotic change of loyalties. Under subpoena, he identified Alger Hiss as one of his former communist associates. By contrast, Hiss struck an imposing image as a well groomed, tall and handsome man from the upper class, with an impressive record of achievement in key government posts.

At the time, Hiss was head of the **Carnegie Endowment for International Peace**, and it was astonishing to many how a man of this distinction could possibly betray his country. In the first round of questioning by the committee, Hiss denied to even knowing Chambers, but in the second round of hearings admitted to knowing him under another name. It was further revealed that Chambers had stayed in Hiss' Washing-

1940-1949

ton home, and had also been generously provided with a used car by the accused.

When the NBC program "**Meet the Press**" aired Chambers' allegations, Hiss sued the station for libel. In retaliation, Chambers produced various papers Hiss had passed on to him eleven years earlier that included State Department documents both in handwriting and typed on a typewriter, which were traced to Hiss. The culmination of evidence was produced by Chambers on his Maryland farm when he with then Representative Richard M. Nixon, dramatically pulled out rolls of microfilm from a hollowed-out pumpkin, which later came to be known as the "**pumpkin papers**." The Hiss proceedings went to federal court, where Supreme Court Justice Felix Frankfurter and other distinguished public servants testified on Hiss' behalf, calling Chambers the traitor. The "pumpkin papers" eventually caused Hiss to be found guilty, and he was sentenced to five years' imprisonment on January 21, 1950. Hiss staunchly maintained his innocence even though his case was considered proof that communist infiltration of the government was indeed a reality and a threat to national security. Chambers continued for a while on the staff of *Time* magazine, but later left.

In September 1949 it was determined that the Soviets had also developed the atomic bomb. It was assumed that communist spies had relayed the bomb technology to the Soviet Union. Print and radio news media reported real and fictitious communist invasions in film, education and government. Broadcasting enabled live documentation of events, and politicians had to learn to use the medium wisely. President Truman began meeting with press secretary **Charles G. Ross** and others of his staff for pre-conference briefings, where carefully prepared opening statements were arranged in advance. As news conferences became increasingly regular during the Truman administration, the president needed to execute greater control over what was reported by arriving better prepared and responding to questions with greater caution.

News commentators provided verbal editorials interpreting and analyzing the comments made by the president at the news conferences. Truman responded harshly to continuing criticism of himself and his administration by news sources and strongly denounced the media. Truman lashed out at "the kept press and the paid radio." He attacked what he called the "confusion of fact with mere

WEWS news truck, Cleveland, OH

speculation by which readers and listeners were undoubtedly misguided and intentionally deceived."

CROSS-MEDIA OWNERSHIP OF NEWSPAPERS, RADIO AND TELEVISION

In the early Forties, the issue of newspapers owning radio stations began to surface. By 1941, 30 percent of AM stations were owned by newspapers, and newspapers had applied for 28 of the first 60 television licenses. Radio enthusiasts argued that media outlets should be owned by different types of companies, so different opinions and groups could be represented. At that time there was no power of limitation for cross-ownership of media.

A federal court ruling in 1942 held that the **Federal Communications Commission** (FCC), a government entity created to ensure that licenses serve the "public interest, convenience and necessity," could inquire into the media ownership issue. The FCC did not have the power to deny a license to a petitioner based solely on the fact of media cross-owner-ship. The FCC ended its examination of cross-media ownership in 1944, and newspapers won licenses without much difficulty. The trend toward ownership of publishing, broadcasting and other business interests under one corporate entity began at this time. As newspaper sales decreased, cross-media ownership allowed publishers such as the *Chicago Tribune*, owner of radio station WGN, to take advantage of the new consumer preference for radio.

Some argued that cross-media ownership did not allow for private citizens, minority, or even majority interest groups to equally express their views. Many people assumed that what they heard over radio, saw on television, or read in the newspaper reflected three different viewpoints, when in fact one media conglomerate may own two or even all three of these media sources. In the United States broadcasting is free from government control. Media ownership is a private, not a public or governmental, concern. This ensures media owners great freedom to set policy for public programming, and to determine which programs serve the public good.

In 1949, a ruling made in 1941 and known as the "**Mayflower decision**" was overturned. The original ruling by the Federal Communication Commission stated that "broadcasters cannot be advocates." By 1949 this was changed to what is called the **Fairness Doctrine** —meaning broadcasters had the right to "editorialize with fairness." Editorialize means to express an opinion, as in a newspaper editorial, or to present an opinion in the guise of an objective report. The Fairness Doctrine contained three rules: (1) A broadcaster must give adequate coverage to public issues; (2) this coverage must be fair and offer opposing views; and (3) coverage must be afforded at the broadcaster's own expense, even if commercial sponsorship was unavailable. With the new right to editorialize broadcasters found it easy to live with "fairness" as it applied to editorials, but found it inhibiting when applied to straight news or documentaries, which prohibited outspoken opinions on social issues for fear of appearing unfair or biased.

1940-1949

THE FUTURE OF TELEVISION

The futuristic magic of television, which stimulated the minds of the public at the opening of the New York World's Fair in 1939, marked the beginning of a major medium of televised broadcast. The 1940 Geneva Conventions were televised. A 90-minute documentary on the national reaction to the bombing of Pearl Harbor was televised in 1941, increasing domestic support for the war. World War II brought the further development of television to a halt, and in 1942 the manufacturing of receivers was stopped and programming curtailed. In 1948, **Community Antenna Television**, or **CATV** began. Most television stations were located in large cities such as Philadelphia and New York. New York City appliance-store owner John Walson installed a large utility pole topped with an antenna. Television signals from Philadelphia 90 miles away were received through it and Walson's TV sales soared.

By 1948 the number of TV sets in the United States had increased to roughly one million. The postwar era was one of progress and growth. A devil-may-care, let's-try-anything sentiment prevailed and very few people wanted to be left out or behind. The middle class of America suddenly had disposable income to afford new technologies such as televisions.

Most early television programs imitated radio formats with vaudeville comedy sketches, music, news and commentary. Both CBS and NBC developed nightly news programs shortly after they started regular programs. In 1948, NBC introduced the "**Camel News Caravan**" with John Cameron Swayze. CBS started "**Douglas Edwards with the News**."

1949 Zenith TV

Most of the film used on these shows were purchased from newsreel companies, as networks had very few film crews of their own. Many stories had no film, so Edwards displayed still photographs gathered through a wire service. Swayze would "hopscotch the world for headlines," simply telling viewers what was happening around the world, as if he were reading headlines.

In 1946 there were 10 television stations in the entire country, linked only in the East. It wasn't until the development of the **coaxial cable** in 1949, that television broadcasting signals were able to extend their range. At the time there were two ways to send television pictures through the air: on the **Very High Frequency (VHF)** and the **Ultra High Frequency (UHF)**. While the

Media in the 20th Century

technical distinction concerns the number of cycles per second completed by the the waves, the functional distinction is that there are far more UHF than VHF channels available. In 1945 the Federal Communications Commission approved the licenses for 13 new carrier frequencies in the VHF range, set up as channels 1 through 13 for television use. As a practical matter, because some of these channels interfered with adjacent channels, this meant a maximum of seven VHF outlets for large areas such as Los Angeles and New York. In contrast, the UHF channels, ranging from 14 to 48, would have potentially provided a wide-ranging set of alternatives for educational television and community access offerings.

Commercial development began on the VHF band, with the first UHF station broadcasting in the fall of 1952. As a result, television became technically segregated into UHF and VHF. The commercial networks, which were viewable almost exclusively on the VHF stations, attracted roughly 90 percent of all viewers. Viewers could not easily pass through the UHF alternatives while going around the channel dial, as it merely contained a "U" instead of numbers, and required an additional rotating antennae to capture these signals. VHF provided a stronger signal that limited actual telecasting to the established broadcasting giants, NBC and CBS. It took ABC until 1970 to catch up and attract equal numbers of viewers. Unlike radio, television was never seen as a possession of the people. Television was a purely commercial enterprise right from the start.

Early commercial broadcasts were all in black and white. As early as 1929 Bell Telephone Laboratories had achieved color television transmission. Throughout the war, RCA and CBS were experimenting with color broadcasts. Unfortunately, the black-and-white television sets in use were incompatible with color transmission as they did not come equipped with a "color wheel" (a spinning disc in both cameras and home sets). In 1946, CBS had developed a "color wheel" system which it used to broadcast its "colorcast" images from New York City to Nyack, New York, to impress the members of the Federal Communications Commission. CBS expected that the mass marketing of television sets would be halted until the regulatory commission worked out the essentials of color broadcast. Instead, the FCC held off any decision, and black-and-white sets (incompatible with color broadcasts) continued to be sold.

RCA was developing a color system that could be received by the existing black-and-white sets; however, the color quality was poor. As the decision was delayed, more and more black-and-white sets flooded the market and the challenge was to develop a color system that could be picked up by the black-and-white sets. RCA, the largest manufacturer of television sets, was adamantly opposed to the CBS color system. Later, when CBS inventor **Peter Goldmark** developed a converter that could be linked to existing black-and-white sets, RCA continued to oppose the idea. Finally, in 1953, the FCC approved the RCA all-electronic system, which used three electron guns to scan for reds, blues and greens, the primary colors in color television. Had the FCC approved the CBS system in 1947, when fewer than 250,000 existing color sets were in use, America probably would have never had an era of black-and-white television. Even more than black-and-white television, color programs provided a new level of realism for viewers to enjoy.

1940-1949

CHANGES IN ADVERTISING AND PUBLISHING

In the Forties, most advertising adopted a pro-American, pro-war-effort theme. Many ads featured men and women in uniform, with themes of patriotism and self-sacrifice. The advertising industry's magazine, *Advertising Age*, celebrated its tenth anniversary in 1940. Although war manufacturing increased and the economy grew during the war, some publications folded as print advertising revenues decreased. Yet the new growth of radio caused advertising to develop a strong audio presence. While the majority of radio advertising consisted of "sponsored by" announcements by the radio hosts, some commercials featured live music and singers.

New publications of the decade were influenced by radio or television. Movie stars were always popular, but during the war, scientists, military strategists and politicians became famous too, as people were highly aware of their importance to the war effort. The magazine *Current Biography*, premiered in 1940 as a rather stuffy reference source, developed into a colorful publication with an excellent format. It featured 36 biographical essays per issue and appealed to readers with an interest in particular individuals currently in the news. One important publication, which began in the Forties but did not last was *Yank* magazine. *Yank* began publication on June 17, 1942, under Colonel **Egbert White** with assistance from noted publishing professionals. White worked as a sergeant in 1918 on the *Stars & Stripes*, a newspaper for military personnel. *Yank* was also for soldiers and benefited from some of the decade's best people in the newspaper and magazine publishing business such as *New York Times* publisher **Adolph S. Ochs**, *Saturday Evening Post* editor **Robert M. Fuoss**, and *Liberty* magazine art editor **Alfred Strasser**.

Advertisement from the 1940's

MEDIA IN THE 20th CENTURY

First TV in Sears Catalog, 1949

At the war's end, *Commentary*, which called itself a "journal of significant thought and opinion on contemporary issues," was established in 1945. This publication discussed Jewish concerns in America and abroad. It was unique among Jewish periodicals in that it presented a moderate, rather than liberal, point of view, and covered topics of general interest and also featured Jewish fiction. *Commentary* addressed issues of religious tolerance and freedom, and was intended to unite Jewish people together and prevent prejudice against them. After the revelations of the horrors of the Holocaust, *Commentary* was a needed voice to help begin the healing of wounds inflicted on Jews and humankind.

The growth of television spawned *Television Index*. A weekly publication that covered the major networks with listings of writers, talent, production personnel and advertisers for news broadcasts, special programming, public affairs and sports. *Television Index* allowed viewers to learn more about what they were watching and gave professionals within the fledgling industry their own trade journal. *Nieman Reports*, an elite publication introduced in 1947, was intended for journalists, public figures and editors who were members of the Nieman Fellowship at Harvard University. This quarterly provided a forum for media-related issues, emphasizing in-depth global analysis.

For print media (and later radio and television) career people, *MIN/Media Industry Newsletter* (formerly *Magazine Industry Newsletter*) was founded in 1947. Typical coverage included personnel changes, statistics on the number of ad pages sold by national and regional newspapers and magazines, and industry news of company startups, takeovers and failures. Writing with an "insider" style, it included gossip, industry trends and techniques. Industry data was collected from a variety of sources, including Crain Communications, the publishers of *Advertising Age* and other media publications.

As the Forties closed, the fears of war remained. Communism and the threat of nuclear war loomed. Yet radio and television offered hope, laughter and distraction, in addition to news. In the Fifties, a conventionalism would develop that soothed people and did not confront them with situations which were different and perhaps threatening. Television would expand dramatically into enjoyable programming and informational news in the next decade. It would later be referred to as television's "Golden Age."

MEDIA
chapter 6
1950-1959
The Golden Age of Television

1957 Space Command TV

Media in the 20th Century

Television was poised to dominate the communication industry in 1950. By June of that year, over 100 TV stations were operating in 38 states. The decade would later be named "The Golden Age of Television." The Fifties were also remembered as the Cold War decade, characterized by fear of nuclear destruction and takeovers by the communists. Media in this decade were influenced by the politics of fear and suspicion, and helped to create a climate of mistrust of politicians, entertainers, and fellow citizens. Television gave a close-up and personal view into the lives of politicians, escalating the emphasis on "image" as a way to determine the character of our leaders. Politicians that were viewed as lenient on communism were committing political suicide. Television helped spread these fears across the nation. As the obsession to eradicate communism mounted, some broadcasters failed to report objectively. One broadcaster, Edward R. Murrow, would combat the dubious accusations against members of the State Department by U.S. Senator Joseph R. McCarthy.

News Anchor Lee Kinnard, WFMY TV, Greensboro, N.C.

> "If the television craze continues with the present level of programs, we are destined to have a nation of morons."
>
> Boston University President Daniel Marsh, 1950

The 1952 presidential candidacy of Dwight Eisenhower and his running mate, Senator Richard Nixon, was the first to test the waters of television as a political medium to influence public opinion. Nixon was rocked by scandal through a *New York* Post article with the headline "Secret Nixon Fund," which maintained that he kept a secret political fund. The fund of $18,000 did exist, and was really no secret, as it was specifically designated for Nixon's fight against communism. Republicans were worried, and some suggested that Nixon withdraw from the race, but he decided to take his case directly to the American people through television. An audience of 55 million people watched the famous "Checkers Speech" on September 24, 1952, as Nixon reviewed the so-called secret fund and denied any misuse of the money.

Declaring that he was not a quitter, Nixon claimed in his television address

1950-1959

> "We will not be driven by fear into an age of unreason if we...remember that we are not descended from fearful men, not from men who feared to write, to speak, to associate and to defend causes which were, for the moment, unpopular."
>
> Edward R. Murrow

that the contributions he had received were used for expenses and other purposes, as he put it, "to permit me to carry on my fight against communism and corruption beyond my official duties in Washington." He also laid out his own personal finances for public inspection, emphasizing the fact that he was not a rich man. He owned a 1950 Oldsmobile and was paying mortgages on two houses and told the audience that his wife wore "a respectable Republican cloth coat." The heart-wrencher was his admission that he had accepted a dog as a gift from a well-wisher, but "the kids...love the dog named 'Checkers' and regardless of what they say about it, we're going to keep it." Within hours of the telecast Republican headquarters was swamped with supportive telegrams. Nixon's appeal as the "common man" not only saved his own candidacy, but gave the whole campaign a boost.

Television encouraged a new form of advertising and brought about the use of advertising agencies to produce political campaigns and sell a presidential candidate. Radio and print media were forced to compete with television, which seemed to provide the best of both those media to its audience and its advertisers. Television also altered the look of newsstands, as magazines had to specialize in order to reach specific markets television did not.

POLITICS VIEWED

Under the threat and fear of communism and potential nuclear war, Senator **Joseph R. McCarthy** emerged as a demagogue; someone who appeals to people's fears and prejudices in an attempt to gain power. He instinctively

US delegate at UN Security Council holds Russian-made gun captured from North Korea, 1951

111

Media in the 20th Century

Senator Joseph McCarthy

knew how to manipulate the media, especially television, playing upon the anxieties of both politicians and the public. On February 3, 1950, British physicist **Klaus Fuchs** confessed to the nation that he had passed atomic secrets to the Soviet Union. The announcement acted as a catalyst for McCarthy to capture the attention of a shocked public. Four days after Fuch's confession, McCarthy addressed a women's club in Wheeling, West Virginia, waving a sheet of paper in the air and claiming that he held a list of 205 names of known communists who were "working and shaping the policy of the State Department." Refusing to prove his allegations, McCarthy positioned himself as the leader of a national crusade against communism. The charges were printed on the front pages of the major national newspapers.

Klaus Fuchs later implicated others, among them an American couple, **Julius** and **Ethel Rosenberg**, who were charged with spying for the Soviet Union. The Rosenberg case dragged on endlessly through the courts, with each appeal maintaining the original conviction of the death penalty. Papers such as the *Los Angeles Times* and New York's *Daily News* carried the story of the alleged betrayal of America by the couple in relinquishing atomic-bomb information to the Soviet Union. The defenders of the Rosenbergs claimed that they were framed and convicted in an atmosphere of anti-communist frenzy, serving as examples to scare the public into blind obedience. The government wanted to make the Rosenbergs symbols of anti-communist fervor, and the media's glamorization of McCarthy and his campaign assisted in the plot. At any point during their long and arduous investigation the couple could have pleaded guilty in an attempt to save themselves from the death penalty. Until the very end, however, they proclaimed their innocence and wrote to their sons: "Always remember that we

> "If television and radio are to be used for the entertainment of all people all of the time, we have come perilously close to discovering the real opiate of the people."
>
> Edward R. Murrow: host of CBS "See It Now"

1950-1959

> **JARGON**
>
> **Tail Gunner Joe:** The term refers to a person who gains glory from someone else's accomplishments. It derives from the false claims of Senator Joseph R. McCarthy that he was a tail gunner on American bombers during World War II.

are innocent and could not wrong our conscience." They were executed on June 19, 1953, amid a wave of protest on their behalf.

McCarthy became the champion of anti-communism in the United States. McCarthy surrounded himself with a loyal following including millionaires, beautiful women, broadcasting stars, politicians, clergy, and his hand-picked team of investigators. *Look* magazine described them as "a heady mixture." These loyalists fed McCarthy and his associates information on people suspected of suspicious behavior. Perhaps the most dangerous of McCarthy's followers were the broadcasting figures whose repeated cries of "traitors," "pinkos," "subversives" over the air greatly added to the hysteria and provided McCarthy with credibility. **Fulton Lewis Jr.** of the Mutual Broadcasting Company and **George Sokolsky** of the American Broadcasting Company (ABC) were two of the many media personalities who constantly pushed McCarthy's agenda into the homes of million of Americans.

> The first color TV sets were sold for $1,000 by RCA in 1954.

Anyone who opposed McCarthy and his supporters was to be "**blacklisted**," that is, ostracized from the community and from one's profession. McCarthy, hiding under senatorial immunity, charged those in the entertainment industry—radio, motion pictures, and television—of conspiracy. Following on the anti-communist crusade initiated by McCarthy, the paperback book *Red Channels*, written by U.S. Naval Intelligence officer **Vincent Hartnett**, but

Ethel and Julius Rosenberg

MEDIA IN THE 20th CENTURY

published anonymously, led to hearings against actors, writers, producers, and others accused of employing the media as vehicles for communist propaganda. Some of the accused cooperated out of fear of being blacklisted; others refused and were either imprisoned or had their careers and personal lives destroyed.

In 1950 there were 3.1 million television sets in American homes.

McCarthy's power was felt all the way up to the White House. To further exacerbate the infiltration of "McCarthyism" into the mainline of media, President Eisenhower, widely rumored to dislike Senator McCarthy, appointed those loyal to McCarthy to manage the **Federal Communications Commission (FCC)** in efforts to subdue the tirades of the young senator. The first of these new FCC members was **John C. Doerfer**, who accused those television stations not carrying McCarthy's speeches of perhaps being communist sympathizers. As a commissioner of the FCC, Doerfer spent several years and taxpayer money trying to substantiate the accusation. Again in 1953, Eisenhower appointed another of McCarthy's friends whom *Look* magazine identified as a member of the senator's intimate circle of investigators. **Robert E. Lee**, a former FBI agent, was rumored to have identified members of the State Department and the Voice of America as subversives to be included on McCarthy's blacklist.

Although the FCC was caught in the web of combating communism on behalf of Senator McCarthy, it also made advances on behalf of the public. FCC Commissioner **Frieda B. Hennock** had lobbied in support of educational broadcasting since her appointment in 1948 by President Harry Truman. In 1951 the work of Hennock and other visionaries was realized when the FCC reserved 209 television channels exclusively for public education. Through these stations, educational and non-commercial programming would be available, which would later include critiques of the U.S. government, criticism that was not tolerated during this decade.

THE POWER OF TELEVISION

Television soon discovered that however much the news operation wanted to remain separate from entertainment, it was difficult to completely maintain such a separation. Broadcasters knew that audiences watched television mostly for entertainment. Television news in the Fifties was broadcast a few moments out of each day in between shows from "I Love Lucy" to "Studio One." Broadcasters also realized the importance of those appearing every night bringing America the news. They had to be someone the viewer felt as if he or she knew, trusted, liked and believed in. Viewers weren't likely to watch the newscaster who could best explain the federal budget, but more likely the type of person whom they trusted and respected. News executives knew then that the bearer of news was as important, if not more important, than the news itself. **Edward R. Murrow**, with his deep voice and handsome features, was a newscaster that the public responded to.

The thirty minute documentary program "**See It Now**," produced by CBS and hosted by Edward R. Murrow, would

1950-1959

initiate responsible television news and the era of solid journalism. The program would assert television's potential to connect the nation in universal causes.

"See It Now" began its first telecast with a live camera picture of the Atlantic Ocean and the Brooklyn Bridge in New York, followed by a live shot of the Pacific Ocean and the Golden Gate Bridge in San Francisco. After the presentation of the images, Murrow stated in a dramatic tone, "We are impressed by the medium through which a man sitting in his living room had been able for the first time to look at two oceans at once... no journalistic age was ever given a weapon for truth with quite the scope of this fledgling television." From its debut on November 18, 1951, to its last program on July 7, 1958, Murrow used the show as a weapon for truth and accuracy by reporting on news issues relevant to the nation.

The show was conceived with producer **Fred W. Friendly** and covered the globe. During one show, Murrow attended night school with a 40-year-old African-American who wanted to learn how to read. In 1952 Murrow took a film crew to Korea for a full hour show that was an extraordinary documentary on the war. After testing the audience with solemn stories, Murrow went on to fight McCarthyism. The story of Air Force reserve officer **Milo Radulovich** would give notice to the world about the power of television.

Murrow made a deliberate attempt to read newspapers from around the country, so as not to isolate his views. While reading the *Detroit News* he learned of the plight of the 26-year-old Radulovich, who was about to have his commission as a lieutenant in the Air Force revoked. The Air Force, tainted by

Murrow on set of "See it Now"

> **"Sincerity is the quality that comes through television."**
>
> Richard M. Nixon, 1955.

Media in the 20th Century

the spread of McCarthyism, requested the resignation of the lieutenant on security grounds because his father subscribed to a Serbian-language newspaper. Murrow took an interest in the case because of its underlying importance. The show's forthright nature had upset some executives at CBS, and the network refused to promote the upcoming telecast. Adamant in their journalistic integrity, Murrow and Friendly funded the project with their own money, paying $1,500 to advertise the show in the *New York Times*. They deliberately challenged the CBS policy that forbade taking sides in political controversy. The simple ad in the *New York Times* read: "Tonight at 10:30 p.m. on 'See It Now,' a report on Senator Joseph R. McCarthy over Channel 2. Fred W. Friendly and Edward R. Murrow, co-producers."

On October 20, 1953, Murrow began the show in his own words: "We propose to examine... the case of Lieutenant Radulovich." On the show Murrow gave Radulovich the opportunity to defend himself, which the government had not done. Murrow concluded the program by making an appeal to the doctrines of democracy: "We believe that the son shall not bear the iniquity of his father, even though the iniquity be proved; in this case it was not." Five weeks later on the show, the secretary of the Air Force was shown restoring Radulovich to duty.

The TV critic for the *New York Times*, **Jack Gould**, commented, "For the first time a major network consented to a program taking a vigorous editorial stand... a long step forward." The report established television journalism as a major influence on the public, more so than any other news medium. Murrow had used television to challenge the willingness of the country to discard the principles of democracy. The telecast set him on a collision course with the man who had begun the national hysteria, Senator Joseph McCarthy.

Murrow would use the persuasive power of television in a direct confrontation with McCarthy. He was aware of the circumstantial evidence McCarthy had against him—evidence that was not substantial, but in the possession of McCarthy was sufficient to ruin anyone's career. Murrow had been a member of the National Advisory Committee, headed by Columbia University professor George S. Counts. The committee had been involved in coordinating a teacher exchange with the Soviet Union in 1935. The *Pittsburgh Sun Telegraph*, a newspaper in the chain owned by William Randolph Hearst, ran an article on February 18, 1935, stating, "American Professors Trained by Soviet, Teach in U.S. Schools." The article implied that American educators were sending teachers to Russian institutions to be trained as "adept communist propagandists." Although the article was speculative and full of innuendoes, it was the type of ammunition that was used against innocent people in the name of patriotism by people like McCarthy. Murrow accepted the possible fallout from his involvement in the program and planned to break McCarthy's hold on the public.

Murrow directed his staff to collect all existing news footage of McCarthy and to begin filming his public appearances. A tentative date for broadcast was set for March 9, 1954. Promoting the program was going to be difficult once again. CBS executives instructed Murrow and Friendly that they wanted no participation in the telecast, would not sponsor an ad, and that any advertisements could not employ the network logo. The date for the broadcast

1950-1959

remained firm and as scheduled. Murrow addressed the television audience, "Good evening. Tonight 'See It Now' devotes its entire half hour to report on Senator Joseph McCarthy, told mainly in his own words and pictures. If the senator believes we have done violence to his words or pictures and desires to speak—to answer himself—an opportunity will be afforded him on this program." With that said, Murrow went on to show footage of McCarthy acting as a one-man committee investigating supposed conspirators against America and democracy. Viewers witnessed McCarthy's temper tantrums in an overwhelming and all-encompassing barrage. Close-ups of the senator conducting interviews, interrogating terrified citizens, conducting hearings, and his general accusatory demeanor were broadcast to America.

Murrow attacked McCarthy point by point, using television to document his editorial comments. As usual Murrow used a sparse studio setting as his background. This simple tactic was effective in maintaining the attention of the audience on the subject of each program.

Two days after the broadcast, McCarthy started yet another investigation to expose an alleged communist employee in the Pentagon code room. Murrow dispatched a cameraman and reporter to the hearings of the accused **Annie Lee Moss**, a middle-aged African-American woman whose job was to feed already-coded tapes into a transmitting machine. It turned out that McCarthy had made a false assumption and erroneously accused her of decoding messages. After his interrogation was crushed, McCarthy abruptly left the

Fred Friendly before taping a conference, "The Presidency and the Constitution"

Media in the 20th Century

1955 Political Cartoon

proceedings, making excuses of needing to attend an engagement. Meanwhile, the staff of "See It Now" had recorded the entire hearing, and continued to pan the camera to McCarthy's conspicuously empty chair. It was to be broadcast at a later date.

That same evening McCarthy appeared on the Mutual Broadcasting System with conservative broadcaster Fulton Lewis Jr. to defend himself against Murrow's broadcast of March 9. McCarthy immediately berated his critics, and predictably produced a copy of the 1935 *Pittsburgh Sun Telegraph* story in an attempt to incriminate Murrow as a communist sympathizer. Lewis asked McCarthy whether he had viewed the program aired by Murrow, to which he replied, "I have little difficulty answering the specific attack he made, because I never listen to the extreme left-wing bleeding-heart element of radio and television." "See It Now" was broadcast right after Lewis's show, and Murrow was caught off guard by McCarthy's comments. He responded by stating, "My personal reaction will have to wait for another time."

The following evening, Murrow addressed all the charges made on his character by McCarthy. Six days later, McCarthy accepted the offer to appear on "See It Now" to respond. Before McCarthy's scheduled appearance "See It Now" devoted its full half-hour format to airing the footage and story of Annie Lee Moss. McCarthy was angry and evoking the **Fairness Doctrine** approached CBS and informed it that it was responsible for subsidizing his rebuttal. CBS readily agreed and awarded him $6,336.99 with which to produce his own show to counter-attack Murrow. Murrow worried about losing the show. In his anxiety, he accepted the offer to purchase a copy of McCarthy's pre-recorded broadcast from Hearst Movietone News, which was producing McCarthy's rebuttal. For $100, Murrow had an advance screening and a transcript of McCarthy's charges against him. Murrow worked with the network's lawyers preparing his answers to the denunciation of his character that McCarthy made on the tape.

McCarthy appeared on "See It Now"

1950-1959

on April 6, 1954, with an introduction by Murrow stating that the half hour belonged to McCarthy and that no restriction had been placed on the content of the show. McCarthy used information on Murrow's past membership in the Institute of International Education in an attempt to condemn him to the audience. He also quoted from the March 9, 1954, issue of the communist newspaper the *Daily Worker*, which said, "Mr. Murrow's program is one of tonight's best bets on TV." As promised, Murrow kept quiet during the show. Once off the air Murrow held a press conference where he gave each reporter a written seven-page point-by-point rebuttal of McCarthy charges. Murrow had the courage to use television to defeat McCarthy at his own game. He had taken the medium of television, which cringed from controversy and relished entertainment, and used it to discuss the most provocative controversial news item of the time. Aided by Murrow's programs, the public began to understand how McCarthy's views were harming innocent people and damaging the nation's democratic ideals. Eventually McCarthy lost all his support and faded from view.

NEWS AS ENTERTAINMENT

The trend toward news as entertainment was furthered by another CBS show hosted by Murrow. "**Person to Person**" debuted October 2, 1953 and was an instant success. The format of a celebrity interview program took viewers into the homes of the rich and famous while Murrow asked questions from a studio set. Shows featured luminaries such as movie star Marilyn Monroe, novelist John Steinbeck, and other musicians, artists, actors, inventors, and more. When asked if he considered this to be news, Murrow candidly responded that he hated the show but that it was necessary to do it. He stated: "To do the show I want to do, I have to do the show I don't want to do." It was this kind of honesty that earned Murrow the trust that the public understood and embraced. CBS executives thought that "Person to Person" would help to shape Murrow's image as a more easygoing, less-serious personality.

The popularity of the show was astounding, with an initial audience of 1.8 million households at its premiere, and growing to 8.3 million by 1958. The show was not permitted to encourage any dissent or political controversy. In a interview in 1956 with the screen actress Shelley Winters, Murrow posed the question: "What kind of world do you hope your little girl will grow up in?" Winters replied, "I hope she grows up in a world dedicated to the principles of Franklin D. Roosevelt." Murrow warned her that the remark was inappropriate for the program, and under the Fairness Doctrine he would be forced to grant another guest the equal time to state his or her political platform, as it was an election year.

The show was influential as to how it personalized the celebrities by bringing the audience into their homes. It satisfied people's curiosity about how others live. The show provided excitement to television audiences and an alternative image of Murrow as the tough newscaster on his other program, "See It Now." From the outset, "Person to Person" was scheduled on prime-time slots and never lacked sponsorship. The last telecast of the show was on September 15, 1961.

Media in the 20th Century

Chet Huntley and David Brinkley, 1956

MARKETING CANDIDATES ON TELEVISION

Other experiments using television to ingratiate newscasters as personalities to the television audience occurred at the 1956 national presidential conventions. NBC approved the team of two relatively unknown reporters **Chet Huntley** and **David Brinkley** to cover both conventions and attempt to attract an audience in a topic considered mundane. At that time, news anchors were revered as stars, much like Hollywood actors. The new duo were an immediate success, using charm and wit to alleviate the dull atmosphere of the conventions. They were praised in the print media, especially the *New York Times*, for "injecting much-needed humor in the commentary." The press commented that the two had imposing, but not commanding, voices, which gave a quality of assurance in their presentation. Between the lulls in the conventions, the two would discuss everything from the appearances of the candidates to some of the more outlandish policies and resolutions circulating on the convention floor. The program was a triumph of style and established the precedent for the format of news, adding a footnote commentary to the stories helping the audience to digest otherwise complex or boring events. At the time, the news was still allotted only 15 minutes to broadcast between popular entertainment shows. However, the entertainment value of the news and its newscasters was beginning to become more evident to the network executives.

More so than either radio or print media, television added a human quality to news, and audiences looked for that personal feeling from its anchors. Chet Huntley and David Brinkley were so enveloped in popular culture that during the inaugural celebration for President John F. Kennedy in 1960, singer/actor Frank Sinatra sang a parody of the song "Love and Marriage" with the words "Huntley, Brinkley, Huntley, Brinkley, one is glum, the other twinkly..." With all the attention received by the pair, other networks were encouraged to increase their output of news.

As part of its responsibility of informing the public, television provided the office of the president with unprecedented power. Network news covered almost any action by the president, whether it represented "real" news or not. These "pseudo-events" served no other purpose than to attract the attention of the media. In 1956 CBS broadcast a cabinet meeting right before the election. CBS was under the impression that the cabinet meeting was legitimate, and welcomed the opportunity to be the first network to televise the proceedings to the public. However, the meeting was carefully staged by the Eisenhower administration, with the president calling on each member of the cabinet, each of whom gave prepared speeches on the progress of the administration and its plans for the future. The entire broadcast fit neatly into the hour time slot, which in the world of television required a great deal of planning and rehearsing. Democrats were outraged, as the telecast was clearly free advertising for the Republican administration just eight days before the presidential election. Democratic candidate **Adlai E. Stevenson**, running against Eisenhower, had to buy media coverage, which he did in a 30 minute presentation that was obviously unrehearsed. He was often still speaking when the screen faded to black. Stevenson did not perform well under the scrutiny of television, and viewers were left with the impression that he was undisciplined and lacked leadership, particularly in contrast to Eisenhower's earlier polished performance. The Democrats could have invoked the Fairness Doctrine to obtain equal coverage on television, but they decided not to pursue the issue. Political candidates and television itself quickly learned that television did not simply transmit reality, but actually had the power to create it.

ADVERTISING

Television was quickly becoming the hot new medium in which companies could advertise their products. Access

Eisenhower broadcast about sending troops to Lebanon

MEDIA IN THE 20th CENTURY

to this powerful forum was determined exclusively by money and a company's desire to spend that money on advertising a product. Like magazines and radio before it, television advertisers communicated fantasies about the product and how people needed it to be successful and happy. Commercials became carefully prepared, elaborately produced and more frequently seen than any program on television. Advertising became a powerful tool in presenting lifestyles that were "acceptable" and normal. The Texaco gas station commercial featuring an attendant cheerfully cleaning the windows of a spanking new Cadillac with a family of four, impeccably dressed, smiling pleasantly on their way to a picnic was what the American family was told they should aspire to become. The goal of advertising was to sell a product by associating it with a vision of how life should be.

Advertisers became sponsors of specific programs and hoped to gain the gratitude of the viewers to purchase their products. In the Fifties, sponsors and advertisers often shared the responsibility for packaging television programs with the networks. With that power came frequent demands on the content of the program. Advertisers tried to avoid sponsoring any show that harbored any sort of controversial or scandalous material. However, it was not beneath sponsors to sometimes exercise unethical behavior in order to increase the number of viewers for their show. When the quiz-show scandals erupted, juries heard testimony that advertisers had played a large role in controlling the shows so that the more "attractive" contestants won, so as to boost ratings. The show **"The $64,000 Question"** first aired

George Burns advertisement for Zenith TV

1950-1959

on June 7, 1955 on CBS, and was sponsored by Revlon, the women's cosmetic company. It offered contestants the opportunity to win up to $64,000 by providing answers to complex questions on a subject they professed to have expertise. Revlon needed players who would engage the audience by their appearance and personality and keep America tuned in as they continued the climb at winning the $64,000. The sponsors saw the contestants as entertainers whose pretensions at honesty were as harmless as those of the actors on dramatic soap operas. After the scandal erupted, the networks took more control over managing programs.

> **"It is pretty obvious that the debasement of the human mind caused by a constant flow of fraudulent advertising is no trivial thing. There is more than one way to conquer a country."**
>
> Raymond Chandler, U.S. author.

In 1952, for the first time, television advertising played a role in affecting the presidential election. The Republican party hired the advertising agency Batten, Barton, Durstine & Osborn to neatly package and market Eisenhower's presidency to the public. A new political advertising style began with that ad campaign. Instead of buying a block of time to present a speech, repeated 30-and 60-second commercial spots featured cartoons, jingles and Eisenhower's one-sentence answers to problems of national security and inflation. The campaign changed the course for all future candidates, who relied on advertising as an integral part of the election process. Television advertising would prove to be a major force in American politics as it evolved into a more powerful platform than the more one-dimensional radio or print ads. Political campaigns of the future would now have television in the "media mix."

NEW PUBLICATIONS ON THE NEWSSTANDS

Playboy's bold beginning in 1953 forever changed men's magazines. Revolutionizing publishing and challenging moral boundaries, it featured photographs of female nudity, including the famous *Playboy* centerfold. It also offered exceptional fiction, celebrity interviews and feature articles by renowned writers, much like it does today. *Playboy* quickly made its founder and publisher **Hugh Hefner** into a public figure.

GQ: Gentlemen's Quarterly began publication in 1957. A socially conscious men's magazine, it featured fashions for the man on the go. It emphasized clothing, fashion, travel, dining, and interviews with trend-setting celebrities, *GQ* maintained its success with young, "in" men.

The Village Voice, the newspaper tabloid, began in 1955, and was written from a New Yorker's viewpoint. The publication originated as a crusader for the arts. Over the years it has become more conservative. It featured gossip columns on the various arts, including dance and theater, plus coverage of national celebrities, it was filled with advertisements, political news and at least one in-depth commentary.

Several new publications emerged in the Fifties dealing with world politics.

World Health: The Magazine of the World Health Organization, started in 1958. An attractive, easy-to-read publication filled with generous illustrations, it contained short articles describing WHO projects, such as success stories and areas that needed help. World Health addressed global concerns such as disease, hunger, polio, vaccination campaigns, and maternal and child health, and was published in at least eight languages.

The publication of *Monthly Vital Statistics Report* was begun in 1952 by the federal government. It contained data compiled by the National Center for Health Statistics, such as births, deaths, marriages, infant mortality, divorce, and causes of death, for various time periods and regions of the U.S.

As Americans in the Fifties focused on the family, it's interesting to note two other publications dealing with family issues from different perspectives. *Family Relations: The Journal of Applied Family and Child Studies* (formerly *Family Coordinator*) began publication in 1952. The official publication of the National Council on Family Relations, it was designed for therapists, counselors, public-policy specialists and researchers. *Family Relations* published applied research and emphasized family relationships. Currently, it covers issues such as family violence and alcoholism in addition to standard research.

Ironically, even as the Fifties focused on the ideal Norman Rockwell-style family, one of the major publications dealing with single parenthood debuted. *The Single Parent* began publication in 1958. It covered topics such as stress, spending the holidays alone and how to cope with the death of a spouse or child, it also provided legal information on child support and tax bills.

Several humor magazines emerged during this decade as well. The wonderfully conceived *Mad* magazine burst on the scene in 1952. Filled with juvenile humor, it was unique in that it had no advertising. Offering parodies of modern culture, contemporary situations, and celebrities, it featured the famous big-eared "**Alfred E. Neuman**" on every cover.

Changing business practices created market demand for new publications. *Business & Incentives* (formerly *Premium Incentive Business*) began in 1950. Colorfully illustrated, this journal presented ads from companies that supply premiums and incentives. Focusing on marketing and promotions tools, it also covered employee incentives and motivation.

Now an American institution, *TV Guide* started publication in 1953. Designed to condense all television programming information into a small digest-sized periodical, it also offered highlights of television shows, gossip, celebrity profiles and general information about the medium. *TV Guide* has been one of the most popular magazines in U.S. history, and today has one of the highest circulation of any magazine.

MEDIA
chapter 7
1960-1969
Social Activism and Countercultures, TV's Effects & New Journalism

JFK News Conference

Media in the 20th Century

The Sixties challenged and changed America culturally, socially, politically and psychologically. The unity and conformity celebrated in the Fifties gave way to various countercultures and cult movements as Americans were confronted with civil rights issues; the Vietnam War; student protests; and more, all covered by national news-gathering organizations, and most immediately by television. Television had become the most dominant form of media. Its effect upon politics, advertising and the public perception continued to grow. For the first time, people admitted that they received more news from television than from any other media source. While it united America in times of grief, such as during the assassinations of President John F. Kennedy and the Reverend Martin Luther King, Jr., critics complained that television also trivialized large, complex issues in its struggle to make them "marketable" and "entertaining."

The Sixties was a pivotal decade for television news. The advent of the half-hour newscast, replaced the previous 15-minute time slots allocated between shows. Newspapers and radio found it difficult to compete with the immediacy of network television news. The launching of the communications satellite *Telstar I* in 1962, followed by others, made it possible to transmit televised news reports from around the world directly to a network broadcast center. Television gained an unprecedented power to communicate major events to the entire nation. America was witness to the assassinations of political and civil rights leaders as cameras recorded the events as they occurred. The Vietnam War was telecast directly into the homes of viewers, and Americans experienced the realities of war through the dramatic broadcasts. Protest movements, civil rights marches, and student riots were communicated with drama and immediacy. America was besieged with images of conflict and unrest that many wanted to

First all-transistor TV from Sony, 1960

Facts and Figures

As the decade began in 1960, the world population topped 3 billion, up from 2 billion in 1930. In 1960, 141 world cities boasted populations exceeding 1 million people, up from 16 in 1900. Some of those cities were Tokyo, with 9.6 million; New York and London, with 7.7 million people each; Shanghai, China, 6.2 million; Moscow, 5 million; Mexico City, 4.8 million; Buenos Aires, Argentina, 4.5 million; and Bombay, India, 4.1 million.

1960-1969

ignore. However there was no way to ignore the power of television news and the stories that it covered.

The American public became more familiar with the names and faces of broadcasters such as Walter Cronkite, than with their senators, congressional representatives, or school board members.

TV FACTS AND FIGURES

In 1968, 11.4 million new television sets were manufactured in the U.S. Around 2.7 million color television sets were sold in 1965 alone, more than double the figure for 1964. About 1 million homes were wired for cable television by 1960.

Cronkite became a revered figure, the epitome of the trusted and reliable newscaster. As a pioneer of television news, he strove to establish the same high journalistic standards of accuracy in television that he had practiced in his years as a newspaper and wire-service reporter. His serious approach to delivering news earned him the evening news anchor spot for CBS in 1962. Cronkite transported the nation directly to the heart of Vietnam and other headline events by reporting live on location and delivering an impartial accounts of controversial subjects.

Although some observers predicted that print media would disappear as television dominated the news, the contrary occurred. Instead, "new journalism" breathed vitality into books and magazines as writers turned to socially relevant topics. This new form of reporting, which later became known as nonfiction reportage, emphasized interviewing techniques to obtain information directly from the source. Its focus was on the writing style and the quality of the description of the news. In order to compete with the drama of television, print journalists investigated stories, issues, politics and people in much greater depth than the TV format allowed. Not since the muckraking days of the first decade of the century, had journalism been so interested in analyzing American culture and righting the wrongs of government and big business.

BROADCAST NEWS

By the early Sixties, television came of age as the preferred medium for news and information. A November 1963 **Roper Poll**, a political census report founded in 1933 by **Elmo Burns Roper Jr.**, indicated that 36 percent of Americans believed TV to be the most reliable media source, compared to only 24 percent who favored print over TV. Many people complained that print journalists and publishers were biased and influenced how news stories were reported, while television granted a

FACTS AND FIGURES IN THE 1960s

Daily paper: 5¢
Sunday newspaper: 25¢
AM-FM radio: $79.95
17 inch portable TV: $139.95
Hardcover novel: $5.75
LP record: $2.98

Media in the 20th Century

The JFK-Nixon debates, 1960

more direct access to the news by providing a visual and more realistic account of an event. Perhaps many people ignored the fact that the news stations chose which images to present, the amount of time allotted to a particular story, and the order in which stories were broadcast. The networks even began to use "**the crawl**"– updates that ran across the bottom of the screen – to bring viewers late breaking news while other programs continued uninterrupted.

Following the style of the Fifties television show "See It Now" came the development of other television news programs. On October 11, 1961 NBC began the weekly program "**David Brinkley's Journal**." The subject matter ranged from entertaining pieces such as the opening of a Broadway musical in New York to more serious issues concerning national and international politics. Brinkley's own personal anecdotes and informative observations lent the program a unique appeal. The show received positive critical reviews, but it did not attract a large number of viewers, and was off the air by 1963.

The CBS program "**60 Minutes**," described as a news magazine show, debuted on September 24, 1968 with hosts **Mike Wallace** and **Harry Reasoner**. The weekly investigative reporting show was an immediate success, using a straightforward format to present a wide spectrum of topics such as national and international politics, personality profiles, human interest stories, and advancements in technology. The real meat of the show was in its exposés of fraud, corruption, greed, deceit and worse. Towards the end of the century the show still enjoyed immense popularity and high ratings.

The success of "60 Minutes" set the pace for the emergence of other investigative reporting television news shows. ABC set out to compete with their own news show titled "**20/20**," first telecast on June 6, 1978. The program's first show was hosted by **Harold Hayes** and **Robert Hughes**, and also featured personality profiles, investigative reports, and more, but met with bad reviews. *Variety* magazine compared it to the popular tabloid magazine *National Enquirer* due to its superficial reporting. After the first show, Hayes and Hughes were dismissed and **Hugh Downs** took over as host, and was later joined by Barbara Walters as co-host. The proceeding shows improved and soon "20/20" developed an audience of its own.

1960-1969

A NEW FRONTIER FOR PUBLICIZING POLITICS

Television's influence on politics increased during the Sixties. The first-ever live broadcast of presidential debates on television and radio involved Senator **John F. Kennedy** and Vice President **Richard M. Nixon** on September 26, 1960. The candidates later participated in two additional broadcast debates. Television gave Kennedy the edge he needed to defeat Nixon by fewer than 120,000 votes. Although radio listeners believed Nixon won the debates, television viewers were impressed by Kennedy's appearance and manner. Nixon looked like he needed a shave and seemed less at ease under the hot lights and in front of the camera. The first debate featured questions on domestic affairs, which was Kennedy's strong suit; Nixon was acknowledged as being more experienced in international affairs. Kennedy received a jump in the polls due to the first debate, although the race was still very close.

On television, Kennedy, who had been labeled as too young and inexperienced by some in the press, appeared equal to his opponent. While responding to questions, Kennedy looked directly at the camera, appearing as if he were addressing the mass audience, while Nixon looked at the moderator, the studio audience and everywhere else except into the lens. Kennedy appeared youthful and vibrant. In contrast Nixon appeared haggard, his face was darkened by a "five o'clock shadow," shunning TV makeup. Interestingly, the television audience responded more to the images the can-

Jackie Kennedy and Charles Collingwood tour the White House, 1962

didates projected and less to their ideas and debating skills. It was a lesson that future politicians never forgot. Kennedy, at 43, became the youngest president ever elected, narrowly defeating Nixon.

Kennedy's domestic program, the **New Frontier**, called for tax reform, federal aid to education, medical care for the aged under Social Security, and the extension of civil rights. Many of his reforms, however, stalled in Congress, and foreign-affairs crises occupied much of his time. He was criticized in the press for his approval of the Cuban **Bay of Pigs** invasion of April 17, 1961, in which the U.S. aided Cuban rebels who attempted to overthrow Cuba's communist government.

Then on October 14, 1962, American reconnaissance planes discovered Soviet Union missile bases, capable of attacking the United States with nuclear warheads, in Cuba. In what became known as the **Cuban Missile Crisis**, Kennedy used television as an instrument for

Media in the 20th Century

President and Mrs. Kennedy and Vice President Lyndon Johnson (left) view TV coverage of space flight, 1961

international negotiations. On October 22, 1962, the drama of potential war played out in the homes of America. Kennedy broadcast a televised demand that the Soviet Union remove all its nuclear weapons from Cuba along with reconnaissance pictures as proof of their existence. He magnified his demand by using television, sending a message to the world that he would not accept any other agreement.

The American public anxiously watched its television sets for the latest news breaks. The networks, which frequently employed the drama of breaking into scheduled programs exploited the event. NBC telecast 94 bulletins and 13 specials between October 22 and 28. While Soviet ships carrying nuclear missiles to Cuba closed in on the U.S. naval blockade, America held its collective breath. To the relief of everyone, on October 28, the Soviet Union announced it would comply with Kennedy's demands. The following year the United States and the Soviet Union signed the first limited treaty banning nuclear tests.

John F. Kennedy became the first president to incorporate live television and broadcasting into presidential press conferences. On television he demonstrated his wit and keen awareness of issues to a scrutinizing audience. When asked how he viewed his treatment in the press, he replied, "Well, I'm reading more and enjoying it less." Kennedy and his press secretary Pierre Salinger were masters at manipulating the media. Most of his press conferences were held in the afternoon, allowing the evening television news anchors to replay the highlights and add commentary.

Even those who disliked his policies or ideas could not help admiring Kennedy's charm and grace. His administration, later dubbed **"Camelot"** for its fairytale quality, emitted an image of vitality, youth, culture and fresh hope. His wife, **Jacqueline Bouvier Kennedy**, added to the presidential mystique and glamour. Demonstrating impeccable style and charm, she personally guided Charles Collingwood and television cameras on a tour of the White House while 48 million viewers watched in awe. John

1960-1969

F. Kennedy was aware of the importance of image and the ability of television to promote ideas and sway public opinion. Exuding confidence and trust, he was entertaining, and the public responded favorably.

On November 22, 1963, President Kennedy was shot and killed in Dallas, Texas, and the news flashed around the world. First to break the news to America was **Walter Cronkite**, broadcasting directly from the CBS newsroom. During the next four days, television demonstrated its power to communicate live events to the entire nation and world via satellite. Millions of Americans witnessed the dramatic scenes that unfolded during those four days, seeming more like fiction than reality. Tens of millions watched the funeral and various tributes on television. To further add to the tragedy, television viewers witnessed the murder of **Lee Harvey Oswald**, Kennedy's suspected assassin, by **Jack Ruby**, a nightclub owner who claimed to be an ardent Kennedy admirer. Vice President **Lyndon B. Johnson** became the new president. He continued many of Kennedy's policies including civil rights legislation that barred discrimination against minorities in employment and in public accommodations.

Television news had become a catalyst of the political process. Politicians who had an eye for major offices began to recognize that access to television, either through free television coverage, heavy political advertising, or a combination of both, could provide them with political power. A politician could quickly overcome obscurity and gain national public attention even without first gaining the support of their political party.

Improved technology enabled television to cover politicians in the home, factory, or any place that would help them reach voters they hoped to impress. Traditional forms of campaigning faded into the background as candidates jumped on the bandwagon. The media, often referred to as the "gatekeepers" or "watchdogs" of the traditional political process, now became a platform of the political process and were hard-pressed to maintain their role as objective observers.

A Johnson news conference at the White House

STRIKES AND CIVIL RIGHTS MAKE NEWS

Along with the political dramas acted out on television, racial riots, civil rights demonstrations and marches against segregation occupied starring roles in television news coverage. The general consensus among historians and journalists since 1960 is that many people would not have believed the violent way that the police treated African-American protesters if they hadn't seen the brutality for themselves on television. Without these undeniable moving scenes, the **Civil Rights Act** of 1964 that ended segregation in schools and public places and the **Voting Rights Act** of 1965, which outlawed literacy tests as a prerequisite for the right to vote, would not have been instituted.

The leaders of the civil rights movement were conscious of the power television had to capture public attention. The **Reverend Martin Luther King, Jr.**, the leader of the nonviolent civil rights movement, campaigned for equal rights for all, and used television to expose corrupt police and government officials. In May 1963, he instigated a demonstration in Birmingham, Alabama, which he called "the most segregated city in the U.S." Knowing that the city police commissioner, **T. Eugene "Bull" Connor**, would use force to subdue the peaceful protesters, King made sure that television crews covered the demonstration. Connor ordered the arrest of hundreds of protesters, including children and the Reverend King. As the protest continued toward downtown Birmingham, Connor's police confronted the group with attack dogs and firehoses. An audience of millions witnessed the firehoses tearing the clothes off people's backs as they stood defenseless. Without viewing these scenes personally, government officials might not have pushed for desegregation. In such instances, the media has the power to control people's emotions and values through the stories they choose to cover, the pictures they show, and the facts they present. Television revealed a reality that other media could not compete with in the minds of the viewing public.

Three months later, in August 1963, over 200,000 civil rights advocates participated in the televised **March on Washington**, organized by civil rights leaders who sought nonviolent ways to eliminate segregation. The Reverend King gave his famous "**I Have a Dream**" speech to a crowd that remained patient and composed throughout. The impact of viewing peaceful demonstrators on television placed African-Americans in a positive light.

LBJ talks with Reverend Martin Luther King, Jr., 1963

1960-1969

Despite his dedication to non-violence, the Reverend Martin Luther King, Jr. was shot and killed on April 4, 1968 in Memphis, Tennessee. After the shooting, riots occurred in 63 cities as the grief and anger felt by the black community was unleashed.

As television was becoming America's primary source of information, it was also the advocate for the nation's values. Television documented mans inhumanity to man in an undeniable way and provided a tangible source of information for an audience that demanded news they could see for themselves.

LBJ greets troops in Vietnam

VIETNAM WAR LIVE IN AMERICA

The war in **Vietnam** escalated in 1965, and networks brought the war into the homes of Americans. The issue of biased television coverage exploded when the images of war were broadcast live for the first time.

Two of the most infamous incidents televised were the torching of the village of **Cam Ne** in August 1965 by American troops and the execution of a suspected spy by a South Vietnamese police chief, **Nguyen Ngoc Loan**, in 1968. Images of children burned and scarred by napalm, prisoners threatened by torture, and more were telecast from Southeast Asia The horrors of war became uncomfortably common images difficult for viewers to endure. Television is sometimes criticized for presenting news as entertainment or exaggerating events to an extreme to make them news worthy. In this instance television confronted America with a horrifyingly realistic picture of war and all that it entails. Many Americans who were accustomed to fighting enemies in the name of democracy, were left confused and demoralized by what they saw happening in Vietnam. The televised war divided Americans into two factions, those who favored the escalation of the conflict and those who urged a peaceful settlement. Opposition to and support for the war were covered by the televised reports, creating uncertainty for Americans who had previously depended on newspapers to tell them what they should believe. The most severe criticism of the news media during that time was its failure to provide a historical perspective of the Vietnam War to the public. Correspondents

MEDIA IN THE 20th CENTURY

Moon cameras sent back pictures of Neil Armstrong's first steps on the moon

witnessed in 1968. Television coverage of the anti-war protests forced America to acknowledge dissent and violence in its own neighborhoods and around the world. Television also gave people the power to enact changes and have their voices heard. Leaders, politicians, and advocacy groups realized that television could send their messages across the nation and create an awareness of issues previously hidden in the back pages of the newspapers. At the 1968 **Democratic National Convention** in Chicago, the **Youth International Party,** or "**Yippies**," a group of radically liberal student activists, clashed with Mayor Richard Daley's police force. Daley posted 12,000 police officers around the city, expecting radical groups to lead a protest at the convention. A riot ensued as the police attempted to disperse the protesters. The officers used tear gas and other violent means to subdue any protesters, innocent bystanders, reporters and anyone else who were in the way. The brutality of the police was shown on the evening news along with the news of the convention itself.

Led by **Abbie Hoffman, Jerry Rubin** and **Tom Hayden,** founder of the **Students for a Democratic Society,** or SDS, the Yippies called for a "revolutionary change in the American structure" and a "participatory democracy." The three men, along with five other members, were jailed and charged with

often reported the day's events— as fragmented incidents— without explaining the forces and causes behind them.

Also telecast into the homes of millions of Americans were student uprisings and demonstrations that protested the war, military presences on campuses, and defense-related university research. In April 1965, 20,000 students gathered in Washington, D.C. to demand an end to U.S. involvement in Vietnam. On October 21, 1967, a total of 75,000 joined a march on the Pentagon to protest the war, an event which inspired **Norman Mailer's** Pulitzer Prize-winning novel *The Armies of the Night* (1968).

CONTINUING PROTESTS

Confirmation that the Vietnam war was far from over provoked the anti-war riots that millions of television viewers

1960-1969

creating a disturbance at the convention. During the trial of what was known as the "Chicago Eight" for the eight leaders of the demonstrations, the defendants read comic books and threw kisses to the jurors in acts of defiance against the proceedings.

Outside on the streets of Chicago, the "**Weathermen**," a radical student group who used violent revolutionary tactics, set off on a **"Day of Rage"** rampage, smashing shop windows and cars and battling the police. By 1969, 448 universities across the nation had been disrupted or temporarily shut down by protesters who stormed administration buildings or staged sit-ins to denounce the war. Although a national opinion poll conducted in December 1967 showed that most Americans wanted to "intensify military pressure within limits and see the war through," the youth of the country would not budge. For them, the war was personal. It was from their ranks that the soldiers were drawn, and most knew someone who had either not survived Vietnam or had difficulty surviving their return to society.

Television news had real violence to report from the battlefields of the war and urban campus riots. Broadcasters also reflected the times by adding violence to entertainment programming. In 1967 the *Christian Science Monitor* newspaper counted 210 violent incidents and 81 killings in just 78 hours of prime time shows. **The National Commission on the Causes and Prevention of Violence**, created after the assassination of the Reverend Martin Luther King, Jr., documented violent incidents on the average of one every 15 minutes on NBC and one every 10 minutes on ABC. ABC had some incident of violence in 91 percent of its evening programming in 1968. Many felt the prevalence of violence on television was contributing to an increase in violent crimes, and that such programs suggested violence was an acceptable outlet for aggression. Most authorities agree that seeing violence on the screen does not necessarily lead to criminal behaviors. However, many believe that it is not constructive to focus so much attention on dehumanizing behavior and the destruction of human life over and over again on television.

Cesar Chavez

In contrast to all of the fighting and violence that was occurring on Earth, televised coverage of human achievement momentarily brought everyone together again and enabled humans around the world to view themselves from a new perspective. On July 16,

Media in the 20th Century

Betty Friedan

1969, the **Apollo 11** landing vehicle known as the **Eagle**, touched down on the surface of the moon. People held their collective breath until they heard **Neil Armstrong** report, "Tranquility base here, the Eagle has landed." The world watched mesmerized as two men, **Edwin "Buzz" Aldrin** and Neil Armstrong, walked on the moon's surface. A television camera mounted on the base of the Eagle recorded the achievement and sent live images back to Earth. Remarkably, television had brought the world closer together with the telecast of the historical accomplishment. In a decade of highs and lows, television sometimes helped to unite Americans and instigate needed change that might otherwise have been unaddressed. Television created a revolution in public response and participation in civil rights causes and other political movements, as people were instilled with the feeling that they could make a difference.

ACKNOWLEDGING OTHER VOICES, BOYCOTTS, AND FEMINISM

Other voices were being covered by television, including the migrant farm workers of California led by **Cesar Chavez**. For some five million Mexican-Americans, Chavez was a savior who promised to restore ethnic pride and win them a share of the American dream. For decades Mexican-Americans had faced discrimination in jobs, wages, education and housing, crowding into urban slums or following the harvest to pick cotton, apricots, lettuce and other produce. Their pay was barely enough to buy food and clothing. Most causes cannot capture the public's attention without the media's help, and the media have a role in bringing important issues to the forefront.

In 1965 a riot broke out between migrant workers and farmers in Delano, California, in the San Joaquin Valley, the heart of grape country. Making public speeches and organizing a national grape boycott, Chavez assumed leadership in a 300-mile march to Sacramento, where a crowd of 10,000 supporters rallied before the state capitol. Winemakers came forward and signed a labor contract, but table-grape growers would not. Chavez's **United Farm Workers** (UFW) continued to fight, shunning violence and relying instead on moral conviction. Calling for a boycott of California table grapes, Chavez embarked on a 25-

1960-1969

day hunger strike to drive the point even further. *New York* magazine reported that many Americans "would rather eat a cyanide pellet than a California grape these days." Grapes rotted in warehouses as stores nationwide refused to carry them. Eventually the grape growers gave in, with most signing contracts by 1970. Chavez then moved on to challenge the lettuce growers. Without television coverage, helped by broadcasters keen interest in the civil rights movement, the public would not have been as aware or as sympathetic to Chavez's cause.

Regardless of the criticisms aimed at television news during this decade of change, there were undeniable voices striving to be heard from every segment of the populace. The feminist movement arose in this decade, demanding improved legal status and better conditions for working women. Women felt they were suffering injustices due to their gender and began to publicly voice these concerns. **Betty Friedan**, a homemaker and the author of *The Feminine Mystique* (1963) and a host of other women began writing books conveying the message of feminism, which demanded equality and access to male-dominated fields of employment. Friedan's book urged women's groups to discuss the fact that the institutions governing society were barring them from pursuing goals outside the realm of the home. Friedan joined others in creating the **National Organization for Women** (NOW) in 1966, a group as persistent as the anti-war protesters. Television and other media followed these activists as well. Women began to question their role in society and how they were portrayed in advertising and entertainment programs. Women's studies courses were instituted on college campuses, offering women a historical perspective of their long struggle to achieve equal status in a world governed by gender bias. The women's movement was a political movement, and the media treated it as such.

It was a female journalist who helped women attain an important legislative goal in the Sixties through the inclusion of women in the Civil Rights Act. **May Craig**, a broadcast journalist with the NBC program "Meet the Press," a show in which a panel of reporters question a leading public figure, interviewed U.S. Representative **Howard W. Smith** of

Walter Cronkite

Virginia. She asked if he would consider revising the Civil Rights Act to include women. He replied that he might do so—hoping, actually, to defeat the entire bill by adding women to the list of minorities the act would protect. When Smith proposed the inclusion of women to the bill before the House, laughter broke out on the floor. However, when the Civil Rights Act did pass, its Title VII section was also enacted, prohibiting discrimination in employment on the basis of gender. The **Equal Employment Opportunity Commission** (EEOC) was established to enforce the law, but it would take eight years of legal maneuvering before the Equal Employment Opportunity Act was passed and the EEOC had any real power.

RISE OF THE NEWS ANCHOR AS HERO

The basic form of nightly news broadcasts began to take shape in the Sixties. The 30-minute newscast, minus the commercial messages, left 22 minutes to examine the events of the world. **Walter Cronkite**, perhaps the best-loved commentator ever to grace the television screen, emerged to reassure America throughout one of its most exciting and turbulent decades. Cronkite's career as a CBS newscaster took a giant leap forward on November 22, 1963, when he was the only anchor present to broadcast the wire service cable announcing the death of President John F. Kennedy. Cronkite did not become a revered national institution overnight. It was also a while before he was able to control his news program, although he took the title of managing editor to convey that he was a journalist and not a mere performer. Cronkite's approach to television news was based on his previous position as a wire service reporter for United Press International, which demanded accuracy and the straightforward delivery of news. In his quest for facts, Cronkite flew in a jet that bombed the jungle near Da Nang in Vietnam in 1965. In 1968 he went to Vietnam again to cover the war and was so convinced of the futility of the situation that he concluded one broadcast on the evening news with "To say we are mired in stalemate seems the only realistic, yet unsatisfactory conclusion. . . the only rational way out will be to negotiate, and not as victors." It was the first and only time that he had offered a personal reaction to a news story.

Walter Cronkite emitted a special quality of warmth and unpretentiousness that made viewers feel that they could trust him. The promotion of news presenters, sometimes referred to as "**anchormen**," was the tactic used to ingratiate viewers to specific stations. The term anchor derived from the world of sport, referring to the last runner of a relay team, whose final effort determines the outcome of the race.

Cronkite captured America's allegiance by following a news story to its end. His competitive drive to beat out the other networks, ABC and NBC, drove him to polish his stories. On the TV screen, Cronkite emerged as a man concerned with the common good and was conventional in his approach to news. As his popularity grew, he earned the right to have the final say about the stories that made the evening news, and thus he validated issues as important by his choice to include them. His approach to news was seldom controversial, and he was adamant in his belief that news should be an impartial account of the day's events.

1960-1969

On his newscasts he televised all opinions on the Vietnam war, both positive and negative. Cronkite helped create a shift in television's relationship to government. Taking his lead, the media no longer unconditionally supported the government's censorship of news about Vietnam. Prior to then the news media had mostly adhered to government requests to censor information. President Lyndon B. Johnson told his press secretary at one point that if he had "lost Cronkite, [he had] lost the country."

Walter Cronkite had this to say about the promotion of "personalities" in TV news:

"I think that it would be absolutely splendid if you got rid of the anchorperson entirely and found some other way — subtitles or voice-overs—to do the broadcast. The reason I say that is because of what has happened to the anchorman, this over-glorification. There are a lot of reasons that is a mistake, but one is the mere suggestion that a person, because he anchors an evening broadcast, might be qualified to run for office. That terrifies me. There's no relation between those two things. It shows how skewed our values have become."

The initial criticism Cronkite received from CBS was about his inability to create controversy and bring excitement to his interviews. CBS criticized him for his failure to get an explanation from Chicago Mayor Richard Daley about the mayor's direction to use force against the protesters and the media at the Democratic National Convention in 1968. Cronkite was aware that his audience expected him to act according to the serene and intelligent character he had created for himself, and he did not want to set his viewers off by reacting in a obtrusive manner. Cronkite won prestige and trust for his composure and the lack of sensationalism in his news presentation.

By the end of the decade, America had experienced a wave of riots and assassinations, an unpopular war, and a loss of confidence in its institutions and leaders. Cronkite helped to fill the void of confidence that America needed. News anchors were viewed as sympathetic intermediaries who strove to make the news understandable and easier to deal with. They took the public to the actual news event and gave the impression that they were providing information that the government might not. Cronkite and others were perceived as heroes who risked their lives to keep the nation informed and aware.

INVESTIGATIVE JOURNALISM

The distinctions between television and newspapers became more pronounced in the Sixties. Television was primarily a "headline" service meant to supplement the newspapers' ability to offer more in-depth coverage and interpretation.

The tumultuous events of the Sixties led to a renewal of the "**muckraking**" journalistic style from the first decade of the century, which focused on exposing corruption in business and government. Prior to the Sixties, the tone of journalism was more placid and non-controversial. World War I, the stock market crash, the Great Depression, World War II, the postwar recovery, the Korean War and the Cold War had clearly identifiable causes. For the most part the wars presented a side that most Americans could rally behind. In those times, the press was much less self-reflective in its coverage. The belief in objectivity had become the principle of most major newspapers, but the memory of the McCarthy era made the press re-examine its principles of objectivity and susceptibility to manipulation by people like McCarthy. The sides of right and wrong was less clearcut during the Sixties, forcing the press to redefine its role in society.

Newspapers began to improve their operations in order to compete with television. *The New York Times'* preeminence was challenged by strong reporting in **Otis Chandler's** *Los Angeles Times*, editor **Thomas Winship's** *Boston Globe*, publisher **Phil Graham's** *Washington Post*, and the *Chicago Tribune*, which left many decisions up to editors and reporters. Newspapers that aspired to national stature were no longer managed as organs that merely expressed the opinions of individual publishers. Investigative reporting in the 1960s offered the public definitive interpretations of the news stories. True investigative reporting was mostly conducted only by the influential and larger newspapers that had the budgets to proceed with lengthy research.

The "organization man" of the previous decade, more passive and dutiful to the publisher's wishes, was replaced by the professionally trained journalist who was attracted to the industry because of the increased pay and prestige. Advertisers were less in control of news content, and most papers offered balanced news and evenhanded political coverage.

Many young reporters who emerged from the Vietnam era and the enormous social changes that rapidly swept the country in the Sixties inherited a distrust of authority. They were given more latitude to explore some of the social and political issues affecting their generation. Stagnant readership, combined with the fierce competition from television news, perhaps made publishers more receptive to their reporters' desires for interpretive and investigative reporting. There was also a recognition among many publishers that the rigid formulas and attitudes of the former press lords were no longer interesting to the public.

A survey conducted in 1968 by the *Chicago Tribune* suggested "prospects of a dwindling audience" because many readers identified the newspaper with "a severe old man preaching rigid and arbitrary lessons as if they were the key to the eternal truth." Newspapers modernized in order to survive and tried to suit the demands of a new audience influenced by the changes of the Sixties. As segments of the population that were previously ignored began to publicly voice concerns over issues of equality or challenging the status quo, newspapers began to respond and reflect some of these voices.

NEW PUBLICATIONS

Adweek (formerly *ANNY*) began publication in 1960. Today it is published in six regional editions, and each carries national articles as well. *Adweek* covered personality and industry news, plus featured topics such as social issues in marketing to minorities. It also carried listings of advertising accounts available and acquired, plus international samples of new ads worth noting.

Family Planning Perspectives started in 1969 as a journal focusing on planned parenthood. All aspects of reproductive health were covered, including adolescent pregnancy, public policy, legal issues, contraceptive practices and abortion. It also included brief information on new research results and news that applied to family planning.

The radical publication *Fifth Estate* began in 1965. This cooperative project between friends shared several bold ideas, including wanting to "deindustrialize the world, eliminate nation states and the capitalist economy and return to decentralized, nature-based communities." It advocated radical ecology by becoming anti-technology and anti-civilization.

Liberal politics starred in *The Washington Monthly*, founded in 1969. It specialized in pointing out the absurdities and often flat-out stupidity of bureaucrats and institutions. It was witty and fearless, primarily written by scholars; its critics often experienced difficulties attempting to effectively refute claims made in *The Washington Monthly*.

The conscientious objection to war based on spiritual or moral principles was popular in the Sixties, and publications popped up to support these schools of thought. *Christian Social Action*, published by the United Methodist Church, began in 1968. It echoed the Methodists' call for consistent policies on peace and social justice.

Although many women's publications would sprout up the next decade, only a few launched during the Sixties would last. *Women's Household: Where Good and Friendly Neighbors Meet* began in 1960. Similar to its sister publication, *Women's Circle*, it proudly declared its traditional bent with its focus on homemaking and female relationships. Two unique features sustained it: Twin Finder (where separated twins could find each other) and its pen-pal service.

Lady's Circle took an approach similar to *Family Circle* and *Woman's Day* magazines. It was started in 1963, and its readers were wholesome, middle-class homemakers. Articles focused on parenting information in a variety of areas (health, nutrition, psychology), celebrities' family lives, cooking and crafts such as needlework, knitting and crocheting. Intended to uplift readers, its fiction often featured people who do good deeds or who are gallant survivors. It also featured a pen-pal service (Friendship Club).

Television's media dominance resulted in several new publications in the Sixties. *Telemedium* (formerly *Better Broadcast News and Better Broadcast Newsletter*) was first introduced in 1963 by the National Telemedia Council. A "nonprofit organization that encouraged the critical evaluation of TV and radio programming toward a media-wise society," *Telemedium* provided a forum for critics to submit their evaluations and recommendations.

In 1963, *Cable Television Business: Business Magazine for the Cable Television Industry* (formerly TVC) came on the scene. It featured updates on sales, industry-association changes, finances, and legislation, plus engineering, personnel and plant-management coverage. The majority of articles focused on the industry's future opportunities, especially in technology.

Telecommunications (North American Edition) was first published in 1967. It covered the technical aspects of global communications, written for broad audience appeal. Many articles dealt with computers, and cutting-edge innovations and technology.

ADVERTISING

The U.S. television industry enjoyed advertising revenues of $2 billion, roughly twice the total of radio advertising revenues, in 1960. Both industries received heavy revenue support from cigarette advertising from American tobacco companies. The ongoing debate over the dangers of cigarette smoking heated up after the U.S. Surgeon General issued a groundbreaking report citing smoking as a health hazard in 1964. In 1967 the FCC applied the **Fairness Doctrine** to cigarette advertisements, granting "equal time" on the air to groups opposed to radio and TV commercials for tobacco products.

As television evolved, advertisers continued to use the medium to link a product with a lifestyle. TV commercials could effectively depict the use of a product improving the life of the consumer. Advertising played to the sentiment of the times in order to appeal to a vast audience.

In 1963 the Congress of Racial Equality's New York chapter convinced Lever Brothers soap company to broadcast a Wisk detergent commercial showing children of different races playing together. An anomaly in network television and advertising, the commercial successfully aired with two boys at play—an African-American and a Caucasian. Most major advertising campaigns featured only white actors and models. Mixed-race or multicultural advertising wouldn't truly take off until the Nineties. The Sixties also witnessed the exploitation of the youth culture, capitalizing on the enormous size of the "baby boomer" market and its need to be noticed. It was a progressive decade in terms of the establishment of civil rights, and at the same time Americans were shaken by changes in their simple lifestyles.

Critics complain that television advertising promotes materialism and fuels the desire to consume. Television is largely dependent on advertisers to support the production costs of programming. Under the Fairness Doctrine, which was finally written into the Communications Act as a law in 1959 by the Federal Communications Commission, a network or station must present all sides of a controversial issue. While the government can keep advertisers from making false claims about their products, it is ultimately up to the individual citizen to evaluate the content of advertising and the products that it is selling.

The decade of the Sixties was a time of radical social movements and changing legislation. Antiestablishment attitudes were strong and manifested themselves in all aspects of society in the form of marches, protests, and boycotts. Television and other media brought news of the world and the nation to people's homes and introduced new causes and issues to the public. Television had a triumphant decade and asserted itself as a medium able to deliver news in an expedient manner, shape public opinion through visual coverage, and unite people in times of sorrow. Television would continue to evolve in the Seventies, and newspapers would once again take a leading role in presenting the news.

MEDIA

chapter 8

1970-1979

Investigative Reporters and the Advent of Television News Programs

Betty Ford's 1975 "60 Minutes" interview with Morley Safer

Media in the 20th Century

The Seventies witnessed America's defeat in the Vietnam War, televised live to the nation, and the country suffered episodes of disillusionment and doubt. "New journalism" underwent further development as reporters took a stronger investigative role in uncovering news. Reporters revealed corruption in government that led all the way to the White House. The story known as the Pentagon Papers heralded a legal battle between the powers of government to protect its secrets and the freedom of the press to print information relevant to the public good. The U.S. Supreme Court upheld the right of the *New York Times* to publish the secret Pentagon study of the Vietnam War. On June 13, 1971, the *Times* ran the first installment of the report with the headline: "Vietnam Archive: Pentagon Study Traces 3 Decades of Growing U.S. Involvement." The story detailed 30 years of deceit, political infighting and ignorance on the part of the United States government. The *Times* reprinted documents, cable messages, position papers, and memos, all tracing American tactics in Vietnam. United States Attorney General John Mitchell attempted to restrain the papers from printing the story, and failed, leading to further investigation of government actions.

By 1970, over one million Americans had fought in the jungles of Vietnam, and over 50,000 American lives had been lost. On April 30, 1970, President Nixon made the stunning announcement on television that he was extending the bombing campaign into Cambodia, a neighboring country to Vietnam. Protests immediately erupted on college campuses across the country. A group of student activists met at Kent State University in Ohio to protest the action. Toward evening, several hundred students followed, throwing bottles and smashing windows in downtown Kent. The following night, campus demonstrators burned down the ROTC building on campus, and the National Guard was called in. The final confrontation occurred on May 4. As guardsmen moved in to break up an anti-war rally on the university commons, an uncontrollable disturbance erupted. Students hurled rocks and insults; guardsmen responded with tear gas. Rifle shots rang out. When the smoke cleared, four students were dead and 10 were seriously wounded. As Canadian communications theorist Marshall McLuhan stated in the *Montreal Gazette* on May 16, 1975, "Vietnam was lost in the living rooms of America, not on the battlefields of Vietnam."

Nixon visits U.S. soldiers in Vietnam

1970-1979

In his second presidential inaugural address in 1973, Richard Nixon promised an end to the Vietnam War. He stated: "The greatest honor history can bestow is the title of peacemaker. This honor now beckons America." Nixon's opponent, Senator George McGovern, also promised a quick end to the war. Popular with youth and the anti-war movement, McGovern came across to the public as a naive idealist when compared to the mature, statesmanlike image Nixon's campaign projected. McGovern's campaign, dubbed by the Republicans as one of "acid, amnesty and abortion," met with dismal failure as Nixon captured 61 percent of the popular vote, the largest victory margin on record.

The "new journalism" examined every aspect of government affairs in its quest for truth. What began as a back-page item about five men being arrested on burglary charges at the Watergate office building, the headquarters to the Democratic National Committee in Washington, D.C., eventually revealed the most widespread political corruption in the nation's history and lead to the resignation of President Richard M. Nixon on August 8, 1974. Cynicism toward government was already high and people were further incensed by the discovery of the president's crimes. Two newspaper reporters from the *Washington Post*, Bob Woodward and Carl Bernstein would follow the story to its fruition and, relying on confidential sources, uncovered the existence of a Republican spying network, a secret fund, and implications of illegal activities on the part of high administration officials. In this instance, newspapers set the stage for television coverage of hearings in the Senate. These incidents shook the foundations of government, leaving many Americans feeling dismayed and betrayed. Television would

Student and soldier at Kent State, May 1970

broadcast the unraveling events of Watergate live to an audience that placed more confidence in the media to inform them than in any other institution. America had lost respect in the integrity and judgment of national leadership.

The "new journalism" with its "quest for truth" reporting style evolved into a more subjective, cynical style of news known as "gonzo journalism," which was usually bizarre or unconventional. Gonzo journalists employed an exaggerated subjective or self-indulgent style of reporting. Noted gonzo journalists included Hunter S. Thompson and Tom Wolfe. As publishers and television producers requested shorter, simpler stories, writers became cynical and frustrated. Like the muckrakers before them, the "new journalists" were not particularly well paid, but felt they contributed an important public service. As stories were edited more liberally to allow room for "fluff" (sidebars, photographs, and charts), some journalists felt under-

MEDIA IN THE 20th CENTURY

PENTAGON PAPERS IN PRINT AND ON THE AIR

Daniel Ellsberg

appreciated, but continued to express their views in thought provoking and earth shattering investigations of American politics and society.

These slogans for the three major networks came into use in 1970:

"It's Happening on NBC!"

"Let's Get It Together on ABC."

"We're Putting It All Together on CBS."

The United States government attempted to restrain the freedom of the press on June 15, 1971, and for 15 days it successfully restrained the **New York Times** from printing a vital news story. In March 1971, the *Times* had acquired a 47 volume report from an unnamed or unknown source, entitled **"History of the U.S. Decision-Making Process on Vietnam Policy."** All the documents were classified "Top Secret" under a 1953 executive order. The report was composed for the Pentagon on the orders of Secretary of Defense Robert McNamara. It was later implied that **Daniel Ellsberg**, a defense analyst at a Washington think tank had "leaked" the reports to the press. Ellsberg had been involved in a project to uncover lessons from America's experience in Vietnam, and had used the report as part of his research. Pentagon records state that Ellsberg was assigned to take ten volumes of the report from the Rand think tank in Washington D.C. to Santa Monica, California on March 3, 1969. On August 29 of the same year, it was arranged for Ellsberg to carry eight more volumes. The contents of the report were historical and non-military in nature, but highly damaging to various government entities. Known as the **Pentagon Papers**, they revealed lies and policy disputes between administrations in the White House and Saigon. Among the notes was a cable from the American embassy in Saigon regarding the planned execution of Prime Minister **Ngo Dinh Diem**, dating weeks before he was ousted from office. Ngo Dinh Diem was assassinated on November

1970-1979

21, 1963 by military officials. There were also memos from President **Lyndon B. Johnson** concerning the sending troops to Vietnam during times he was simultaneously reassuring the country that he had no long-range plans for war in Southeast Asia. The papers did not cover the years of Richard Nixon's presidency.

In the style of the "new journalists" **Neil Sheehan**, a reporter at the *New York Times*, set out to develop the story for the public. The liberty of the press came into debate as Attorney General **John Mitchell**, instructed by President Nixon, attempted to restrain the press from printing the story. Mitchell asked the *New York Times* to stop the series because the disclosure would "cause irreparable injury to the defense interests of the United States." The *Times* refused, assuming the responsibility of informing the public of the corruption in government. Mitchell took the case to a federal district judge, Murray Gurfein, who ordered a temporary restraining order on June 15, 1971, prohibiting the *Times* from printing further incriminating reports, after its third installment. Four days later, the court denied the government's request for a permanent restraining order against the press; the court ruled that the government had failed to prove its point and only wanted to conceal "general embarrassment." Judge Gurfein upheld the temporary restraining order, though, and the *Times* took the matter to the U.S. Court of Appeals on June 23, 1971. The Court of Appeals reversed the decision of Judge Gurfein. Judge Gerhard Gesell of the New York State Appeals Court ruled that "government cannot impose a prior restraint on essentially historical data."

The government however, continued to try to restrain its publication. The case reached the U.S. Supreme Court on June 25, 1971, when the court agreed to continue the temporary order of restraint while it weighed the issue. The lawyers for the paper argued that the government could not prove that national security was jeopardized as a result of the printing of the articles. Surprisingly they did not argue on the basis of the First Amendment's guarantee of the freedom of the press. The Supreme Court overturned the restraining order by a 6-3 vote on June 30, 1971, stating that "any attempt by the government to impose prior restraint on publication of information by newspapers bears a heavy presumption against its constitutional validity under the First Amendment." The decision allowed the *New York Times* and other papers, such as the **Washington Post** and the **Boston Globe**, to publish the articles drawn from the Pentagon

Washington Post **newsroom**

Media in the 20th Century

Washington Post reporters Bob Woodward and Carl Bernstein

Papers. The positive outcome reinforced the importance of the First Amendment to protect freedom of the press. However, the truth shook America's faith in its leaders.

The publication of the Pentagon Papers received strong attention, but it was not the first time the press revealed government manipulation and propaganda. CBS correspondent **Roger Mudd** had broadcast a 60-minute documentary on February 23, 1971, titled, "**The Selling of the Pentagon**," accusing the military of instituting a nationwide propaganda campaign to manipulate the public toward the war effort. Mudd began the show with clips of demonstrations performed by the military in schools, parades, and other occasions, and explained to the television audience that the report was from America and not Vietnam. He made it evident that the report was about "how the U.S. military used taxpayers' money to sell itself to the American public." Supporters of the war were outraged by the criticism, as was the Defense Department.

The material in Mudd's documentary was not new, but it had not received any attention until it was broadcast for the public. In the documentary, the Pentagon admitted to spending an estimated $30 million a year on public relations. Mudd discovered an independent report completed by a foundation known as the Twentieth Century Fund, which claimed that the actual spending on public relations was closer to $190 million. The program aired a short clip of weapons being fired during a public relations demonstration by the military. The display of weaponry was estimated to have cost $2 million. Congressional committees conducted investigations on the accuracy and impartiality of the program in attempts to discredit its findings. Attempts by the government were also made to forbid other portions of the program from being broadcast on a later date. CBS refused to turn over the film, and freedom of the press for television became an issue. CBS won the battle and maintained the right to air further clips at its discretion. The documentary was the first of its kind, a landmark in programming history. Its in-depth investigative style was unlike the usual reporting of the day. It also substantiated the power of television to influence public opinion and affect government action.

CORRUPTION EXPOSED

Political corruption did not end with the Pentagon Papers of course, nor did the investigative reporting of the press. The public had just seen the tip of the iceberg. The **Watergate** scandal, essentially a plan to sabotage the Democratic Party, resulted in the resignation of President Richard Nixon and a Pulitzer Prize for *Washington Post* reporters **Bob Woodward** and **Carl Bernstein**. Distrust between the White House and Congress had grown as a result of the publication of the Pentagon Papers. The distrust spread to the public, and it escalated after President Richard Nixon announced his plans to expand the war into Cambodia, followed by the killing of the four students at Kent State University. The White House was tense, and news leaks flourished. Nixon had to devise a plan to protect himself and ensure his 1972 reelection. He agreed to a proposal by White House aide **Tom Huston**, creating a domestic-security group comprised of representatives from the Federal Bureau of Investigation, the Central Intelligence Agency, and other government agencies.

The committee was authorized by the president to wiretap communication lines, commit burglary, and violate other laws to protect against security leaks and uncover disloyal members within the administration. Nixon established a surveillance team in the White House, later referred to as the "**plumbers**," whose job it was to prevent leaks of classified information to the press. On June 17, 1972, five men were apprehended breaking into the headquarters of the Democratic National Committee in the Watergate office building in Washington. The men were caught placing listening devices and taking documents concerning the party's campaign strategy from the office of Lawrence F. O'Brien, the party's chairman. The burglars were government operatives, and members of the **Committee for the Re-Election of the President**, later dubbed **CREEP**. Arrested were **James W. McCord**, a former agent of the CIA, who was security coordinator for CREEP, and four others who did not know the full implications of the assignment.

> "It was when 'reporters' became 'journalists' and when 'objectivity' gave way to 'searching for truth' that an aura of distrust and fear arose around the New Journalist."
>
> Georgie Anne Geyer, U.S. author, columnist.

The *Washington Post* assigned reporters Bob Woodward, 29, and Carl Bernstein, 28, to the story. What seemed at first to be an ordinary burglary became more and more complex and disturbing. Assisted by an unknown informant known as "**Deep Throat**," the two reporters began to crack open the Watergate affair, working 12 to 18 hours a day, seven days a week. On August 1, 1972, they reported a financial link between the Watergate break-in and the Committee for the Re-Election of the President (CREEP). This breakthrough story claimed that $25,000 was deposit-

MEDIA IN THE 20th CENTURY

ed into a bank account of **Bernard Barker**, one of the men arrested in the Watergate break-in. On September 16 they reported that campaign finance chairman **Maurice H. Stans** and CREEP aides controlled a "secret fund" that supported CREEP activities. The next day they discovered withdrawals from the fund by CREEP executive **Jeb Stuart Magruder** and his aide **Herbert L. Porter**. Twelve days later, on September 29, they reported that former Attorney General John N. Mitchell actually controlled the fund.

Their ground-breaking story in the October 10, 1972 *Washington Post* read: "FBI agents have established that the Watergate bugging incident stemmed from a massive campaign of political spying and sabotage conducted on behalf of President Nixon's reelection and directed by officials of the White House and the Committee for the Re-Election of the President." Identified as being involved in the illegal operation were

What did Americans spend to read the newspapers?
(dollars in thousands)

Year	Weekday	Sunday	Total:
1970	1,921,404	712,998	2,634,402
1975	2,888,978	1,034,537	3,921,515

John Mitchell, former attorney general, and the director of CREEP; Jeb Stuart Magruder, deputy campaign director of CREEP; G. Gordon Liddy, finance counselor of CREEP; E. Howard Hunt, a former White House consultant; John Ehrlichman, domestic adviser to the president; Charles Colson, special counsel to the president; and John W. Dean III, presidential legal counsel. A White House spokesmen denounced the *Post* stories as "shabby journalism," "mud-slinging," "unfounded and unsubstantiated allegations," and "a political effort by the *Washington Post*, well conceived and coordinated, to discredit this administration and individuals in it." On October 25, Woodward and Bernstein reported that a White House aide, Hugh Sloan, had testified in a Washington courtroom that White House chief of staff H.R. Haldeman was authorized to dispense money from a secret cash account to fund political spying. The trail had led Woodward and Bernstein right into the Oval Office. Despite denials of involvement by Nixon and his staff, the

Richard Nixon's resignation on TV, 1974

1970-1979

Post was awarded the gold Pulitzer Prize medal in 1973 for "meritorious public service," yet Republican senators continued to denounce the paper for printing "rumors and innuendo."

In 1972 a study was conducted to evaluate the coverage of the Watergate story. Surprisingly, it revealed that little attention was actually paid to the story by the public. Woodward and Bernstein established *The Washington Post* as the lead runner of the story. In August 1972 *Time* magazine had broken a major story identifying the "plumbers" involved in the burglary, but did not follow up on the investigation. It was calculated that of the 433 Washington-based reporters, only 15 were assigned to the Watergate story. Out of the 500 political columns written in the press between June and November, fewer than 24 were on Watergate.

The initial television coverage of the Watergate story was handled in a routine manner. Over the course of seven weeks, starting on September 14, CBS devoted 71 total minutes to the story, NBC allotted 42 minutes and ABC gave just 41 minutes of news time. Many of the stories were less than a minute in length, thus it was no surprise that an October 1972 Gallup Poll, which measured the nation's political attitudes, showed that only 52 percent of Americans recognized the word Watergate. Nixon was re-elected to the presidency in a landslide, but would resign two years later when the Watergate story was fully revealed in 1973 and television took notice.

The trial of the five men who broke into the Watergate building began in January 1973, presided over by Judge **John**

Ford pardons Nixon, September 8, 1974

J. Sirica. In February, the Senate Select Committee on Presidential Campaign Activities, led by Senator **Sam J. Ervin Jr**. of North Carolina, began to hear testimony.

The American public began a marathon of television viewing. Televised hearings of the Watergate investigations began in May 1973. As the nation watched, the hearings revealed that the White House had been embroiled in wiretapping, forgery and other corrupt business. Nixon's "enemies list" of real and imagined foes, whom he had investigated surfaced. The shocking news culminated when Nixon himself was found to have ordered a cover-up of the break-ins. The facts of the case were uncovered with the help of recorded conversations made by the White House. Nixon had taped most of his meetings, implicating his involvement. The famous missing 20 minute gap of these tapes most likely contained the most damaging facts to link Nixon personally. It seemed that the White House was engaged in a conspiracy to obstruct justice.

Impeachment proceedings against President Nixon began in May 1974. Earlier, on June 25, 1973, John Dean, a White House aide, had testified before the Senate committee that President Nixon authorized payment of "hush money" to the men arrested in the Watergate burglary. On July 16, 1973, Alexander Butterfield, another presidential aide, had testified in court that Nixon had taped his conversations in the White House. From then on Nixon was locked in a battle with the Senate committee to maintain possession of the secret tapes, claiming "national security" and "executive privilege." The Supreme Court ruled that Nixon had to turn over the recordings that might contain evidence of misconduct or he would be admitting his own guilt. Meanwhile, Vice President Spiro Agnew resigned on October 10, 1973.

Among other things, the tapes revealed Nixon saying, "I want you all to stonewall it." Left with no other choice, Nixon choked back tears when he announced his resignation before television on August 8, 1974. An estimated 110 million Americans viewed the historic live telecast from the White House Oval Office. In his farewell speech, Nixon insisted that he acted "in what I believed at the time to be the best interests of the nation," and admitted to having made some "judgments" that "were wrong." Two years before the eve of its 200th birthday, America witnessed for the first time a president resigning from office. Stepping into the role of president was Vice President **Gerald R. Ford**, who, in a televised appearance, quickly granted a complete pardon to former president Nixon. The pardon outraged many and clouded Ford's brief tenure in the nation's highest office. Nixon's relationship with the media had its ups and downs. Television had endeared Nixon to the public in 1952 with the televised "Checkers Speech," but it later worked against him in the 1960 presidential debate with John F. Kennedy. After his failed campaign for the California governorship, his words to the press on November 7, 1962 were, "You won't have Nixon to kick around anymore, because, gentlemen, this is my last press conference." Finally the print and television media brought him down with the Watergate scandal.

GONZO JOURNALISM

The "news journalism's" quest for truth and in-depth investigative reporting was followed by "gonzo journalism's" bizarre, subjective and unconventional style. With the public's faster lifestyle and waning interest in investigative reports of complex issues, cynical reporters such as **Tom Wolfe** and **Hunter S. Thompson** spoke for many. In addition to the public's new attitude, publishers were becoming more corporate and bureaucratic, and reporters' frustration came through in their tone, style and word choices. For example Thompson stated in "Fear and Loathing at the Superbowl" in the February 15, 1973, Rolling Stone magazine, "If I'd written all the truth I knew for the past ten years, about 600 people, including me, would be rotting in prison cells from Rio to Seattle today. Absolute truth is a very rare and dangerous commodity in the context of professional journalism."

Gonzo journalism's influence even extended to Europe. In the September 8,

1988, Paris *International Herald Tribune*, Wolfe stated, "The attitude is we live and let live. This is actually an amazing change in values in a rather short time and it's an example of freedom from religion." One famous statement of Tom Wolfe's, from his 1984 book, *The Bonfire of the Vanities*, is "A liberal is a conservative who has been arrested." This statement epitomized the idea of the Seventies. Many people believed in moral relativism (or "live and let live") until they became a victim of it.

> "Gonzo journalism is a style of 'reporting' based on William Faulkner's idea that the best fiction is far more true than any kind of journalism, and the best journalists have always known this.... True gonzo reporting needs the talents of a master journalist, and the eye of an artist/photographer.... Because the writer must be a participant in the scene, while he's writing it or at least taping it, or even sketching it. Or all three. Probably the closest analogy to the ideal would be a film director/producer who writes his own scripts, does his own camera work and somehow manages to film himself in action, as the protagonist or at least a main character."
>
> Hunter S. Thompson, U.S. journalist. *The Great Shark Hunt*, 1979

NEW PUBLICATIONS

Women's magazines finally came of age in the Seventies. The major difference between these new publications and the previous ones was that most of the new magazines were published by and for women. They addressed real issues of concern and interest such as women's health and female spirituality from new perspectives.

Today's Christian Woman debuted in 1978. Still in publication, its articles often related to spiritual development, parenting and controlling anger. It described itself as "a positive, practical magazine designed for contemporary Christian women of all ages, single or married, who seek to live out biblical values in their houses, workplaces and communities." It was subsidized not by mainstream advertisers but by Christian bookstores, educational institutions and therapy programs. The covers usually featured Christian role models, such as singer Amy Grant.

Daughters of Sarah: The Magazine for Christian Feminists began in 1974 as a Bible study group's newsletter, evolving into an interdenominational journal for Christian women. It defined itself as both feminist and Christian, which the editors believe were inseparable.

Women's Studies in Communication started publishing in 1977. It was the official journal of the Organization for Research on Women and Communication. "Communication" was interpreted broadly to include interpersonal, small group and organizational communication, as well as mass media. Its contents were primarily research papers by substantially established professionals, on such topics as "TV Rape: Communication of Cultural Attitudes Toward Rape" and "The Rela-

Media in the 20th Century

tionship between Communications and Marital Uncertainty: Is 'Her' Marriage Different from 'His' Marriage?"

In July of 1972, *Ms.* magazine began publication. A former staff editor for *Look* magazine, **Patricia Carbine**, was the publisher and feminist journalist **Gloria Steinem** was its editor. *Ms.* primarily served as a forum for women's liberation. Often criticized by conservatives as "too feminist," *Ms.* journalists interviewed some of the world's most powerful women of the Seventies and continues to do so today.

In 1973, *Playgirl: Entertainment for Women* was seen as a novelty; critics never expected it to last beyond a few years. Most of its features were either advice columns, reader responses or articles with sexual themes. Inspired by *Playboy*, it featured photos of men.

ADVERTISING

Concern over the connections between children's programming and advertising arose in the early Seventies. Former Nixon administration food consultant **Robert Burnett Choate, Jr.** testified before a Senate subcommittee that 40 of the top 60 dry breakfast cereals have little nutritional content. "The worst cereals are hucksered to children on television," he said. His findings helped the Federal Trade Commission to enforce the policy of "truth in advertising." The FTC monitored advertisers to represent the truth about a product, including its appearance. For example, they targeted cereal advertisers who used glue instead of milk to make the product appear richer. In the late Sixties and early Seventies the demand for government controls and advertiser accountability was heard. Children's programming on commercial television came under greater scrutiny by new groups of concerned citizens. Quality educational programming for children began in 1969 with the debut of Public Broadcasting System's "**Sesame Street**." This kind of high-quality alternative programming helped children and adults understand the differences between educational and commercial content, and offered shows that wouldn't bombard impressionable children with advertising. The interest group

Gloria Steinem, editor of *Ms.*

1970-1979

Action for Children's Television (ACT) forced a reduction in advertising during commercial children's programming in 1970. The group successfully pressured the networks to limit the advertising of food products and toys on Saturday-morning cartoon programs. The group argued that the advertising didn't just contain the marketing of a product, but gave the children other messages that took advantage of their innocence. By 1972 the networks and the **National Association of Broadcasters** (NAB) agreed to reduce the time devoted to commercials in children's weekend television shows from 16 minutes for a one hour show to 12 minutes, to be officially effective as of January 1, 1973. Further pressure was placed on the networks as the ACT worked to limit "**tie-ins**" in programs. Tie-ins referred to the mention of a product within the context of a program, using cartoon characters or the program host to promote the product. For example, the group did not want popular program hosts such as Captain Kangaroo selling ideas of what was desirable, to their children

Commercial television is an effective medium with which to sell all kinds of products. In 1969 tobacco companies proposed a three-year plan to phase out cigarette ads on radio and television. Britain's Royal College of Physicians had reported that cigarette smoking had become a cause of death comparable to the great epidemics of typhoid and cholera in the 19th century. On January 2, 1970, the ban on radio and television cigarette advertising took effect, taking with it almost $220 million in advertising. Still, U.S. cigarette sales had reached $547.2 billion in the early Seventies, in spite of the advertising ban. With the exception of beer and wine, liquor advertising has always remained voluntarily off the airwaves.

Not all people joined the fight for controlled advertising. In April 1973, *Variety* magazine reported that roughly one in five Americans find television commercials as "a fair price to pay for being able to view the program." The majority of the population disagreed and control of advertising was enforced by the FCC

A 1975 advertisement for Cadillac

MEDIA IN THE 20th CENTURY

PBS's Sesame Street

and the National Association of Broadcasters. Advertising has proved to be adaptable to the regulations imposed on media and maintained its success by following trends.

The Seventies was a turbulent decade with media constantly challenging boundaries as in the attempt to prohibit the publication of the Pentagon Papers. In the wake of political corruption, media asserted itself as the champion of the people by exposing President Richard Nixon and his involvement in the Watergate scandal. News on the air became more believable as television was able to provide immediate and live news reports. People were often more inclined to identify with a event that they could witness as it occurred, rather than hearing about an event on the radio or reading it in the print media.

Television would continue to grow in the next decade as new networks began and satellite TV would become the news craze, allowing events from around the world to be broadcast in real time.

MEDIA

chapter 9

1980-1989

Scandals, Mergers and Cable TV

3.8 Meter Satellite Dish

Media in the 20th Century

The Eighties was a time of explosive growth for media, especially television. Many newspapers disappeared during this decade due to the rising costs of materials and labor, and the rise of cable 24-hour news stations. Many cities became "one newspaper" towns, leaving only one print voice to service a multitude of people. Political and financial scandals would dominate news topics of this decade. Corporate mergers and takeovers exploded in many industries, including media. As media conglomerates became larger, they formed alliances with advertisers and movie studios.

Satellite TV would report events happening across the world available in real time. As cable news rose in popularity, network television pushed the boundaries of acceptability in order to remain competitive. Subscriber-supported cable TV could air more graphic violence and sex, including R- and X-rated movies. Drawn to the "theater in your living room," cable subscriptions and viewing increased, while network viewing decreased. Like early print media, cable TV was subscription-driven and originally contained no advertising. Later, cable would follow print's lead and sell advertising time, that targeted specific types of viewers.

According to market research studies of consumer buying patterns, in-depth investigative reporting did not always appeal to consumers in the Eighties. Survey participants complained about stories being too long and negative, and wanted to hear good news for a change. Bold, colorful and national in coverage, Gannett Corporation's newspaper *USA Today* burst on the scene in 1982, delivering topical and non-controversial national news coverage.

THE PRESS

In media and other large industries, mergers became common as larger corporations acquired companies weakened through poor investments, competition or lawsuits. Large publishers of dominant newspapers targeted smaller competitive newspapers for takeovers; with the goal of total domination in their markets. Cities large and small across America, such as Salem, Massachusetts and Little Rock, Arkansas were left with only one paper. No competition between publications meant one publication could control advertising rates, as well as coverage of local and national issues. In cities such as Detroit, where two newspapers remained after a bitter "news war," a joint operating agreement involving **Gannett's** *Detroit News* and **Knight-Ridder's** *Free Press* allowed both papers to co-exist while sharing staff and resources. Joint operating agreements were intended to help financially insecure publications survive. Sometimes this survival tactic resulted in two editorial voices that echoed the same views instead of expressing contrasting opinions.

In his book *The Chain Gang—One Newspaper versus the Gannett Empire*, **Richard McCord** (a former reporter for the Long Island newspaper *Newsday*, then editor and publisher of the *Santa Fe Reporter* in New Mexico), revealed the experiences small community newspapers had with large media conglomerates, particularly Gannett. **Frank Wood**, the editor/publisher of the *Green Bay News-Chronicle* in Wisconsin, asked McCord, who had experienced Gannett's takeover techniques while at the *Santa Fe Reporter*, for his assistance to prevent the Gannett paper from forcing him into bankruptcy. McCord's

1980-1989

research and notes, taken from trial and court transcripts in the case *Community Publications Inc. v. Gannett Co.* included several memos from top Gannett people. In this case *Community Press*, a weekly, sued Gannett for "unfair and illegal anti-competitive and monopolistic practices... in Salem that drove it out of business there." Those practices included Operation Demolition, a 13-week ad program designed to woo away current *Community Press* advertisers. One Gannett memo explained that the whole idea of the program "is to reduce or eliminate each of the advertisers... while at the same time you keep additional advertisers from advertising in the *Community Press*."

McCord's research in Green Bay led him to believe Gannett would pursue a similar program in Green Bay with the intention of "demolishing" the *News-Chronicle*. With McCord's eight-page investigative report, the *News-Chronicle* made advertisers and consumers aware of Gannett's possible intentions. In closing, he outlined how they, the consumers, with their subscription and advertising dollars, would decide whether or not Green Bay remained a true two-newspaper town or part of a chain. Although the *News-Chronicle* still struggles financially, the people of Green Bay decided to support both papers.

The larger media companies, such as Gannett, took advantage of their "best" reporters and syndicated them within the other papers they owned. This meant other Gannett papers could access and

USA Today's first issue, September 15, 1982

use a large pool of columns from around the country in addition to those generated by their own local reporters. This internal reuse of articles put many reporters (and some smaller papers) out of the work. Many reporters shifted to working in advertising departments in order to stay in the publishing field.

The creator of Gannett's *USA Today* was **Allen H. Neuharth**. As publisher of *USA Today*, Al Neuharth marketed Gannett to Wall Street to increase Gannett's financial and professional reputation. He pointed out why newspapers were a still-vital media source, as well as a good investment. In the majority of communities, the daily newspaper was then and is still the advertising vehicle of choice for local merchants. Without competition their publishers can raise the subscription prices of papers as well as the ad rates to generate more revenue as needed. While consumers may search and channel-surf through a variety of television stations, they are more closely connected to their local newspapers. Neuharth's intent with *USA Today* was to create a national newspaper that the growing ranks of traveling business people, transferred families and other less-rooted Americans would support. *USA Today*'s look, feel and approach to news influenced regional newspapers throughout the country. The increased use of color photography, multiple color graphs and colorized weather maps were incorporated into most successful papers of the late Eighties and Nineties. Gannett's aggressive consumer marketing of *USA Today* through street kiosks, airlines and other means was an expensive and large scale undertaking on a national scale. Gannett supported *USA Today* through years of financial loss.

One small trend that began in the 1980s and would expand in the 1990s was the return to "civic newspapers." Even as many small community papers were taken over or eliminated, consumers still wanted to be connected to their community through their local newspaper. Large papers added new sections directed to different groups or geographical regions within their markets, such as the Warren, Ohio, *Tribune-Chronicle*'s Saturday tabloid "Neighbors." The *Dallas Morning News* added a weekly "True Romances" feature to the bridal page in 1982. Another innovation that began in the Eighties were foreign-language editions for large ethnic groups, such as the Spanish version of the *Miami Herald*.

NATIONAL AND INTERNATIONAL POLITICS AND THE IRAN-CONTRA AFFAIR

War between **Iran** and **Iraq** added fuel to an already tense situation in the Middle East. In September 1980, Iraq seized back 90 square miles (230 square kilometers) of Iranian territory in the Shatt al-Arab area which Iran had recently been given partial control over. Iran did not win a quick victory, and a bloody war ensued from 1980 to 1988. Iran received covert aid in the form of U.S. arms and aircraft replacement parts, primarily by way of Israel. In November, a Beirut, Lebanon, magazine revealed that the United States had sent spare parts and ammunition to Iran in the hopes that "moderates" there could help obtain the release of U.S. hostages held by terrorists in Iran's capital. Further investigations revealed government fraud, deceit and corruption. The profits from the Iranian arms sales were used by the United States to fund the "Contra" forces

MEDIA ACQUISITIONS

Purchaser	Acquisition	Amount ($)	Year
Time	Warner Communications	13.9 billion	1989
Capital Cities Comm.	ABC Broadcasting	3.5 billion	1985
Sony	Columbia Pictures	3.4 billion	1989
National Amusements	Viacom	3.4 billion	1987
McCaw Cellular	LIN Broadcasting	3.3 billion	1989

1980-1989

(rebels against the existing Nicaraguan government). This funding was in direct violation of U.S. law. Marine Lieutenant Colonel **Oliver L. North** and National Security Council adviser Vice Admiral **John F. Poindexter** refused to answer questions concerning the matter and resigned their positions.

Unlike Watergate in 1973, the Iran-Contra affair did not bring down the presidency. As a former movie actor and friend of many powerful media executives and celebrities, President **Ronald Reagan** enjoyed a warmer relationship with the media than many past presidents. Reagan, who was still "one of media's own," didn't seem the type to be involved in such complex political arrangements. After Nixon's resignation in 1974, America felt a real loss of an international elder statesman, and the media were a bit wary of destroying another president. Reagan himself was quoted in the September 1986 issue of *Fortune* magazine, "Surround yourself with the best people you can find, delegate authority, and don't interfere." Many felt that he lived by that policy and did not truly comprehend the scope of the Iran-Contra dealings

Although National Security Council figures Poindexter and North were heavily involved, investigators and reporters were unable to discover how involved higher officials, especially President Reagan and Vice President **George Bush**, were. The televised Senate investigation drew millions of viewers daily, although not with the same urgency and interest as had been the case with Watergate.

President Ronald Reagan, was also called "The Great Communicator"

The intricacies of foreign politics were difficult to follow and understand. While North said he believed Reagan was aware of the secret arrangement, Reagan himself repeatedly claimed, "I don't recall" and "I don't know" during vigorous questioning by the Senate investigative committee. Reagan's continued inability to remember earned him the nickname the "**Teflon President**," meaning that nothing, including the Iran-Contra mess, stuck to him.

The Tower Report, commissioned by

Media in the 20th Century

Oliver North at Iran-Contra Senate Hearings

the Senate, documented the distribution of nearly $48 million from arms sales to the Contra forces. During the trial, it was disclosed that Oliver North instructed his secretary, Fawn Hall, to stay overtime and shred thousands of pages of documents. Oliver North conducted himself as a "good soldier" and was willing to be the scapegoat. Even if he was wrong, much of the public respected North's patriotic statements that he "did it for his country" and was willing to accept the blame. The Tower Report issued a wrist-slap to the president, saying that he bore the "ultimate responsibility" for the behavior of his staff.

Deception by officials, mismanagement, and law breaking were obvious. North and Poindexter were both found guilty but their convictions were later dropped on technicalities. By this time, the public had tired of the whole Iran-Contra affair. Still, television and radio talk shows debated the issue of whether doing the wrong thing for the right reason was acceptable, and, if so, whether that person should be punished. Central Intelligence Agency officials pleaded guilty in 1991 to withholding information about the Contra aid from Congress. Acting CIA Director William Casey was charged as well, but in 1992 George Bush magnanimously pardoned Casey

1980-1989

and the other government officials indicted or convicted for their participation in the Iran-Contra affair. Casey died shortly after that, taking any other secrets with him to his grave. The 1994 independent prosecutor's report said President Reagan and Vice President Bush had some knowledge of the affair and/or its cover up. But with no evidence directly connecting them with a crime, no charges could be pressed.

NEW PUBLICATIONS FOR ALL

Specialty publications, in a multitude of forms, both trade and consumer, bloomed in the Eighties. Along with the men's and New Age movements came new magazines for them. Family themes were popular, especially due to the increasing divorce rate; the new families needed to know they were not alone and find support. As computers and technology continued to evolve, more specialized publications developed along with them for both consumers and people in the emerging industries. Although newspapers decreased the space they devoted to news, and changed in format and content, people still read them. In some markets the community paper became more popular than the large metropolitan paper. All in all, people still read, but mainly to learn how to cope in a changing world and get ahead financially.

The number of women's magazines continued to increase, although not at the furious rate of the Seventies. Several, such as *Lear's* and *Mirabella*, were funded by wealthy, well connected women. With more career women in the workplace, it was natural that trade magazines specifically for women appeared. In 1981,

> **"Society drives people crazy with lust and calls it advertising."**
> John Lahr, U.S. drama critic, quoted in *The Guardian*, London, August 2, 1989.

Tradeswomen: A Quarterly Magazine for Women in Blue-Collar Work entered the scene, "dedicated to securing a permanent place for women in the blue-collar work force." A national publication, it included interviews, articles and features by and about women in a variety of trades, as well as a networking column. *Entrepreneurial Woman* began in 1989 as an offshoot of *Entrepreneur*. It featured motivation and information for women who were considering going into business for themselves. Articles focused on the practical aspects of owning and operating a small business, as well as inspirational success stories of women entrepreneurs.

ADVERTISING

Professional sports had always been linked to advertising and media coverage, especially the large sporting events such as the Super Bowl, the World Series, and the like. In the Eighties, advertising sponsorship of sporting events and endorsements of their products by sports figures reached multimillion-dollar heights. The February 6, 1984 *Advertising Age* revealed that basketball star Julius "Dr. J." Erving would receive $2.5 million for commercials and personal appearances on behalf of Coca-Cola from 1984 to 1988. Beginning a trend that would continue and escalate into the Nineties and the 21st century. People of the Eighties longed for heroes; and it seemed

MEDIA IN THE 20th CENTURY

the only heroes left were athletes. Major sports apparel manufacturers weren't the only type of advertiser that went after athletes to endorse specific products. It was not unusual to see tennis players appear in ads for electronic companies or baseball stars selling automobiles. Advertisers even named products after athletes, such as Nike's Air Jordan, named for basketball great Michael Jordan.

As the millions paid to sports stars for endorsements rose, the cost of sports ad campaigns rose, and ultimately the prices of the advertised products rose. Soon $100 sports shoes became common. Advertisers possessing multi-million-dollar budgets for these campaigns had the power to influence many forms of the advertising-driven media. Athletes endorsing specific products were also expected or contractually obligated to wear or use the products, where they could be photographed.

Not satisfied with simply advertising their products during sporting events, some of the larger corporations began underwriting and sponsoring sporting events, such as college football bowl games, with a new twist. Instead of the traditional "sponsored by" tag line, sponsors paid to have their names attached to the events. The former Sun Bowl (1936-1986) became the John Hancock Sun Bowl in 1987 and 1988, then the John Hancock Bowl from 1989 to 1993, and then the Northwest Bank Bowl in 1996. The Orange Bowl (1935-1988) became the Federal Express Orange Bowl in 1989. This type of major sponsorship would expand and reach new heights in the Nineties, with corporations even underwriting baseball stadiums; San Francisco's famous Candlestick Park was renamed 3Com Park in 1995 after the Silicon Valley computer company paid a few million dollars for the exposure.

One of the decade's most ironic television programming sponsorship was the tabloid *National Enquirer's* sponsorship of a "CBS Morning News" show in early 1984. As reported in *Advertising Age's*, January 16, 1984, issue, "CBS Morning News" had once referred to the *National Enquirer* as a "scandal sheet of questionable news validity." After the *Enquirer's* sponsorship was announced during the show, the program went on to interview **Harold Evans**, the author of **Good Times, Bad Times**. Evans' book criticized the *Enquirer's* rival, *Star* publisher Rupert Murdoch.

The Eighties was the "name brand" decade. The economy was skyrocketing. The baby boomers had come of age and their children had an even more voracious appetite for the consumption of products advertised in media. With the rising popularity of cable's Music Television station (MTV), music video-style commercials emerged. MTV changed the music industry and how people listen to music. The visual part of the music package became almost as important as the sound.

TECHNOLOGY/ NETWORK & CABLE TV/COMPUTER ANIMATION

Cable television was a form of pay-TV broadcasting. It sent programs to paying subscribers through coaxial and/or fiber-optic cables instead of via the public airwaves. Originally developed to reach areas where reception was poor or nonexistent, it expanded in the Seventies

1980-1989

and Eighties. In the early 1980s, the U.S. government decided to deregulate the industry, freeing it from government restrictions, theoretically allowing competing companies to respond directly to consumer demands. Cable TV marketed its services by offering additional programming not available on network TV.

In addition to the basic cable channels, cable also offered premium channels for which customers paid for over and beyond the basic service. Premium channels cover a wide range of programming from the Disney Channel's G-rated movies and cartoons, movie stations such as HBO (Home Box Office, owned by Time Inc.), Showtime, Playboy and Adam & Eve offered PG, PG-13, R-rated, and X-rated movies respectively. Exclusive pay-per-view sporting events became available, such as the $80 world heavyweight championship fight between Evander Holyfield and Mike Tyson in 1997.

Top Ten Cable Advertisers in 1985

1.	Procter & Gamble Co.	$30,487,371
2.	Philip Morris Cos.	$21,061,420
3.	Anheuser-Busch Cos.	$15,345,131
4.	General Mills	$12,144,905
5.	Time Inc.	$11,006,706
6.	Mars Inc.	$8,163,657
7.	RJR/Nabisco	$7,530,852
8.	Thompson Medical Co.	$7,060,414
9.	Ford Motor Co.	$6,159,088
10.	Kellogg Co.	$4,554,186

The early success of pay-per-view sporting events led to pay-per-view movies, featuring a variety of films fresh out of the theaters, but not yet released for rental or purchase. Home-shopping services flourished, where consumers in the comfort of their own home could "for a limited time only" call the toll-free number on the screen and order the products displayed at a bargain price. Home shopping channels sold everything around the clock from jewelry and clothes to books and artificial flowers. The Eighties also saw the rise of the **Infomercial**— a televised commercial packaged as entertainment. A whole new industry was created almost overnight.

As part of the 1984 **Cable Act**, public access to television was guaranteed for nonprofit organizations, communities, and private citizens, and required cable companies to provide free studio space and equipment. Although the goal was to avoid monopolies in cable TV programming, by consumer accounts it did not succeed. But cable's popularity forced network television out of its complacency to become competitive again. Cable showed movies with more graphic content and adult language and network television began doing the same in a quest to keep viewers.

Some cable channels succeeded by

> "I still believe that if your aim is to change the world, journalism is a more immediate short-term weapon."
>
> Tom Stoppard, British playwright. *The Guardian*, London, March 18, 1988

Media in the 20th Century

focusing on one type of programming. **Ted Turner** introduced **CNN (Cable News Network)** on June 1, 1980, offering 24-hour news. While many predicted failure, CNN carved a niche for itself, especially in war and crises, such as the Iran hostage crisis, the shooting of President Reagan, and later during the Persian Gulf War in 1991. The popularity of stations such as CNN and ESPN (a 24-hour sports channel) proved there were enough viewers to justify specialty stations.

Another approach to expand television signals to rural and remote areas was by satellite TV. Communications satellites provide worldwide links to radio and television station transmissions and telephone service. Satellites eliminate the limitations of ground-based communications systems. The first communications satellite was NASA's *Echo 1*, launched on August 12, 1960, which reflected radio signals back to Earth. Later satellites could receive, amplify and rebroadcast signals back to Earth. Examples were NASA's Relay and AT&T's *Telstar* satellites. Many governments, including the U.S., USSR, and Canada, launched satellites, as did private and public companies. By directing a receiver or "dish" (originally a huge dish 6 feet or larger in diameter), viewers could access all types of satellite communications, including cable premium stations' programming and "video feeds" of live studios awaiting broadcast— without paying cable companies for the service. Satellite TV technology would improve in the 1990s, allowing an 18-inch dish to do the work of the original 6-foot dish. By the Eighties, a network of sophisticated, highly reliable communications satellites was bringing news and entertainment from

TV photojournalist and reporter for KVUE-TV, Austin, TX, 1987

1980-1989

around the world directly into American homes.

Cable TV was originally funded completely by subscription fees. Thus one of the benefits and selling points of cable was its lack of commercials. As cable television grew and increased in popularity, advertisers saw cable could be an "exclusive" market where their ads could have greater potential impact. Advertisers also used cable stations to regionally test the effectiveness of a particular ad campaign and fine-tune it before rolling it out nationally. In the December 1, 1986, issue of *Advertising Age*, writer Judann Dagnoll described how the regional tests were assessed by media and advertising research companies. "ERIM tests media plans for clients and measures results with scanner information at supermarkets. "Basically, we are testing a commercial response in relationship to household purchases," says Laurence Gold, vice president for Nielsen Market Research." Regional and target marketing efforts were assisted by cable TV's ability to segment market in new and different ways —from lifestyles to locations to age and more. Cable and network television programmers and advertisers also began actively marketing

Ted Turner

themselves to teenagers and children. "I want my MTV!" became the demand of the youth culture. In August 1981, MTV (Music TeleVision) emerged, offering rock-and-roll videos. At first there were only about an hour or two of videos, which repeated often, rather like radio in its beginnings. Punk and modern rock exploded and created some of the best music in years, and fans hungered to see

Media in the 20th Century

Camera operator at WXIA-Atlanta, 1988

and hear their favorite groups. New styles of photography, computer animation and videotape composing turned the music video into a new art form, although it wasn't to everyone's taste. Singer Michael Jackson's music and expensive, high-concept "Thriller" video revolutionized the genre. Filled with excellent dancers, videography and special effects, it even generated its own "Making of Thriller" videotape. Another pioneer on MTV was Peter Gabriel with his "Sledgehammer" video. It featured the artist's face shifting through thousands of computer-animated graphics "expressions."

Later, films such as Disney's "Who Framed Roger Rabbit" and other programs and commercials experimented with new video-imaging and computer modeling art forms, creating cutting-edge effects that appealed to young viewers. Video game sales exploded due to the exciting new technology, with Sega's "Super Mario Brothers" game becoming both a cartoon show and feature-length film. The trade magazine *Advertising Age* even devoted special issues on how to effectively market to children and youth, with their shorter attention spans and limited vocabulary and comprehension. Programming in the Eighties provided more action and less dialogue. Children's cartoon shows such as "Teen-Age Mutant Ninja Turtles" spawned multimillion dollar sales of toys and merchandise.

In 1986, **Rupert Murdoch**, best known as the publisher of the tabloid newspaper *Star*, launched the **Fox Broadcasting** network, which broadcasts to over 200 affiliate stations. The Fox network was the first new network

1980-1989

in the U.S. since 1948 when both ABC and CBS established themselves (NBC became a network in 1946).

In order to compete with the already existing networks, the Fox network introduced many innovative shows including the entertainment news show "**A Current Affair**" in 1986. Hosted by **Maury Povich**, the show quickly gained mass appeal and was syndicated a year later. The show was ground breaking in its tabloid style of news reporting, which the show's producers termed "reality television."

Some of the viewing public felt that the program was too graphic in content and launched a campaign to take it off the air. The Reverend Donald Windmon of Mississippi led a group in monitoring the show, among others, for lurid content. According to the April 23, 1989 issue of the New York Times, the Reverend Windmon succeeded to some degree and major advertisers cancelled commercial spots on "A Current Affair" and others.

In spite of the Reverend's crusade, the popularity of the show remained undaunted. At the 1989 **National Association of Television Program Executives** (NATPE), the show was a leader in sales to program buyers from television stations in the nation. As an independent network, Fox was not required to abide by FCC rules. At the time, the Fox network was not considered a full-fledged fourth network by its competitors, but as it continues to expand and become more competitive, it earned their respect.

Parents concerned about the escalating violence and sexual content on television and radio, specifically MTV and rock-and-roll radio stations, formed the non-profit **PMRC** (Parents Music Resource Center). Led by Tipper Gore (then-Senator Al Gore's wife), the group politely reminded recording and programming producers of their responsibilities to the general public and requested labels on records and notices on programming to alert parents to their actual contents. They were rebuffed as censors by members of the National Association of Recording Arts & Sciences (producers of the Grammy awards), although Tipper Gore said she was pleased to debate the issue with them and exercise her First Amendment rights.

In Gore's book, *Raising PG Kids in an X-Rated Society*, she detailed PMRC's mostly negative experiences with the television programming and radio broadcasting community. However, the cries of the PMRC were heard by the National Association of Broadcasters president **Eddie Fritts**, who wrote a letter to 800 radio station owners alerting them to parental concern over the "porn rock" situation. He wrote, "The lyrics of some recent rock records and the tone of their related music videos are fast becoming a matter of public debate. The subject has drawn national attention through articles in publications like *Newsweek* and *USA Today* and feature reports on TV programs like 'Good Morning, America.' Many state that they are extremely troubled by the sexually explicit and violent language of some of today's songs ... which at least one writer has dubbed 'porn rock.' ... It is, of course, up to each broadcast licensee to make its own decisions as to the manner in which it carries out its programming responsibilities under the Communications Act."

Fritts followed up that letter two weeks later with one addressed to 45 major record company executives: "At its May meeting, NAB's Executive Committee asked that I write you to request that all recordings made available to broadcasters in the future be accompanied by copies of the songs' lyrics. It appears that providing this material to broadcasters would place very little burden on the recording industry, while greatly assisting the decision making of broadcast management and programming staff." Lenny Waronker, president of Warner Brothers, told the *Los Angeles Times*, "It smells of censorship." Reluctantly, many records companies decided to voluntarily comply by publishing lyrics and/or using "Warning: Explicit Lyrics" labels to avoid industry regulation and a government-mandated rating system.

The country's fascination with sex, scandal and violence was reflected in television programming by the commercial and the mounting number of cable TV stations. A few new uses of television were pioneered in the Eighties. The show "America's Most Wanted" used the power of TV to involve the public in solving real life crimes. It featured re-enactment of crimes, sometimes using actual footage, and asked the viewing public to call any leads into a phone number. The show was an instant success in the ratings and also helped solve a large percentage of the crimes it covered.

Besides computer-animated graphics, another new communication technology arrived: cellular telephones. Mobile phones existed as early as the 1940s, but cities typically had only one transmitter, which for the most part were used for emergencies. In Chicago, the Federal Communications Commission authorized testing a Motorola phone system equipped with low-power transmitters throughout the city, and a computer system to help facilitate passing along the calls to the moving phones. Just in time for Christmas 1983, the costly $3,000 cellular phones were sold in Chicago. In addition to the cost of the phone, lucky drivers paid $150 per month to have the latest technological toy. Eventually the price of cellular phones came down to make them affordable for most people. As a result of their extensive use, everyday people with cellular phones became reporters for the media— from calling in local traffic to their favorite radio stations to eye-witness live accounts of news as it is happening.

One problem with cellular phones and all wireless communications is their lack of security. Wireless, mobile and cellular phones allow unscrupulous reporters, curious neighbors or government investigators to "tap" into telephone conversations and hear the conversations without the speakers' knowledge. Any ham radio operator can pick up and "dial in" to private conversations.

As the Eighties drew to a close, voices debating real issues were often ignored in favor of commentary, sports and confrontational talk shows. Scandals, sex and violence were the focus of news coverage on radio, television and print. Advertising glorified a level of wealth, beauty and success few could achieve and focused on selling to the youth. Journalism gave way to sensational splash journalism and "**infotainment**" (entertainment and publicity posing as information) shows in the 1990s. The massive amounts of information speeding via traditional media and the information superhighway (Internet or World Wide Web) would both excite and overwhelm consumers in the final decade of the 20th century. Everyone was plugging in for what was to come.

MEDIA

chapter 10

1990-1999

The Internet, the Decline of Newspapers and the Emergence of Full-Service Entertainment Conglomerates

Zenith-Diba Internet TV

Media in the 20th Century

The Nineties saw the emergence of talk shows as a new cultural phenomenon. They were part self-help, part advice, and part pseudo-debate, and consumers devoured them like the yellow journalism tabloids of a century before. Talk show hosts enjoyed first-name recognition among viewers— Sally Jessy Raphael, Phil Donahue and Oprah Winfrey. Covering topics such as incest, alcoholism, family relationships and sexual deviations, talk shows enjoyed immense popularity—as well as criticism for their superficial treatment of complex issues.

Traditional newspapers continued their decline during the Nineties. With the expansion of media conglomerates and the standardization of newspapers' formats and coverage, few independent publications remained. The exception were niche papers directed at particular groups, such as African-American men, parents or Catholics.

As the Internet became available in the public sector, electronic publishing and chat rooms opened up forums for individuals to express their views to a large audience around the world. People with only a small amount of technical knowledge could air their views without the huge expense of traditional publishing. Still, advertising lurked nearby, always looking for new ways to use new media with which to promote their products to consumers. Debates arose over copyrights as new technologies and means of communicating evolved. As the next millennium loomed on the horizon, everything was becoming digitized so that it could be easily recorded, manipulated and transmitted. The saying "Pictures never lie," would no longer be true.

"The job of the press is to encourage debate, not to supply the public with information."

Christopher Lasch, U.S. historian. *Gannett Center Journal*, Spring 1990.

"We now have a whole culture based on the assumption that people know nothing, and so anything can be said to them."

Stephen Vizinczey, Hungarian novelist, *Observer Review*, London, June 24, 1990.

"Journalism could be described as turning one's enemies into money."

Craig Brown, British journalist. *Daily Telegraph*, London, September 28, 1990.

"The lowest form of popular culture—lack of information, misinformation, disinformation, and a contempt for the truth or the reality of most people's lives—has overrun real journalism. Today, ordinary Americans are being stuffed with garbage."

Carl Bernstein, U.S. journalist. *The Guardian*, London, June 3, 1992.

"The corporate grip on opinion in the United States is one of the wonders of the Western World. No First World country has ever managed to eliminate so entirely from its media all objectivity—much less dissent."

Gore Vidal, U.S. novelist, critic. *A View from the Diner's Club*, 1991.

1990-1999

MEDIA SPOTLIGHT

In 1990, the U.S. Senate was asked to approve President Bush's choice for Associate Justice of the Supreme Court, an African-American judge named **Clarence Thomas**. A former colleague and employee of Thomas', **Anita Hill**, met while they were employed by the Equal Employment Opportunity Commission (EEOC), which enforced federal laws against employment bias and sexual harassment. Hill, a law professor at the University of Oklahoma, testified before the Senate Judiciary Committee that Thomas had sexually harassed her and others during their employment together in 1981 to 1983. The widely covered and televised hearing in October 1990 captured the attention of a huge television audience. Vermont's Senator Patrick J. Leahy echoed the sentiments of millions when he said, "They are both credible, intelligent, well educated, both lawyers, both testifying under oath, and one is lying .... Which one it is, I don't know." The Thomas-Hill hearings were televised from the same Senate Caucus Room as the 1954 McCarthy and the 1972 Watergate hearings. The hearings left questions unanswered. Although the Senate confirmed Thomas, 52 to 48, the issue of sexual harassment was brought to the nation's attention as a large social problem for many women and a few men.

On March 5, 1991, an amateur videotape, made two days earlier, was broadcast during the nightly news on station KTLA in Los Angeles, California. The story centered on police brutality and showed four police officers brutally kicking and beating **Rodney King**, an apparently unarmed black man. CNN picked up the story and ran it on March 6. The shocking tape angered the nation, and many people demanded that the police officers be severely punished and that Los Angeles Police Chief **Daryl Gates** be summarily dismissed from duty. Black leaders encouraged the masses to wait for justice to be done. When a mostly white jury acquitted the Los Angeles policemen, the verdict triggered some of the worst violence and looting in American history. The riots caused more than $1 billion in damages, 52 were killed, 2,000 injured and 50 square miles of south-central Los Angeles was left devastated. The extensive news coverage of the riots was chilling. At a retrial in 1993 a federal jury found two of the officers, Sgt. Stacey Koon and Officer Laurence Powell, guilty of violating King's civil rights. They were both convicted and sentenced to two years in prison.

The enraging footage of King being savagely beaten set an example of the power of amateur videotapes and their

Anita Hill testifying at the Senate hearings, 1990

Media in the 20th Century

An O.J. Simpson trial news conference

use in the media and the courts. As *Newsweek's* TV analyst Jonathan Alter asked, "What happens when anyone anywhere in the world has the power to be a TV reporter?" **Ted Koppel** of ABC offered an ominous answer: "The world is in the early stages of a revolution that it has barely begun to understand: Television has begun falling into the hands of the people."

In June 1994, a baffled nation watched as the National Basketball Association's playoff game between the Houston Rockets and New York Knicks was interrupted for a news bulletin. The telecast showed a former pro football star, **"O.J." (Orenthal James) Simpson**, slowly being driven in a white Ford bronco down a California freeway with police chasing him. His companion, Al Cowlings, said Simpson was suicidal. At a hastily arranged press conference, his attorney Robert Shapiro, and Simpson's friend Renart Kardasean, read a note written by Simpson and pleaded over the air for him to turn himself over to the police. The televised live coverage was mesmerizing and the NBA championship game was demoted in importance to a footnote on the TV screen. Saddened and shocked, the public had earlier learned that Simpson was supposed to turn himself in for the murder of his ex-wife Nicole and her friend Ronald Goldman. The media coverage of the trial in print, radio and television was almost non-stop. Talk shows hotly debated the issues of racism and spousal abuse, while legal analysts offered daily opinions. The Simpson criminal trial was televised and broadcast live, escalating the drama and creating a media frenzy and circus-like atmosphere. In 1995 Simpson was acquitted in the criminal trial. The families of the murder victims took him to civil court in 1996 and won the case in an untelevised trial finding Simpson liable in the deaths and requiring him to pay millions of dollars in damages.

1990-1999

WAR AND TALK

On February 24, 1991, America turned to CNN for coverage on the **Persian Gulf War**, code-named **Operation Desert Storm**. Several months before, Iraq had invaded the small, oil-rich country of Kuwait. U.S. President George Bush assembled a coalition of countries, including Great Britain, France, and Saudi Arabia, to force Iraq out of Kuwait. After attempts at diplomacy and economic sanctions failed, the allied forces began weeks of punishing and relentless bombing and missile attacks against **Saddam Hussein's** Iraqi troops and strategic military and communication

EDUCATION, LANGUAGE AND POPULATION

Tuition and total expenses at Harvard, Yale, Stanford, and other first-rank American colleges exceeds $30,000 per year. As 1989 ended, 76.9 percent of the population had completed high school and 21.1 percent had graduated from college. According to the 1990 census, over 31.8 million Americans (almost 14 percent) spoke languages besides English; compared with 23.1 million (11 percent) in 1980. After English, the most commonly spoken languages are Spanish (spoken by over half of non-English-speaking Americans), French, German, Italian, and Chinese. As the last decade of the 20th century began, the total U.S. population totaled 248,709,873, averaging 70.3 people per square mile of land.

"This week with David Brinkley"
(l to r.) George Will, David Brinkley, Sam Donaldson

installations. U.S. General **H. Norman Schwarzkopf** then executed a devastating combined air and ground attack, which swept 270,000 troops around the Iraqis' western flank.

The media and in particular CNN, successfully brought the events of the war directly to people in America and around the world. The evening of the first bombing raids on Iraq's capital of Baghdad were broadcast live from the

Media in the 20th Century

Al Rasheed hotel in the city's downtown area. CNN reporters **John Holliman**, **Peter Arnatt** and **Bernard Shaw** gave live blow by blow reports as the bombs were dropping all around them. Viewers could only watch and listen in amazement at the events unfolding in front of them. CNN's successful live video coverage of Operation Desert Storm was made possible by portable video uplinks for satellite transmission. Audio coverage was provided courtesy of a four-wire overseas phone connection, which did not require operators, switching connections or local electricity. At one time CNN had 150 people stationed in the Gulf — technicians, support staff and broadcasters, plus another 1,500 people working on the story throughout the world. The successful (and short) war unified the country through media and made CNN a respected household name.

"**Infotainment**" and talk shows became bigger and bolder during the Nineties. Talk shows invited members of the home audience to call in and participate in the dialogue of a show much like radio talk shows. Combining elements of tabloid journalism, talk radio and social confrontation, the often controversial talk shows commanded large market shares and, best of all, were inexpensive for media companies to produce. "Infotainment" shows such as "Entertainment Tonight" offered bits of information designed to keep people watching.

KPIX television news room, San Francisco

1990-1999

CONTRACTIONS IN NEWSPAPER PUBLISHING

In the Nineties, people overwhelmingly preferred and trusted TV news over the news reported in the print media. A Center for Media and Public Affairs study conducted in November 1996 found that of the 3,004 people polled, the majority believed that the news media usually "get the facts right." Filmed footage of events were easier for the public to assimilate and believe as compared with the printed reports by unknown print reporters. The disheartening trend of diminished newspaper reading that began in the mid-Seventies and Eighties continued throughout the Nineties as network and cable news programs gained more viewers. As of February 1, 1994, the total number of daily newspapers was 1,556, a net loss of 14 (1 percent) in one year. In the previous year 26 dailies ceased to exist.

Morning distribution of newspapers was strongly preferred to afternoon distribution: many evening dailies converted to morning distribution during the early part of the decade. In attempts to maintain subscribers, newspapers frequently used the value of the coupons and advertising specials typically included in the Sunday editions as a marketing tool.

As more metropolitan papers were bought up by conglomerates such as **Gannett** and **Knight-Ridder**, people looked more to independent community papers for news that had meaning to them. Increasingly standard formats, while popular with focus groups, didn't always generate the same reader response. As the Internet came on-line, people found they could subscribe directly to news agencies. The rise of customized news pages, where consumers chose exactly what kinds of news they wanted further distanced consumers' away from traditional news sources.

PUBLISHING & PRINTING

1996 sales

Times Mirror	3,714,000
Gannett	3,642,000
Reader's Digest Assn.	2,869,000
Knight-Ridder	2,451,000
McGraw-Hill	2,195,000
New York Times	2,020,000
Tribune	1,953,000
Dow Jones	1,932,000
American Greetings	1,672,000

REPORTING ON RELIGION

Most major print and broadcast media do not provide much coverage of religious groups. There is mutual suspicion between religious leaders and media people. Religious people fear being labeled intolerant or hypocritical if their words are taken out of context. Past religious leaders from Jim Baker to Jimmy Swaggert that had been disclosed by the media as felons or worse, had cast a shadow of uncertainty over high profile televangelist religious leaders. Media people by nature are skeptical: they question and doubt, searching for facts, not feelings. Yet the Internet is changing that relationship with bulletin boards, chat rooms and home pages devoted to a variety of specialized sites on religion and spirituality.

Roman Catholic **Pope John Paul II's** Web site contains his traveling schedule, press releases and writings, which are being translated into six languages. An Orthodox Jewish site, **Yaale Va' Yavo**, delivers e-mailed prayer requests to Jerusalem's Wailing Wall, where they are folded and placed in the stones, just as Jewish pilgrims have done for years.

THE RISE OF NICHE-MARKET PRINT PUBLICATIONS

Most new publications in the Nineties were directed to niche (narrowly focused) markets. Community newspapers, freely circulated "alternative" papers and parenting publications became popular with consumers, cutting into the advertising revenues of large newspaper chains. The intellectual cynicism and dark humor of "Generation X" (people born from 1965 to 1975) showed up in many forms of media and advertising, including animated TV shows like Fox's "The Simpsons" and MTV's "Beavis and Butthead." Not as status-conscious and brand name oriented as the baby boomers, Gen-Xers value social responsibility, are highly independent, and would rather do work they enjoy than earn more money at a boring job.

Celebrity lifestyles remained a popular media subject in the Nineties. *Entertainment Weekly* began publication on February 12, 1990. Time Warner spent $150 million launching the new magazine, its first new magazine since *People* began in 1974. A hybrid between *People* and *TV Guide*, it focuses mostly on current celebrities and their professional careers.

RADIO ON THE NET

**BBC
(British Broadcasting Corporation)**
http://www.bbc.co.uk

Virtual News Talk Radio
http://www.aa.net/~radiobzz/index.html

National Public Radio
http://www.npr.org

Radio On The Internet (Home of the "Geek of the Week" Internet-based interview show)
http://town.hall.org/radio

Radio Stations On The Internet (a list of links to radio stations and networks)
http://cavern.nmsu.edu/~rebel/radio1.html

**Voice of America
(radio broadcast to 92 million listeners in 47 languages)**
gopher://gopher.voa.gov

Vintage Fashions: Fashion Treasures of Yesteryear, which also started in 1990, captured the past. Described as a "clearinghouse for information on vintage clothing, jewelry, and fashion accessories," it interested collectors and hobbyists.

Men's magazines expanded in scope as well. *Journeymen: Exploring Men's Issues* started in 1991. It addressed father-son relationships, friendship, men's health, divorce, and intimacy. Sensitive and sensible, it described itself as "a participatory networking publication intended to help men make connections with each other." Another niche market magazine was *Today's Black Father*, which emerged in 1991. This journal's intention was to expand African-American men's consciousness regarding family life and responsibilities through advice and profiles of good examples. The quarterly featured articles on coping with unwanted pregnancy, weekend parenting, relationships, finance and all other aspects of fatherhood.

Community-parenting publications exploded in the 1990s. While only a handful existed in the early 1980s, as of 1997 there were 119 parenting publications to serve communities nationwide, according to Parenting Publications of America. Many are in the newspaper tabloid format and distributed free within the communities they serve. Some are truly magazines, while others have made a transition to what Robert McClory, associate professor at the Medill School of Journalism, dubbed "magazoids" and "tabazines" —hybrids with elements of each.

For the strictly fashionable woman, *Allure* began publishing in 1991. Unashamedly a fashion and beauty magazine, it featured intelligent journalists covering fashion. It had bold graphics, lots of photographs and a non-traditional approach to beauty. *American Woman*, launched in 1990 focused on male-female relationships, its articles covered all aspects of sexuality, including fantasies, affairs and flirting. Its provocative photos primarily showed the under-40 single and married people who form the magazine's target audience.

ADVERTISING

The strong influences and styles of Generation X and MTV colored the advertising landscape. Advertisers and marketers looked to youth-oriented media for inspiration, from MTV to *Wired* magazine. Commercials often featured cutting-edge animation and graphics along with "in your face" music. Some overly stylish ads left consumers scratching their heads, wondering what the message was.

Life in the Nineties became too fast and full for consumers. Advertisers needed to work harder at getting the attention of the consumer and were challenged by the consumers ability to exercise the power of the remote control to zap their commercials off the screen.

At the 1997 Parenting Publications of America annual conference, Dr. Patricia Alvey, director of Texas Creative Advertising at the University of Texas-Austin, told the assembled publishers, "Ninety percent of the advertising out there is bad. What we try to do in our program is elevate advertising to an art form. When advertising is well crafted, it meets consumer and advertiser needs." Good advertising is memorable: It has a concept, thematic strength, readable print style, understandable copy and a reward. The Milk Advisory Board print and television campaigns are a good example. The ads clearly remind people of a need they have and the satisfaction they get from filling it. The Humane Society's campaign (Dog: "You throw, I fetch. I'll fetch anything. I'm a fetching machine.") shows consumers the value of Humane Society animals as pleasurable companions. The newspaper chain Knight-Ridder's literacy campaigns is another example of a well crafted public service as program: half page ads with extra-large type claimed: "No matter how big we make this, 400,000 people in Kentucky still can't read it."

Children's advocates claim that advertisements for adult products, such as cigarettes and liquor, encourage under-age smoking and drinking. According to a

Media in the 20th Century

Best-Selling U.S. Magazines 1995

	Magazine	Circulation
1.	Reader's Digest	16,261,968
2.	TV Guide	14,122,915
3.	National Geographic	9,390,787
4.	Better Homes & Gardens	7,600,960
5.	Good Housekeeping	5,162,597
6.	Ladies' Home Journal	5,153,565
7.	Family Circle	5,114,030
8.	Woman's Day	4,858,625
9.	McCall's	4,605,441

January 1997 *USA Today* report on 534 6th through 12th-grade students, the majority recognized and liked several image advertising campaigns, although it did not necessarily mean that they purchased those products. Results from the survey showed that 95 percent knew who Joe Camel was and 65 percent liked the ads. Budweiser's frogs campaign (three frogs vocalizing one syllable each: Bud- Wei-Ser) was 99 percent recognized, and 92 percent of the students surveyed liked them.

In late 1996, Anthony Faiola of the *Washington Post* wrote a report headlined "Liquor firms abandoning 48-year ban on TV ads." The voluntary ban had been in place since 1936 for radio and 1948 for television. The article quoted a report from the Distilled Spirits Council of the United States which said "it would lift the ban ... to compete head-on with wine-and beer-makers who have been guzzling market share for the past decade." The group maintained it would attempt to target adult consumers through the content and placement of its ads. Although the council claims it will only target adults, it's likely the ads will also influence children and teens. While CBS, NBC and ABC have long refused ads for hard liquor, affiliates and cable stations began accepting the commercials from at least one major liquor company.

The use of market surveys and focus-groups by advertisers expanded in the late 1980s and into the 1990s. Focus groups are used to gain additional input on consumer opinions about ad campaigns, TV programs and political polls.

Originally used to gather information about consumer products, the use of focus groups has expanded into other areas including political campaigns. The October 14, 1996, *Weekly Standard's* article on focus groups featured an interview with President George Bush's former 1992 campaign manager, **Sean Fitzpatrick**. Fitzpatrick explained his frustration with the campaign's extensive use of focus groups: "In politics people often don't know what they think. But you're asking them to be instant experts. And once they're in that role of expert, they're no longer useful to you. They're no longer reacting as normal voters."

Changing Boundaries in Advertising, Editorials, Reporting and Censorship

Publishers often walk a fine line between editorial content and pleasing their advertisers. One new advertising hybrid to take hold in the Nineties was the "**advertorial**." Usually designed to resemble a regular column or feature, in reality they are biased advertisements made to look like unbiased editorials.

Cross-marketing and the effects of media consolidation have become more widespread in the last decade. For example, a network station owned by Disney began having more of its talk and infotainment shows visit Disneyland or mention Disney films. Movie tie-ins with fast-food chains and breakfast cereals dominate advertising during children's programming on television.

Media conglomerates make possible much of the print, radio and television programming available. These conglomerates' power over outside advertisers may appear to be strong, however, advertisers do have considerable power over media. Berkeley, California filmmakers **Beth Sanders** and **Randy Baker** decided to make a documentary on the subject. Two major PBS studios turned them down, unwilling to potentially lose any corporate sponsorship. Finally San Jose Channel 54, KTEH, agreed to air their film, "**Fear and Favor in the Newsroom**," on January 27, 1997. Sanders and Baker documented advertising pressure tactics such as the 1994 automobile dealer ad boycott of Knight-Ridder's *San Jose Mercury News*. It was spurred by a business section story by reporter Mark Schwanhausser, called "A Car Buyer's Guide to Sanity," which seemed to be basic consumer-friendly advice. Claiming they were unfairly portrayed as dishonest, the dealers withdrew their advertising until the *Mercury News* ran its own full-page ad citing the top 10 reasons to buy or lease a car from a factory-authorized dealer. One million dollars poorer due to lost ad revenue, the *Mercury News* found that its ad helped woo the dealers back, and the ad dollars returned. Another example was a Pulitzer Prize-winning series in the *Atlanta Journal and Constitution*, detailing how financially African-Americans were five times less likely than whites to be approved for bank loans. The banks in the area withdrew millions of dollars worth of advertising in response.

The media are supposed to question large corporations (including themselves), when evidence points to wrongdoing. If the media don't, who will? Yet the threat of lawsuits over story content and handling are a real threat to good investigative journalism. In a January 25, 1997 *San Jose Mercury News* column by **Murray Frymer** entitled "**Does Public Really Want Media To Let Up?**" Frymer detailed the fallout from an excellent ABC "Prime Time Live" investigation into the Food Lion supermarket

MEDIA ACQUISITIONS

Purchaser	Acquisition	Amount ($)	Year
GTE	Contel	6.2 billion	1990
Matsushita	MCA	6.5 billion	1990
AT&T	NCR	7.4 billion	1991
A T & T	McCaw Cellular	12.6 billion	1993
Viacom	Blockbuster	7.7 billion	1994
Viacom	Paramount	9.7 billion	1994
Viacom	Blockbuster	7.7 billion	1994

MEDIA IN THE 20th CENTURY

chain. "Prime Time" reporters followed the example of 19th century muckraking journalist Nellie Bly to get the story: they went undercover to get inside an institution to reveal the truth. Once the reporters were in and working as employees at Food Lion, they witnessed major violations of public health laws including the selling rat-gnawed cheese, as well as expired meat. Food Lion lawyers retaliated and sued ABC for broadcasting the story. A Greensboro, North Carolina, jury awarded Food Lion $5.5 million to be paid by ABC for lying to the supermarket chain in order to be hired. When police do the same thing, it's a "sting," and when journalists did it in earlier decades it was called an exposé. Today it's considered "outside the bounds of fairness." As Frymer stated, "If punishing the messengers serves to shut doors, will that serve the public good?" Past exposés resulted in improved mental health care, prison reform, and legislation to prevent monopolies. Journalists and the public deserve the right to discover and present the truth, whether the stories involve large corporations or individuals who have the power and financial resources to harm unwitting consumers.

The public needs and expects its institutions, particularly those that involve public health, to conduct themselves in a consistent and honorable manner—whether or not they are being watched.

Newsrack of tabloids at check-out counter

TELEVISION — WINDOW INTO THE FUTURE

According to a Nielsen Media Research in May 1994, 98 percent of all American households owned at least one TV set. Of the households with televisions, 99 percent had color sets, 38 percent owned two or more sets, and 28 percent have three or more sets. Beyond that, 63 percent received at least basic cable, 28 percent received pay cable and 79 percent owned VCRs. Clearly, TV is a major part of the American media and news scene. It is estimated that the average American of the Nineties spends 20 to 25 percent of his or her waking hours with the television on.

As in the Eighties, parents continue to question the value and appropriateness of media programming for children of various ages. Tipper Gore and the PMRC

1990-1999

ABC News anchor Peter Jennings

(Parents Music Resource Center) forced music industry compliance with self-imposed product labeling to help parents judge material.

In January 1997, a self-enforced system rating programs was instituted by many major network and cable channels, with the exception of HBO (Home Box Office) and BET (Black Entertainment Television). HBO announced its plans to keep its 10-point system, which includes notes about adult language, graphic language, mild violence, violence, graphic violence, brief nudity, nudity, adult content, strong sexual content and rape in its shows. BET's chairman, Robert Johnson, said his the channel will wait for a better system. The ratings are: **TV-Y** (recommended for youth of all ages), **TV-Y7** (for youth 7 and up), **TV-G** (general audience), **TV-PG** (parental guidance suggested), **TV-14** (for audiences 14 and up), and **TV-M** (for mature audiences). Later in July of that year, a revamped system was announced to add more detail about a shows content. The new symbols to be combined with those in use were: **S** (sexual depictions), **V** (violence), **L** (coarse language), **D** (suggestive dialogue), **FV** (fantasy violence in children's shows). In response to the new rating system, NBC announced it would not comply and stated, "While we believe that more information is useful to parents, NBC is concerned that the ultimate aim of the current system's critics is to dictate programming content."

Products in development in the late Nineties included **HDTV (High Definition Television)** and **WebTV** (a way

Media in the 20th Century

to access the Internet through existing television and telephone lines). HDTV offers almost film-like television quality. One potential drawback is that current screen sizes are too square to fully contain the images, so programming will be viewed like many of today's videotapes: "modified to fit your screen." HDTV images promise to be more lifelike, as the colors are more true and defined.

WebTV requires special software and hardware designed for the integration with existing television sets and telephone lines (for modems, which are used to call the Internet Service Provider, or ISP, to access web sites). While this is an unproven concept, it remains to be seen how it can handle the massive amount of information traveling on the Internet through standard analog phone lines, which are meant to carry audio information. As with any type of computer or electronic device, the integration of modern technology with older technology tends to be problematic and slow. With more media sources expanding onto the Web, and new electronic journals and information available solely on the Net, television may truly provide an interactive window into the 21st century.

GLOBAL COMMUNICATIONS AND WIRELESS TECHNOLOGY

Wireless communications continued to develop in the 1990s. Cordless phones, pagers and mobile or cellular phones became common. By 1997 over 65 percent of U.S. households had a cordless phone, about 35 percent had a cellular phone and 28 percent owned a pager. When AT&T announced on August 16, 1993 that it would purchase McCaw Cellular Communications, the nation's largest cellular-phone company, questions arose. If wireless phones could replace wired lines, AT&T could bypass the regional telephone companies and eliminate billions of dollars in fees each year. Cellular telephones were just the beginning. The Nineties also saw the introduction of wireless computer networks, direct-broadcast satellite television, digital wireless cable TV networks, and even global telephone service. New

Barbara Walters and Hugh Downs on "20/20" set

184

1990-1999

global positioning systems using satellites can locate an individual within a few inches anywhere in the world. As we enter the 21st century technology is in development to make these systems cheaper, more reliable, and easier to use.

The impact of these new communication tools upon media was enormous. Reporters now have the ability to file a live report of a breaking news event from any place on the Earth. Even the average citizen can potentially become a key participant in reporting important news event. Concerns over security issues have the FCC and various groups vying over who will control this new technology. Important media questions regarding information access are still being hammered out as wireless technology evolves.

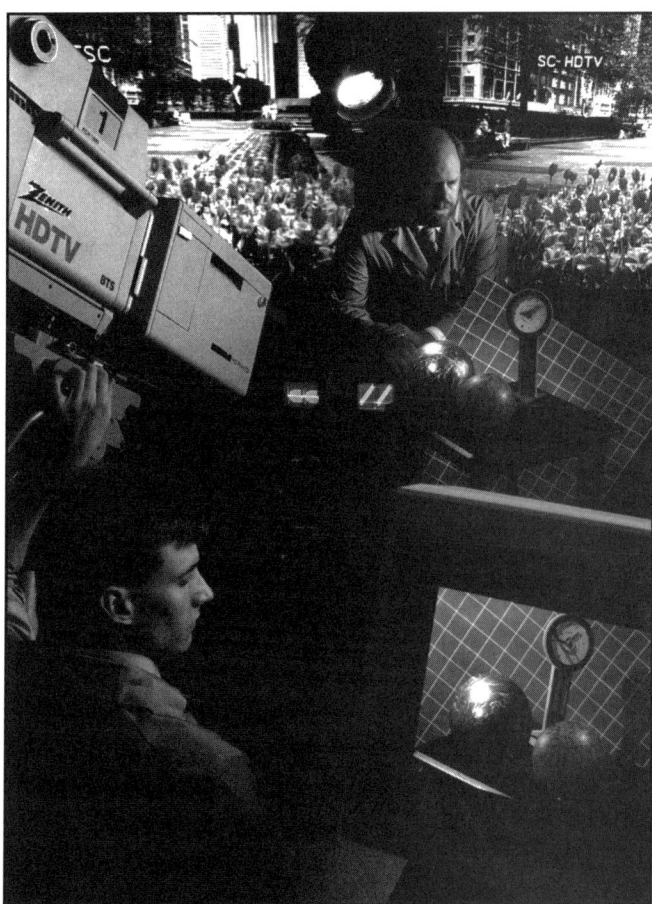

HDTV

THE INTERNET

As the 20th century began to draw to a close a new media was born— the **Internet**. It links people together through their computer terminals with modems connected to telephones lines. **ISDN (Information Service Data Network)** lines are designed to handle the large amounts of graphics and data on the Web at faster transmission speeds. Corporations that have worked with the government and/or high-end graphics content, such as movie animators, were previously the main ISDN utilizers. Once inside the "Net," a web of networks and software allows users from all walks of life all over the world to communicate with one another. Among the services available through the Internet are Telnet, which grants users access to more powerful comput-

Media in the 20th Century

Remote control

the **National Science Foundation**, which controls the Internet's core computer network. Although advertisers would love to get a true count of the number of people currently accessing the Internet at any given time, it's incalculable. Estimates in early 1997 say approximately 15 million people in the U.S. and 25 million worldwide regularly access the Internet. Public libraries and even popular coffee houses began to offer consumers access to the Internet. The majority of users tend to be university and corporate researchers, government officials, students, scientists and of course reporters and journalists.

Electronic publishing on the Internet began in the late 1980s. By late 1996, over 3,000 "**e-zines**" (electronic magazines) were available on the Net, with more arriving daily. Suddenly, anyone could publish and electronically distribute news and information. Electronic journals are broadly defined as any type of electronic periodical available over the Internet, including journals, magazines, e-zines, webzines and newsletters. Several sites, including **CICNet** (http://www.cedar.cic.net) and the **Catalogue of Projects in Electronic Text**

ers; Usenet news groups, allowing open discussion between users; electronic mail, whereby a person may send and receive "mail" on the Net; and the World Wide Web (or "Web"), which displays pages of text and images.

Originally developed in the Fifties for military purposes by the Pentagon, the Internet is now open to the world. Currently it is subsidized by

Video disk player

1990-1999

Free Internet software

(http:www.tku.edu.tw/orgn/other/catalog/c/cept.htm) offer listings of electronic journals. Another useful site is The Media List, containing E-mail addresses for a variety of publications and programs. Once an amateur or professional publisher has developed a Web page or publication, they can distribute it by being linked to an infinite number sites and indexes. Publications can be as general or specific in scope as the publisher desires, depending on whether he or she wants to reach a broad or a niche market. The debate over content and public access of Web sites will continue into the 21st century. The First Amendment has been successfully defended in early test cases.

Forward-thinking companies developed their own Web pages (sites potential consumers could visit in cyberspace) or hired "Webmasters" (experts in designing home pages, complete with links and graphics) beginning in the early Nineties. Sites were designed with color graphics, offers of free information and samples connected by links (highlighted and underlined words programmed to take the viewer to another site). At **ClariNet** and other services, subscribers could customize a "personal" electronic newspaper by selecting their preferred news topics. ClariNet would send stories on the selected topics gathered from wire and Internet sources daily. All major publishers have a presence on the Net, including the *Wall Street Journal*, the *Los Angeles Times* and *USA Today*. The broadcasters are there as well: CBS, NBC, PBS, ABC, CNN, the Discovery Channel, and others all have sites that people can visit.

Media forms continue to evolve and change, as they try to deliver the news and entertainment. With the Internet, more voices are being heard. In a diverse world such as ours, there is room for all of us to be heard. **Marshall McLuhan**, famous for his statement, "The medium is the message," also said this in 1967, "The new electronic interdependence creates the world in the image of a global village."

TELEVISION ON THE NET

ABC: American Broadcasting Corporation
http://www.abc.com
CBS: Columbia Broadcasting System, Inc.
http://www.cbs.com
CNBC: Consumer News and Business Channel
http://www.cnbc.com
CNN: Cable News Network
http://www.cnn.com
NBC: National Broadcasting Company
http://www.nbc.com
NICK: Nickelodeon/Nick at Nite
http://nick-at-nite.viacom.com
PBS: Public Broadcasting Service
http://www.pbs.org/

Media in the 20th Century

$64,000 Question 123
17th Amendment 45
20/20 128
3Com Park 164
60 Minutes 128
accident theory 42
Action for Children's Television 155
Advertising Age 108, 163
advertorial 181
Adweek 140
Agricultural Adjustment Administration (AAA) 83
Al Rasheed 176
Aldrin, Edwin "Buzz" 136
Allure 179
America's Most Wanted 170
American Broadcasting Company 113, 174, 182
American Magazine 46
American Marconi Company 49, 61
American Mercury 66
American Telephone & Telegraph (AT&T) 71, 72, 74
Amos 'n' Andy Show 90
anchormen 138
Apollo 11 136
Arlin, Harold W. 71
Armstrong, Neil 136
Arnatt, Peter 176
Associated Press 47, 97
Baird, John L. 76
Baker, Randy 181
ballot initiative 45
Baltimore Sun 66, 67

Barker, Bernard 150
Bay of Pigs 129
Bernstein, Carl 149, 150
Bierce, Ambrose 41
blacklisted 113
Blue Network 99
Bly, Nellie (Elizabeth Cochrane) 36
Bolshevik Party 54
Boston Globe 147
Braun, Karl F. 50
Brinkley, David 120
Britain, Battle of 94
British Broadcasting Corporation (BBC) 99
Bryan, William Jennings 40
Bryan, Wright 99
Buccaneer 36
Bunyan, John 44
Bush, George 161
Cable Act 165
Cable News Network 166, 173, 175
cable television 164
Calmer, Ned 98
Camelot 130
Carbine, Patricia 154
Catalogue of Projects in Electronic Text 186
cellular phones 170
Censorship Board 58
Central Committee 55
Chain Gang—One Newspaper v. Gannett Empire 158
Chamberlin, Ernest 42
Chamberlin, Neville 86
Chambers, Whittaker 102
Chandler, Otis 140

Chavez, Cesar 136
Checkers 110
Chicago Tribune 78, 83
Choate, Robert, Burnett Jr. 154
CICNet 186
Civil Rights Act 132
ClariNet 187
Clark, Herbert 99
coaxial cable 105
Columbia Broadcasting System (CBS) 73, 78, 86, 88, 90, 98, 106, 116, 121, 148, 164
Commentary 108
Committee for the Re-Election of the President 149
Committee of Public Information 56
communism 100
Communist Party 53
Community Antenna Television 105
Community Press 159
composographs 59
Connor, T. Eugene "Bull" 132
Cosmopolitan 45
Craig, May 137
crawl 128
Creel, George 57
Cronkite, Walter 99, 131, 138
crystal sets 50, 64
Cuba 41
Cuban Missile Crisis 129
Current Affair 169
Current Biography 107
D-Day 98
Daily Graphic 67, 68
Daily Mirror 59, 67

INDEX

Daladier, Edouard 86
David Brinkley's Journal 128
Davis, Elmer 94
Davis, Richard Harding 42
Day of Infamy 97
Day of Rage 135
De Forest, Lee 61
Deep Throat 149
Democratic National Convention 134
Detroit News 70
Doerfer, John C. 114
Does Public Really Want Media To Let Up? 181
Downs, Hugh 128
Dupuy, Richard 99
e-zines 186
Eagle 136
Echo I 166
Edwards, Douglas 105
Eisenhower, Dwight D. 121
Ellsberg, Daniel 146
Engels, Friedrich 54
Entertainment Tonight 176
Entertainment Weekly 178
Entrepreneurial Woman 163
Equal Employment Opportunity Commission 138, 173
Ervin, Sam J. 151
Erving, Julius "Dr. J" 163
Espionage Act 57
ESPN 166
Evans, Harrold 164
Fairness Doctrine 104, 118, 119, 121, 142

Fall, Albert B. 65
Fear and Favor in the Newsroom 181
Federal Communications Act 90
Federal Communications Commission (FCC) 104, 114
Federal Radio Commission 60, 72, 154
Feminine Mystique 137
Ferdinand, Archduke Francis 56
Fessenden, Reginald A. 49
fireside chats 79, 85
Fitzgerald, F. Scott 67
Fitzpatrick, Sean 180
Food Lion 182
Ford, Gerald R. 152
four minute men 57
Fox Broadcasting 168
Friedan, Betty 137
Friendly, Fred 115
Fritts, Eddie 169
Frymer, Murray 181
Fuchs, Klaus 112
Fuoss, Robert M. 107
Gallup Poll 84, 151
Gannett 158, 177
Gates, Daryl 173
Gauvreau, Emile 67
General Electric 74
Gentlemen's Quarterly 123
Gibbons, Floyd 72
Golden Age 110
Goldmark, Peter 106
gonzo journalism 145, 152

Good Times, Bad Times 164
Gore, Tipper 169, 182
Gould, Jack 116
Graham, Phil 140
Great Depression 78
Green Bay News 158, 159
Harding, Warren G. 65
Harnsworth, Alfred 59
Hartnett, Vincent 114
Hatfield, Henry 90
Hattersley machine 59
Hayes, Harrold 128
Hearst, William Randolph 36, 39, 41, 47, 58, 67, 78, 80, 82, 83, 84
Hennock, Frieda B. 114
Herrold, Dr. Charles 50
Hicks, George 99
High Definition Television 183
Hill, Anita 173
Hiroshima 100
Hiss, Alger 102
Hitler, Adolf 85
Hoffman, Abbie 134
Hogan's Alley 38
Hollman, John 176
Hoover, Herbert 72, 74, 78
House Beautiful 70
House Committee on Un-American Activities (HUAC) 101
Howard, Tom 68
Hughes, Robert 128
Huntley, Chet 120
Huston, Tom 149

189

Media in the 20th Century

I Have A Dream 132
Illustrated Daily News 59, 67, 68
infomercial 165
Information Service Data Network 185
infotainment 170, 176
International News Service 47, 97
Internet 177, 185
Invasion from Mars 87
investigative journalism 44
Iran 160
Iraq 160
Jack Benny Show 90
jazz journalism 53, 59, 66
jingle 89
Johnson, Lyndon B. 131, 147
Jungle, The 46
Kaltenborn, H.V. 87
Kansas City Times 75
Kastenbein machine 59
KCBS 50
KDKA 71
Kennedy, Jacqueline Bouvier 130
Kennedy, John F. 129
Kent State 144
Keston, Paul 89
King, Reverend Martin Luther Jr. 132
King, Rodney 173
Knight-Ridder 158, 177
Koppel, Ted 174
KQW 50
Lady's Circle 141
Lanston, Tolbert 60
Lasker, Albert 90
Lear's 163
Lee, Robert E. 114
Lenin, Vladimir 54, 55

Lewis, Fulton Jr. 113, 118
Lindbergh, Charles A. 64
Linotype 38, 59
Luks, George B. 40
Lusitania 56
MacFadden, Bernarr 67
Mad 124
Magruder, Jeb Stuart 150
March on Washington 132
Marconi, Guglielmo 49, 61
Marshall, Howard 99
Marx, Karl 54
Mayflower decision 104
McCarthy, Joseph R. 110, 111, 112, 113, 118
McClure's 45, 70
McClure, S.S. 45
McCord, James W. 149
McCord, Richard 158
McCormick, Robert R. 59, 67, 78, 80, 82, 83, 84
McDonough, John 98
McKinley, William 40
McLuhan. Marshall 187
McNamara, Robert 146
McNamee, Graham 72
Meet the Press 103
Mencken, Henry Louis 66
Menshevik Party 54
MIN/Media Industry Newsletter 108
Mirabella 163

Mitchell, John 147
Monotype 59
Moss, Annie Lee 117
Motorola 170
Ms. 154
muckraking 38, 44, 139
Mudd, Roger 148
Munich crisis 86
Murdoch, Rupert 168
Murow, Edward R. 86, 94, 110, 114, 116, 118
Music TeleVision 167, 179
Mutual Broadcasting System 118
Nagasaki 100
Nathan, George Jean 66
National Association of Broadcasters 155
National Association of Television Program Executives 169
National Broadcasting Company (NBC) 72, 73, 78, 87, 106, 183
National Commission on the Causes and Prevention of Violence 135
National Organization for Women 137
National Recovery Administration (NRA) 83
National Science Foundation 186
Neuharth, Allen H. 159
Neuman, Alfred E. 124
New Deal 79, 83
New Frontier, 129

INDEX

new journalism 145
New York Journal 39, 43
New York Post 110
New York Times 71, 78, 94, 116, 120, 146
New York Tribune 58
New York World 36, 37, 39, 42, 43
Newby, Ray 50
Newspapers Enterprise Association 47
newsreels 91
Newsweek 169
Ngo Dinh Diem 146
Nguyen Ngoc Loan 133
Nicholas II 53, 54
Nieman Reports 108
Nixon, Richard M. 110, 129, 145, 149, 151, 152
North, Oliver 161, 162
Northwest Bank Bowl 162
Ochs, Adolph, S. 107
Operation Demolition 159
Operation Desert Storm 175
Orange Bowl 164
Orson Welles 88
Oswald, Lee Harvey 131
Outcault, Richard F. 39
Paley, William S. 73, 90
Parents Music Resource Center 169, 182
Patterson, Joseph M. 59, 67
Pearl Harbor 96

Pentagon Papers 144, 146
People 178
Persian Gulf War 175
Person to Person 119
Phillips, David G. 45
Pilgrim's Progress 44
Pittsburgh Sun Telegram 116
Playboy 123
plumbers 149
Poindexter, John F. 161
Pope John Paul II 178
Porter, Herbert L. 150
Povich, Maury 169
Pravda 52, 53, 54, 55
pre-empting 73
propaganda 56
public relations officers 98
Publisher's Press 47
Pulitzer Prizes 37
Pulitzer, Joseph 37, 39, 41
pumpkin papers 103
Pure Food and Drug Act 47
Pyle, Ernie 94, 95
radio 49, 61, 70, 85, 104
Radio Act 72
Radio Corporation of America 49, 71, 106
Radio Free Europe 101
Radio Liberty 101
Radulovich, Milo 115
rating 183
Reader's Digest 69, 78
Reagan, Ronald 161
Reasoner, Harry 128
recall 45

Red Channels 114
referendums 45
Remington, Frederic 42
Rockefeller, John D. 46
Roosevelt, Franklin D. 79, 81, 84, 97, 98
Roosevelt, Theodore 44
Roper Poll 127
Roper, Elmo Burns Jr. 127
Rosenberg, Ethel 112
Rosenberg, Julius 112
Ross, Charles, G. 103
Rubin, Jerry 134
Ruby, Jack 131
Russian Socialist Party 54
S.S. Titanic 61
San Francisco Examiner 39
Sanders, Beth 181
Santa Fe Report 158
Sarnoff, David 61, 71, 92
satellite 158, 166
Schwarzkopf, H. Norman 175
Scientific America 70, 75
Scovel, Frances 42
Screen Writers Guild 102
Scripps, E.W. 47, 94, 95
Scripps-MacRae Press Association 47
Sedition Act 58
See It Now 115
Selling of the Pentagon 148
Sesame Street 154
Shaw, Bernard 176
Sheehan, Neil 147
Shirer, William L. 86

Media in the 20th Century

Simpson, Orenthal James "O.J." 174
Sinclair, Upton 46, 91
Sirica, John J. 151
smear bureau 84
Smith, Howard W. 137
Sokolsky, George 113
Spanish-American War 42
Stans, Maurice H. 150
Steffens, Lincoln 45
Steinem, Gloria 154
Stevenson, Adlai E. 121
Strasser, Alfred 107
Students for a Democratic Society (SDS) 134
Sun Bowl 164
Supreme Court 83
Swayze, John Cameron 105
tabloid journalism 59, 67
Tarbell, Ida 45
Teapot Dome 65
Teflon president 161
television 75, 105
Television Index 108
Thomas, Clarence 173
Thompson, H.O. 96
Thompson, Hunter S. 152
tie-ins 155
Time 69, 78, 82
Tower Report 161
Trading with the Enemy Act 57
triode tube 61
Trotsky, Leon 54
Trout, Bob 98
Truman, Harry S. 100
Turner, Ted 166
TV Guide 124, 178

Ultra High Frequency (UHF) 106
United Farm Workers 136
United Press 47, 97
United Press International 47
USA Today 159, 169, 180
USS Maine 36, 42
Very High Frequency (VHF) 106
Vietnam 133
Vietnam War 144
Village Voice 123
Vizcaya 43
Voice of America 101
Voting Rights Act 132
Wagner, Robert 90
Wallace, DeWitt 69
Wallace, Lila 69
Wallace, Mike 128
Walters, Barbara 128
War of the Worlds 88
Washington Post 147
Watergate 149
WEAF 74
Weathermen 135
Web TV 183
Westinghouse 71, 74
WGY 76
White, Egbert 107
Wilson, Woodrow 56
Winship, Thomas 140
wireless 184
Wolfe, Tom 152
Wood, Frank 158
Woodward, Bob 149, 150
Works Progress Administration (WPA) 83
World War I 52, 56
World War II 85, 95
World Wide Web 186

World's Fair 92
WWJ 70
Yaalev Va'Yavo 178
Yank 107
Yellow Feller 40
yellow journalism 38
Yellow Kid 39
Yippie 134
Youth International Party 134